Hallowed Ground

Stories of the Yale Pioneer Cemetery

IAN BROWN

◆ FriesenPress

Suite 300 - 990 Fort St
Victoria, BC, V8V 3K2
Canada

www.friesenpress.com

Copyright © 2017 by Ian Brown
First Edition — 2017

All rights reserved.

No part of this publication may be reproduced in any form, or by any means, electronic or mechanical, including photocopying, recording, or any information browsing, storage, or retrieval system, without permission in writing from FriesenPress.

St. John the Divine burial register provided by the archives of the Anglican Diocese of New Westminster.

ISBN
978-1-5255-0863-9 (Hardcover)
978-1-5255-0864-6 (Paperback)
978-1-5255-0865-3 (eBook)

1. HISTORY, CANADA

Distributed to the trade by The Ingram Book Company

Table of Contents

Acknowledgments	v
Brief History of the Yale Pioneer Cemetery	1
Early Burials	14
Post 1960 Burials	203
Royal Canadian Air Force Plane Crash	221
About the Author	227
Endnotes	229

Acknowledgments

This book was written between the hours of 8:00 p.m. and 1:00 a.m. beginning in March, 2014 and was finally done in April, 2017. There are a number of people I'd like to thank for helping me transform a passing idea into the book you're holding in your hands. Thanks to Debbie and Allison Zervini who spent the first hours at the British Columbia Archives compiling the original list of names that were used as the basis for this book. Thanks also to Deb and the Yale and District Historical Society board for their encouragement and words of reassurance as the project took shape, and for backing it financially. Thanks to Melanie Delva at the archives of the Diocese of New Westminster - Anglican Church of Canada. Melanie let me hold the St. John the Divine burial record book in my hands. It was a humbling experience to be able to touch that much history. As I did my research, I gained immeasurable respect for the Yale clergymen who dealt with death on such a regular basis. Without the help of Irene Bjerky I wouldn't have been able to detail the lives of her family. They have long called Yale home and have contributed much to its story. Thanks to Kathleen Lloyd, Queenie Fasolino, Margie Wayne and all of those who were willing to share memories of their loved ones through stories and pictures. Thanks go to my old friend Greg Nesteroff for digging up old newspaper articles for me from time to time, I'm glad we could work together one more time. To those who were willing to read a very rough draft and give me their honest opinions and criticism I owe a debt of gratitude. It was a great honour to have my high school English teacher Theresa Crosgrey give up some of her precious retirement to grade one more paper. Thanks for not giving me a letter grade because I know you were tempted, and I think I know what it would have been. Also to my supportive parents Peter and Debby Flynn for reading through it and saying nice things. To my Grandparents Lloyd and Dorothy Brown I owe a debt of gratitude. They have been gone for many years, but they were front and centre in my mind as I wrote. I lament that I couldn't discuss this project with my Grandpa - he would have been a big help. Thanks also to my maternal Grandparents Jack and Betty DeLair for listening and encouraging their grandson as they've always done. Thank you to my wife's parents Peter and Helen Sawatzky for babysitting so I could get out and study. Finally, thanks to my beautiful wife Anita for understanding when I spent all those nights working on "the project." Without your support and encouragement this never would have been finished. To Nathan, Laura and Jillian, thanks for making me appreciate what I have!

Ian Brown
Abbotsford, B.C.

Hallowed Ground

IAN BROWN

Brief History of the Yale Pioneer Cemetery

Established as a stopping point between Fort Langley and Fort Kamloops, British Columbia, Fort Yale was a dot on the map of what was then New Caledonia when it first made an appearance. The town was founded in 1848 by Ovid Allard, a manager with the Hudson's Bay Company, and named after his superior, James Murray Yale. It was a small settlement consisting of a few small buildings, not even warranting fortifications or a garrison. It remained a sleepy stopping point on the rough trade route for ten years, until gold was discovered at Hills Bar, just south of the fort, in 1858. The gold rush was on, the population exploded, the colony that we now know as the British Columbia was created and the name Yale is recorded to this day in history books as one of the foundations of the province.

The creation of the town, the gold rush of 1858-59, the construction and consecration of St. John the Divine Church, and the CPR are all well documented. But there is very little mention of the Yale cemetery. When looked at in a larger context, the pioneer cemetery is not what you could call a "busy" place." Between the first recorded burial in 1859 and the last in the 2000s, approximately 320 people were laid to rest there. This amounts to fewer than two burials per year, and the vast majority of the interments occurred during the CPR construction years of 1880-1884, and the building of the Canadian Northern Railway on the Fraser's east bank between 1912 and 1914.

Just as Yale has experienced its cycles of boom and bust, so, too, in a manner of speaking, has the cemetery. Between 1859 and 1879, there were thirty-four burials in the cemetery, averaging a little fewer than two per year. However, when blasting began and the rails were put down, the "population" of the cemetery grimly expanded. Ninety-two people were laid to rest there between 1880 and 1884, with twenty-eight burials in 1883 alone. The vast majority of those who died in those years were connected to the railway, and there were sure to be unrecorded interments in the cemetery as those numbers only take into account the souls recorded in the St. John the Divine records. Other denominations, the Chinese, and Indians would not be counted, although the latter two groups had their own cemeteries in and around town. Only a handful of those buried on the banks of the river would have been born in Yale.

There have been Indian burials in Yale and the Fraser Canyon as long as they have inhabited the area—an estimated 8,000 to 10,000 years—but the beginnings of the Yale Pioneer Cemetery can be traced to 1858. Almost nothing is recorded of any burials between 1848 and 1858. Perhaps any HBC employee or traveller passing through who happened to die in or around Yale was simply sent home for interment. If they were buried in Yale, there seems to be no record of them.

The story goes that a rudimentary cemetery was established somewhere along Yale Creek, probably sometime in 1858, but it seems that when gold was discovered in the area, the sanctity of the dead became secondary to profit. When four men's burial plots were discovered in the way of the digging operations, the dead were allegedly exhumed and moved to the current site. If this is true, the men's re-burials were not recorded in St. John the Divine's records, and so their names are lost to history.

The first mention of an official cemetery in Yale was in 1859 in a letter from Judge Matthew Baillie Begbie. Arriving from England of the previous year to be the first judge in the new colony of British Columbia, Begbie was "one of a handful of men newly appointed to form the nucleus of the government of the colony."[1] As such, it fell to Begbie to serve not only as judge, but also as lawmaker, a role that was entirely new to him.

Begbie travelled extensively through the interior of the new colony, from New Westminster to the Omineca, north to Cassiar, and nearly every point in between. He often held court in the open air, bringing law and order to a population that included British subjects, First Nations peoples, Americans, and Chinese, among others. He visited the miners at their claims and camped along the way at places like McLeese Lake, Quesnel, and Barkerville. The colony he travelled was a collection of small settlements or mining camps, separated by wilderness and organized very loosely, usually by miners who followed their own codes of recognizing the boundaries of their claims. Begbie, acting as a legislator, sought to bring some kind of order by drafting the Pre-emption Act of 1860, which allowed individuals to claim provincial Crown land for the purpose of settlement and agriculture. The judge also created the Town Lot Leases Relief Act to resolve the many disputes arising from a mix of unextinguished Indian titles, Hudson's Bay holdings, and mining claims. Begbie "had actually laid out plots of land in Lytton in 1859, and probably elsewhere, for settlers, and he was concerned that they should not be dispossessed through some future pre-emption by another person."[2]

It is under this set of circumstances that Begbie wrote to Governor Douglas in late 1859 at the end of his second circuit of British Columbia. He held court at Yale, one of only four settlements surveyed by the Royal Engineers (the others being Fort Hope, Douglas, a settlement at the north end of Harrison Lake, and New Westminster), and it was here that a cemetery for Yale is first mentioned. Writing to Governor Douglas in Victoria, Begbie says:

"There is still two-and-a-half feet of snow, or was last night behind the post office here—but we have had two or three beautiful days and it is fast melting away. Surveying has been (illegible) horrible. I believe McNicol and myself however have agreed in a report to be sent to Col. Moody as to a church site here: behind the court house. There is, as far as we can judge, no good site for a cemetery—but when the surface can be seen, a better judgement can be formed."[3]

After Judge Begbie moved on from Yale at the conclusion of his second circuit, the task of locating and surveying a proper cemetery must have been a low priority for the colonial government, because it was an item left unchecked on its list. Begbie did not ultimately decide where the cemetery would lie; it would be up to the church to decide.

George Hills was installed as the first Church of England bishop for British Columbia in London on January 12, 1859, and was consecrated at Westminster Abbey six weeks later, on February 24. Until the arrival of Hills as a colonial bishop, it was common practice for the Hudson's Bay Company to "hire a chaplain to serve the needs of the employees at company forts."[4] In the new colony, it was clear that this arrangement had become obsolete, as only a bishop could perform ordinations and confirmations. Visiting bishops could perform such functions, but their appearances in British Columbia were few and far between. Bishop Hills landed at Esquimalt in early January 1860, and one of the first changes he made in the diocese was to send Reverend William B. Crickmer from Fort Langley (where it was anticipated the capital of the colony would be established) to Yale, to start a church.

Bishop Hills' diaries offer valuable insight to colonial life in 1860, especially with respect to Hope and Yale. Hills left New Westminster in late May of that year and made his way to Yale, spending a few days at Hope in early June. On June 9, Hills made the eight-hour canoe journey up the Fraser from Hope, arriving at four o'clock in the afternoon, and greeted by Reverend Crickmer and his wife. The next day, Hills and Crickmer opened a temporary church in Yale, located in a former storefront. On a rainy June 11, 1860, Hills made the following entry:

"I went and looked at sites for a burial ground. A romantic ravine with rolling torrent borders the north part of the town. It is quite a study: a picturesque bridge crosses the stream at the town path."[5]

Hills goes on to describe his interactions with the people of Yale over the next few days, from groups of miners leaving town for the gold fields of Barkerville to the town's "principle people."[6] He also witnessed the construction of the Cariboo wagon road, connecting the south of the colony with the interior. His descriptions detail the extreme ruggedness of the country the engineers were trying to conquer, and foreshadow the challenges Andrew Onderdonk would face two decades later while building the Canadian Pacific Railway through the canyon. Tea meetings, remonstrating gamblers and blasphemers, and crossing paths with the notorious Ned McGowan, whom Hills described as "one of the most zealous of the choir," and "a fine young man of superior qualifications,"[7] filled the rest of his days.

Finally, on June 13, 1860, the origin of the Yale Pioneer Cemetery becomes clear:

"I walked today with Mr. Crickmer in search of a burial ground. We selected a spot westward near two streams. Our ramble was pleasant amidst beautiful scenery and flowers in wondrous profusion. We gathered strawberries."[8]

St. John the Divine Church was built in 1863, and the parish register began to tell the story of births, baptisms, marriages, and deaths, with events recorded from 1859 until about 1950.

From that late spring day in 1860 until recent years, the Yale cemetery has seldom seen days of stability. By 1866, locals were appealing to Judge Begbie to improve access to the burial grounds, asserting "that the road leading from Yale to the cemetery is impassable, being blocked up and fenced across, so that a corpse cannot be conveyed there on any vehicle, and only with great difficulty can be carried on men's shoulders or by Indians."[9] In the cemetery's almost 160 years of existence, it has often been treated as an afterthought, and even though it was an active burial ground until the early 2000s, it was often in a state of natural reclamation as the weeds and acacia took over, granite boulders littered the site, and wooden gravemarkers rotted away. That is not to say the locals weren't concerned about the little cemetery, as work parties were occasionally organized to push Mother Nature back, but it was always a losing battle. The first documented example of a concerned citizen putting out the call to honour the burial ground and the memory of its inhabitants came from Michael Hagan, the editor of the *Inland Sentinel* newspaper. The paper had been established by the Irishman in Emory City, speculated to be the hub of CPR construction in the canyon. When it became obvious that Yale, not Emory, would be the company's headquarters, the newspaper was moved upriver. Hagan used the *Inland Sentinel* as a platform to champion the rights of the underdog, especially the Chinese coolies who were dying by the hundreds working on the railway, seemingly unnoticed by Onderdonk and his associates. He wrote in detail in the *Sentinel* about their working conditions, the discrepancy in their wages compared to the white worker, and the general discrimination they faced while working for the CPR. In fact, Hagan was an outspoken and well-known critic of the Canadian Pacific and, in turn, the government, in an effort to bring some accountability through his paper to the citizens of Yale. It's not surprising then, that he took to the pages of the *Sentinel* on May 11, 1882. Reporting on a community meeting, Hagan wrote,

"That whereas the public cemetery—generously donated by a private person for the benefit of this town—will soon become unavailable unless some more of it is cleared, and whereas the government has repeatedly made use of the same free of any charge. Therefore, be it resolved that the members for this district do urge upon the government the placing a sum on the estimates sufficient to carry out this much-needed work. Carried unanimously, moved by W. McGirr, seconded by A. Leamy."[10]

The private donor Hagan mentions is a mystery; it doesn't quite align with Bishop Hills' account of choosing the grounds while on a walk with Reverend

Crickmer. It does prove, however, that the earliest burials took place at the bottom of the slope, near to the river. Dr. M. W. Fifer's burial (and the site of his assassin's execution) are known to have taken place where the railway tracks now run. Ah Chung, the doctor's devoted assistant at his Gold-Rush-era medical practice, returned to pay his respects at the gravesite in 1883, only to find it obliterated by the CPR. Many of the oldest graves can be found in the lower end, while the graves of those such as the immigrant labourers of the Canadian Northern Railway, built between 1912 and 1914 through the canyon, can be found on the upper slope. Hagan's mention of the government's free use of the cemetery would seem to refer to the scores of railway workers who were being killed at work along the line. A local reminisced in the early 1900s:

"I remember once when the powder work three or four miles west of Yale blew up, the men were injured badly and were helped up the hill walking, one was called Mr. Ashdown of Chilliwack. This must have been in 1883. So many men were killed on the railroad that the cemetery at Yale was filled with those killed in these accidents. One wonders who all these men were and where they came from."

Later in the spring of 1882, Michael Hagan wrote of a different kind of decay afflicting Yale's little cemetery:

"Complaints are again made this spring as to the neglected appearance of the cemetery. Even private lots are not safe from the spirit of vandalism. Last year, tokens of affection were stolen from decorated graves in 'the City of the dead.' It is earnestly hop'd flowers the present season will be left alone."

A month later, most of the cemetery, along with a good portion of the town, was under water as the Fraser eclipsed its previous high-water mark set six years before. "This past week has been one of deep anxiety to the people of the whole Fraser River country," wrote the *Inland Sentinel*. The last great flood was in '76, when immense injury was done to property, and already the high-water mark of that year has been covered this week, with the river still rising as we go to press."[11] If the cemetery was affected by the flood of 1882, 1894 would have left the grounds in even worse shape. That summer, a plea went forth from St. John the Divine to clean up the cemetery:

An Appeal!

An effort is being made by the Vicar and people of Yale, British Columbia, to FENCE AND CLEAR THE OLD CEMETARY, now overgrown and open to the depredations of cattle.

As the Relatives of nearly all buried there are non-residents, this appeal is made to you to help PRESERVE THE REMAINS OF YOUR DEAD FROM DESECRATION.

Donations will be gladly received and acknowledged by

> The REV'D. C. CROUCHER,
> WM. TEAGUE, Esq., J. P.,
> or MRS. REVESBECK.

Yale, July 27th, 1894.

The record-breaking Fraser River flood of 1948 submerged the cemetery and laid waste to nearly every burial plot save for the Teague monument. One local recalls that after the water receded, some residents went to the cemetery and put the grave markers back to the best of their ability, but nobody could say for sure that they were in the right place.

In 1965, during his years touring the province interviewing British Columbia's greying pioneers, the CBC's Imbert Orchard made a stop in Yale to speak with Judge Charles Edward Barry, grandson of the famous Ned Stout and a lifelong Yale resident. "I want to point out," said Justice Barry, "that we have one of the oldest cemeteries in British Columbia. And which now has gone to wrack and ruin. It was said that the Anglican Church were the owners of it, but they disclaimed ownership and I don't know, no-one seems to be in control of it. I once saw a stone; it was near the old gate and the mark on it was 1859, and it was laying on the ground. Whether it's there now or not I couldn't say. It's so grown over and washed out with creeks and stuff, that I really wouldn't know."[12]

The Yale Pioneer Cemetery is bordered by All Hallows and Graveyard Creeks. In 1960, one of them overran its banks and again caused immense damage to the cemetery, with some residents claiming to see coffins floating down the Fraser. Unfortunately, many graves were destroyed and a part of the town's history was irretrievably lost. According to the Yale and District Historical Society, a group of local men led by Walter Chrane and Mitch Hodge did some repair work to the cemetery after the flood, and a grant received by the local ratepayers' association helped keep it in at least respectable condition for the next few years, but "gradually, maintenance was discontinued and acacia saplings took over." Due to the damage caused by flooding, the disintegration of wooden grave markers, neglect, and the passage of time, only about one quarter of the graves have some kind of marker. There are over 200 unmarked graves in the Yale Pioneer Cemetery today.

In the late 1960s, the government's senior cemeteries inspector paid a visit to Yale to interview perhaps the town's greatest historian, A. C. Milliken. Finding that Mr. Milliken was not home, the inspector returned to town and spoke with Mitch Hodge, who had done a lot of maintenance work in the cemetery in the past. Hodge spoke of clearing trees twelve inches in diameter, and said that in 1960 the overflowing creek "flooded through the cemetery, gouging a gully from the highway down to the CPR tracks." Hodge also stated that "a number of memorials and gravestones were swept down in the flood."

"The cemetery," wrote the inspector, "is still overgrown with thorny bushes, creeping vines, and trees, and is obviously quite old. It has had fairly extensive use and some of the gravestones show death to have occurred before 1885. The latest use of the cemetery, as far as I could determine in the short time available, was in 1947. However, Mr. Hodge said that he recalled some burials having been performed there about two years ago (mid 1960s)."

The sudden interest in the Yale cemetery in the 1960s hit a dead end when the government admitted it had no knowledge of the cemetery, where the burial records were stored, or who was responsible for its maintenance. The Yale ratepayers' association of the day voted to undertake responsibility for the restoration and care of the cemetery, but it was an immense undertaking, and the inspections that took place in 1968 resulted in the recommended closure of the site to any future interments. "Inspection of the site from a health point of view," wrote the Public Utilities Commission, "discloses that it is not suitable for continued use as a cemetery and must be closed to further burials." In 1969, the government speculated that, because no official title to the cemetery land could be found, it was likely that the land was never formally approved to operate as a cemetery, which would seem to be supported by Crickmer's and Hills' choosing of the site almost on a whim while out for a walk.

In the early 1970s, the cemetery was completely cleaned out by the historical society, but it was then left once again to Mother Nature. Verna Shilson, who was president of the Yale group, stated that every year at least some work was done, but by the next spring, any ground gained had been lost, and interest in the cemetery's upkeep waned again.

In 1980, it was revealed that, although the Public Utilities Commission had recommended closure of the cemetery to future burials, this recommendation was never made official. That same year, the historical society applied for a grant in the amount of $2,000, which it received, the money forwarded by the British Columbia Heritage Trust. The historical society, however, declined to officially take over the restoration work, citing the fact that such a small society, already trying to establish a museum, didn't have the wherewithal to undertake any work on the cemetery. However, later that year, some work was done in the cemetery, with the historical society reporting 428 man hours of volunteer work and the application of $250 from the society to widening paths and removing stumps. Brian Minter, who was well known in the Fraser Valley for the well-manicured Minter Gardens, even came to offer his advice to the society. Nothing came of this renewed interest, however, and, in 1982, a work bee organized to tidy up the grounds attracted only one prospective worker. Writing in 1985, Mrs. Shilson stated that a summer student had at least managed to clear a path around the grounds the previous year, but that nothing was planned for '85, and "we just do not know what will happen this spring." On a positive note, Shilson wrote that families of some of the deceased from Richmond, Coquitlam, and Mission had come to the cemetery to work on their family plots and that the grounds "even had flowers blooming last summer."

In the spring of 1989, a motorcycle accident took the life of Glynnis "Glennie" Chrane. The recent high school graduate had grown up in Yale and her parents, Walter and Clara, still lived there. For the heartbroken family, there was no question of where to bury their daughter. Walter, scowling at the overgrown cemetery littered with rocks, stumps, and weeds, set to work. With the help of Clara, Glennie's sisters, Glady and Irene, and other family members, he dug, filled, and cleared the land. After the work was done, the Chranes kept the grass cut and the grounds as pristine as possible. Jim and Verna Shilson helped to establish the Yale Museum and kept the grounds groomed and the Barry family also did their part. Most of the labour was voluntary; the people of Yale treated the grounds with the respect that had been absent for so many years.

Dr. Keizo Hayashi was a chiropractor who moved to Gordon Creek, just south of Yale, in 1942. While the majority of Japanese and Japanese-Canadian people were sent to internment camps during World War II, the doctor had been released into the custody of the Haskell family. Hayashi and the Haskells purchased a small farm on Gordon Creek, and the doctor opened a practice in Hope, which he ran from 1951 until the 1980s. Hayashi grew to love Yale and was a fixture in the area, always appreciative of its history and natural beauty. Jade collecting was a favourite hobby of Dr. Hayashi, and he scoured the Fraser from Hope to Lytton in search of it. His handcrafted jade jewelry was available for sale for many years throughout the area. When Dr. Hayashi passed away in Chilliwack in 1994 at the age of ninety-two, he expressed his love for his home of nearly fifty years by leaving a third of his estate to the Yale and District Historical Society, which chose to honour his legacy by creating an endowment to fund the upkeep of the Yale Pioneer Cemetery. Today, the endowment ensures that the grass is cut, the headstones are repaired and kept upright, and that the invading bushes on either side are held at bay.

In 1980, a passerby wrote to the Yale and District Historical Society:

"Dear Sir:

On passing through the Fraser Canyon recently we stopped overnight in your town of Yale. Usually, as so many motorists do, I imagine, we travel right on through and miss your local interesting historical value. We saw and loved St. John Church, Lady Franklin Rock, and just the simple peacefulness of the town's location and grand view. But what we were disappointed in was the condition of that graveyard, which is the epitome of British Columbia history, and we feel should never be allowed to deteriorate into such a way we couldn't even find it. Then to see the pioneers who made our province memorialized in the area in which they chose to work their lives away just forgotten with tangled bush overgrowing their monuments. Yale is the focal point of our realistic and romantic history. Its pioneers should be honoured."[13]

Finally, after over 150 years, the Yale Pioneer Cemetery is a place where the dead can be, as the letter writer demanded, honoured. The efforts of the town to preserve its cemetery before Dr. Hayashi's generous gift should not be discounted, but it was simply too monumental a task. However, thanks to the dedication and love for Yale shown by the doctor, the members of the community, and the Yale and District Historical Society, the graveyard on the hill, so chosen on a grey, late-spring day in 1859 by Bishop Hills and Reverend Crickmer, can at last be visited by all.

Clergy of St. John the Divine

Alexander David Pringle
1859

William Burton Crickmer
1860 - 1862

Henry Reeve
1862 - 1865

David Holmes
1868 - 1873

George Ditcham
1876 - 1878

John Booth Good
1878 - 1880

Charles Blanchard
1880 - 1881

R.C. Whiteway
1881 - 1882

Darrell Horlock
1882 - 1885

Edwin Wright
1885 - 1888

Charles Croucher
1890 - 1917

Charles Fitzgerald Yates
1917 - 1931

Heber Hannington Greene
1932 - 1942

George Charles Turner
1943 - 1944

Harold Scudamore
1944 - 1955

William Davis Pope
1955 - 1963

Charles H. Gibbs
1964

Leslie George Chappell
1964 - 1971

Paul McMullan
1971 - 1986

Ed Wilkin

J.S. Barton

Harold Vaughn Thomas

Archie Pell

Fred Tass

Gail Newell

The Grave on the Hill

High up on the hill is a little short mound
That I in my wanderings one summer day found;
The long, tangled grass grew green on the spot
So lonely, neglected, and seemingly forgot;
My mind, when I saw it, with thinking did fill—
I wondered, "Who sleeps in this grave on the hill?"

Oh, who so long here in silence has slept,
And who was the mother that over it wept?
And whose were the words that fell with the clay
That hid it forever from vision away?
How many sad hearts with sorrow did fill
As they turned from this lone little grave on the hill?

There's a stone at its head, but it speaks not a word
Of the long sleeping one beneath it interred;
A bright flower-bed is still blooming where
I know it was planted with tenderest care.
But that hand is gone; no more will it till
And brighten this lone little grave on the hill.

I will plant some sweet flowers on this little grave,
In spring-time to blossom and over it wave;
A white stone will raise at the tiny mound's head
And on its smooth surface shall let it be said—
So that he who then cometh may read if he will—
That some mother's babe is asleep on this hill.

—*Yale Inland Sentinel*, September 6, 1883

Early Burials

These are the stories of those buried in the Yale Pioneer Cemetery's first hundred years, between 1858 and 1960.

Burroughs, Charles
???? - 1858

In 1858, David Higgins, a Canadian-born journalist working in California, sold his interest in the *San Francisco Morning Call* newspaper and was among the first treasure seekers to arrive in Yale in the early days of the Gold Rush. Higgins bought a stake in a claim based in Yale and took a job at Ballou's Express, in addition to acting as a correspondent for a handful of California papers to describe the events taking place in the British-owned territory. Higgins remained in Yale for the next year-and-a-half, and his writings from those days offer a glimpse into the comings and goings of day-to-day life in the town during that frenetic period. He describes the layout of the town, interactions among the townspeople, even a story about getting lost in the mountains around Yale on Christmas Eve, 1858. His recollections about Charles Burroughs are the only surviving account of one of the first men to be buried in Yale, and they are perhaps the most moving because Higgins witnessed the events himself.

"Down on the bar there lived a little English woman named Burroughs. She had two dear little children, a boy and a girl, who were noted for their neat appearance on all occasions. Her husband had gone up the canyons in quest of gold, leaving wife and children in a small tent. A scanty supply of groceries and money which he left behind for their sustenance was exhausted and the family were reduced to great straits. The neighbours on the waterfront did all they could to help the woman, but they were generally poor, too. It was understood that Mrs. Burroughs was too proud to appeal for help."[14]

The Burroughs family relocated to Yale from Lytton in search of fortune, but, as Higgins writes,

"There were sad days in store for Mrs. Burroughs in the tent down on the bar. She was destined to have a great heart trouble. Looking back as I write through all these years that have lapsed since then, I conjure up her frail figure as I last saw it, with her dear little ones pressed to her breast and calling on God to protect and buoy them up in their great sorrow. That picture is one I never can forget."[15]

It turned out that the hardships the family faced living on the sandbars of Yale in the face of winter would have all been worth it, save for one misstep and a tragic accident that took the life of their husband and father.

"One stormy afternoon a miner came into town. He had travelled rapidly over the trail from a bar where his company were located in quest of a surgeon. The story he told was that a stranger on his way down the river trail had shot himself in the thigh while climbing over a tree that had fallen across the path. A doctor was procured and accompanied the man back to Sailor Bar. When they reached there, the stranger was dead—having bled to death. The doctor (Dr. Max Fifer), after pronouncing the man to be dead, asked if he had any effects. Some letters and a bag of gold dust weighing over $700 were handed to him. Every miners' cabin was provided with a pair of gold scales for weighing dust. From the purse, the doctor weighed out $150 as his fee and handed the bag back to the miners. The latter brought the letters and the balance remaining in the bag to Yale, and handed them to the authorities. The letters were addressed to 'Charles Burroughs, Lytton' and bore the Yale postmark."[16]

After much debate and many declining to take the job, a Mrs. Power and Mrs. Felker were given the task of asking Mrs. Burroughs if the objects belonged to her husband, who affirmed that they did. According to Higgins, Burroughs was very much anticipating reaching his family by nightfall, and that he had been whistling and singing a song called "The Girl I Left Behind Me" while using his rifle as a walking staff when the accident occurred.

"Little more remains to be told," writes Higgins. "Mrs. Burroughs had the body brought to Yale and interred in the little cemetery. At the grave, the widow knelt, and with her children pressed to her bosom engaged in silent prayer, while we all drew back and gazed reverently at the affecting scene."[17]

Burroughs' death in 1858 predates the establishment of the Yale cemetery in its current location, which occurred in the spring of the next year. He was likely one of the four bodies buried in the cemetery that were eventually relocated because of the site's intrusion on a potential gold-bearing hotspot. If his body was moved, there remains no record of it, and Charles Burroughs' name appears only in the memoirs of David Higgins.

Smith, John

1810 - 1860

The first burial recorded in the St. John the Divine register was "John Smith," a native of Denmark. He was interred by Bishop William Burton Crickmer on September 4, 1860, and was likely the first burial in the "new" cemetery that had been established by Bishop Hills after the original graveyard was relocated. Crickmer noted that Smith was about fifty years old when he died.

Fifer, Dr. Maximilian William

1822 - 1861

The murder of Dr. Max Fifer and its aftermath are perhaps the most sensational chain of events in Yale's history, the stuff of which movies are made today. Fifer was a German living in the United States when he signed on with the Regiment of New York Volunteers in 1846, which sailed around Cape Horn en route to California to fight in the Mexican American War. The conflict, which resulted in California's cessation to the United States from Mexico, concluded in 1848, at which point the regiment was disbanded in California. This coincided with the events of the California Gold Rush, in which Fifer took part and made his fortune. In the following years, he took his medical training and hung his shingle in San Francisco, where he became prominent in the community.

News of the Fraser Canyon Gold Rush in 1858 convinced the doctor to pull up stakes and head north. He landed in Yale, where he would spend the remainder of his life. It was during those tumultuous days on the Fraser that Fifer became chair of Yale's town council, and, as a doctor, both well-known and well-loved among the town's people. It was also during that time that the doctor treated a Hill's Bar miner named Robert Wall for a unique condition, and events were set in motion that led to Fifer's murder on July 5, 1861.

"Cold Blooded Murder. —On the evening of the 5th inst., the most coldblooded and cowardly murder ever perpetrated in the two Colonies, was committed at Yale. The victim was Dr. Wm. Fifer, an old and respectable resident of that town, and president of the Town Council; the perpetrator was a vagabond known as Robert Wall, who had formerly mined on Hill's Bar but more recently has been loafing about at New Westminster. The circumstances, as nearly as can be gathered from the many accounts furnished us, are these: About six o'clock on the afternoon of the 5th, a man entered Dr. Fifer's drug-store and inquired for that gentleman. The doctor's servant informed him that his employer was in the back-room. Thither the man proceeded, and saluted the doctor, who advanced towards him. The stranger kept his right hand concealed from view in the bosom of his shirt. As the doctor approached, the man held out his left hand, in which was a newspaper partially folded, and said: 'Look at this.' The doctor took the paper from the man, and bent his eyes toward it, when, as quick as a thought, the latter drew a small Derringer pistol from his bosom, and fired.

"The ball entered Dr. Fifer's left breast and passed entirely through his heart. The victim staggered, turned partially around, leaned against the side of the room, and then sank down in a corner. He must have died instantly without a groan. The cowardly murderer surveyed the corpse for an instant and then walked leisurely out of the store, proceeded to a canoe (manned by a white man and two Indians), and jumped in. The canoe was then shoved off, and proceeded downstream at a rapid rate. Mr. Jules David, of this city (Victoria), with several other gentlemen, was seated on a bench in front of the drugstore conversing, and heard an explosion inside, but paid no attention to it. They also saw the murderer walk quietly out immediately afterward, and it was not until his canoe had been shoved off that they were made aware of the horrid deed which had been committed within doors.

"As soon as possible, three canoes were manned and the fugitive followed. At Hope, the parties in pursuit were informed that Wall had left the canoe a short time before and taken the river trail for old Langley. One of the canoes proceeded five miles further down the river and encamped for the night, and before morning, Wall made his appearance at the camp. He was fired upon and fled to the woods, where all trace was lost. The white man who was in the canoe with Wall was arrested the same evening, half a mile back of Hope by a drover named Evans, to whom he had fled for protection. The drover took him in charge and lodged him in the Hope jail. His name is Michael Hagar, a young man, aged about twenty-four years. He denies knowing the object of Wall's visit to Yale. On Monday last, Wall was seen at Old Langley and on the next day was arrested by a posse of police from New Westminster, on the trail between Langley and Semiahmoo, while making his way toward American territory. He surrendered at once. He was taken to New Westminster and lodged in jail.

"Three days after the murder, an inquest was held upon the body of the murdered man; a verdict of 'wilful murder' was rendered, and the remains interred. Dr. Fifer was a native of Germany, a widower, aged about forty years, and leaves a child in San Francisco to mourn his loss. He was for a long time a resident of San Francisco, where he practiced medicine, although it is charged that he was not a regularly educated physician. He had resided at Yale since early in '58 and was much beloved by his friends. On several occasions, it has been asserted that deceased, maltreated patients who came under his care, and about a year ago a violent assault was made upon him by a woman at Yale, who alleged that he had maltreated her child.

"Wall, in a statement made to the officers by whom he was taken into custody, said his reason for killing Dr. Fifer was that he had maltreated him two years ago. He had often been heard to say that he would someday kill the doctor, and Mr. Ballou, of the Express, hearing of these threats, warned deceased half an hour before he was killed that Wall was coming up the river with the avowed intention of murdering him. Deceased, it seems, took no precautions, and hence his melancholy and untimely end. The murderer will be tried at Yale about the 3d proximo."[18]

In 1858, Fifer had treated Wall for an ailment that caused him uncontrollable sexual urges. His multiple visits to local prostitutes resulted in a venereal disease that raised painful, pus-filled sores on his legs that prevented him from walking comfortably. The disease was obvious to those on the street because of the way Wall walked, which led him to Dr. Fifer. The treatment prescribed, according to Wall, eventually caused impotence, resulting in a slow-burning rage that culminated with Fifer's assassination in 1861. On July 16, 1861, the *Colonist* continued with its coverage of the story:

"The Yale Murder. —It is related that when the news of the murder of Dr. Fifer by Wall, at Yale on the 5th inst., reached Hope and New Westminster, coupled with the report that the murderer had fled to Washington Territory for protection, that the American residents dispatched messengers to Whatcom and Semiahmoo, imploring the people at those places to seize and send him back, and not allow their towns to become places of refuge for British Columbian criminals. The people at Whatcom and Semiahmoo stirred themselves accordingly, and had the villain succeeded in reaching either town, he would unquestionably have been handed over to our authorities without an observance of the formula usual in such cases. An attempt is made in some quarters to show that Wall was rendered insane by the malpractice he had sustained at the hands of the deceased. Any unprejudiced man who read the account published by us yesterday cannot fail to see that there was much 'method in his madness.'

"It was proven at the coroner's investigation that Wall hung about Yale for two hours previous to killing Fifer, being deterred from committing the deed by the presence in and around the store of a number of friends of deceased; that his canoe was ready-manned at the beach during all that time; that when he confronted his victim he handed him a newspaper to read and that while the latter was in the act of doing so—his attention being thereby distracted from the person standing before him—he was coolly shot down. The subsequent flight of the murderer and the attendant circumstances go to point out the utter absurdity of the statement that Wall was insane. Added to these conclusive facts, the murderer's antecedents are of the worst description. If he had been maltreated by his victim, he had the laws to appeal to; and if he is allowed, through the influence of false sympathy, to escape a well-merited punishment, no physician's life in the two colonies will in future be worth a straw. The murder appears to us to have been one of the most deliberately planned and coolly executed tragedies that it has ever become our painful duty to record."[19]

Dr. Fifer, about forty when he was murdered, was buried by his friend Reverend William Burton Crickmer in the Yale cemetery. Robert Wall was arrested in New Westminster after a multi-day canoe and foot chase, and was sentenced by Judge Begbie to hang for his crime. The gallows were constructed so that Wall would hang over the grave of Dr. Fifer, and the execution was carried out in view of the public on Friday, August 23, 1861.

"Robert Wall, the murderer of Dr. Fifer, was hanged at Yale on Friday last between ten and eleven o'clock a.m., in the presence of 400 people. Mr. S. Wolf, of this city (Victoria) was present. He walked from jail to the gallows and mounted the scaffold with a firm step, and seemed perfectly unconcerned as to the dreadful fate which awaited him. On the scaffold, he knelt with the Rev. Mr. Crickmer, who offered up a fervent prayer on his behalf. His legs and arms were then pinioned, and he was asked if he had anything to say, upon which he advanced to the front of the platform and spoke as follows: 'Gentlemen, I have but few words to say. I am sorry for what I have done. The treatment that Dr. Fifer used toward me I cannot state here. The medicine he gave me at times entirely ruined my brain; and whenever I made up my mind to do anything, it appeared there was something urged me on. I am sorry for committing the deed; I have never looked into the Bible, and I think if I had and paid attention to it, I would never have committed the deed. I am prepared to meet my doom and hope to be forgiven as I forgive all. I have no more to say. Goodbye.' At the conclusion of the remarks, the doomed man stepped back to the drop; the rope was adjusted about his neck and the fatal cap drawn over his eyes. The trap was then sprung and he fell about five feet. He struggled violently for some minutes, appearing as if his neck was not broken, but in about ten minutes, life was pronounced extinct. After hanging half an hour, the body was cut down and buried by the authorities."[20]

It is never conclusively stated where Wall was buried, and if he was placed in the same cemetery, no location is known. Twenty years after Fifer's death, the Canadian Pacific Railway violated the sanctity of the burial ground, and to the dismay of Dr. Fifer's devoted assistant Ah Chung, the line was built directly over the burial plot, destroying it forever. Hope's Dr. Gerd Asche has written a fascinating account of Dr. Fifer's brief time in Yale in a book entitled, *M. W. Fifer MD—Healer, Prophet, Fool*, which tells the account from Ah Chung's perspective.

Eves, George

1832 - 1862

The burial of George Eves on May 12, 1862, was the third to take place in the relocated Yale cemetery. His was the first interment overseen by Reverend Henry Reeve, who would officially open St. John the Divine the next year. Eves was an American and was twenty-nine years old at his death, the cause of which remains a mystery.

Clarke, John

1815 - 1862

The only information available about John Clarke comes from Reverend Reeve's notation in the Anglican burial records. Clarke was an American and was buried in Yale on July 4, 1862. Clarke was the fourth person buried in the cemetery, and he died before the church was completed; Reeve would officially open it in 1863. The location of Clarke's grave has long been lost.

Kilban, John

1812 - 1862

Reverend Henry Reeve provides all the information available about Kilban. He was an American, about fifty when he died, and he was a carpenter. He likely came to Yale during the gold rush and stayed in town after it had died down. Kilban was the fifth person buried in the Yale Pioneer Cemetery at its current location.

Klein, female

???? - 1863

All that is known of the seventh interment in the Yale cemetery, is that Ms. Klein was buried by Reverend Reeve on April 23, 1863.

Evans, Lillian

1804 - 1863

Little is known about Lillian Evans and what brought her to Yale. The only evidence left is available on her wooden grave marker in the cemetery. It states that she was born in South Wales, and died in 1863 at the age of fifty-nine.

Enderlin, E. F. (Frederick)

1829 - 1866

Enderlin was born in Baden, Switzerland, in 1829 and was living and mining in Boston Bar thirty-seven years later when he met his death.

"Fatal Accident —We regret to have to announce a terrible accident that happened at Boston Bar last week, depriving a fine young man, named Frederick Enderlin, of life. It appears that the deceased and his brother Alexander had been mining at Boston Bar, on the Fraser River, for some years past, and that on Monday last, a cave took place in the bank that carried Frederick into the river, burying him several feet below the surface. His remains were not got out until Thursday, when an inquest was held by Mr. Sanders, JP, and a verdict returned of accidental death. The interment took place on Friday, at which a large number of persons attended, out of respect to the deceased and his surviving brother. The last offices of the Church were performed at the funeral by the Rev. J. B. Good, of this town. Deceased was a native of Switzerland, and we understand it was his intention, had his life been spared, to return home this fall in company with his brother."[21]

The accident occurred on July 15, 1866, and Enderlin was buried five days later on the twentieth. Reverend Good's notation in the St. John's burial records confirms the *Tribune's* account of the accident. He wrote, "killed suddenly whilst bench mining. The body was not recovered for some days."[22] Frederick Enderlin was the eighth person buried in the Yale cemetery after it was moved to its current location. His brother Alexander moved to the United States sometime after the accident. He and his wife Frances lived in Chillicothe, Ohio, where they had a son in 1867. In honour of his lost brother, Alexander named his son Frederick.

Thomas, Charles

c.1828 - 1868

Charles Thomas was a miner who was prospecting in the Cariboo during the gold rush that attracted scores of foreign treasure seekers during the 1860s. Thomas was traveling south on the relatively new Cariboo Wagon Road when he died suddenly on November 9, 1868. Reverend Holmes of St. John the Divine wrote that Thomas was found at the "5 Mile House on his way from the Cariboo. Congestion of the brain."[23] He was laid to rest as the eleventh burial in the Yale cemetery, on November 11, 1868.

Struthers, James
1826 - 1869

Hailing from East Kilbride, Lanarkshire, Scotland, Struthers was a prospector working up and down the Fraser River in the years after the gold rush. He was about forty-three years old when he died in 1869 at "Mariaville," near Hope. According to St. John the Divine's Reverend Holmes, Struthers died of a "lingering consumption" and was interred soon after in Yale. His was the thirteenth recorded burial in the cemetery, and it took place on September 29, 1869.

Goudie, Gilbert
???? - 1870

The life of Gilbert Goudie is a mystery. He died hundreds of miles from Yale, yet he is buried there, and only the inscription in the church record book by Reverend Holmes lends any clue to his identity. Goudie was a London-born merchant who, according to Holmes, "died at Quesnelle and is buried in the cemetery at Yale, British Columbia."

Evans, Charles
1839 - 1871

Evans was a popular figure in Yale in the 1860s, and appeared on the political stage as the colony of British Columbia debated whether to join the Dominion of Canada. He was born in 1839 in Lancashire, England. He immigrated to Canada in the late 1850s and became a bookkeeper in Canada West (now Ontario). He came further west in around 1862 and took employment in Yale at Barnard's Express (also known as the BX), a company that moved freight and passengers between southern British Columbia and the Cariboo gold fields. He met his wife, Jane Wells, while in Yale; they were married on March 9, 1866. The family farmed in the Chilliwack area, and owned an acreage on the banks of Atchelitz Creek. Evans Road, which crosses the Trans-Canada Highway in Chilliwack, is a reminder of Evans's contributions to that community. A supporter of the idea of British Columbia joining the rest of Canada, Evans served as a delegate at the Yale Convention of 1868. The convention was a meeting of Confederation supporters who thought that the colony would benefit from joining the Dominion, though the idea had been previously rejected in Victoria. Evans, a champion of Confederation, would not live to see British Columbia join with the rest of the nation. Husband to Jane and father to John, Henry, and Sarah, Evans also served as a magistrate in Yale during those years. He was a man with a devoted family and a successful career who was loved in his community and was building a solid legacy when he committed suicide on March 14, 1871. Reverend Holmes notes that Evans "died at Yale. Buried in cemetery, Yale, British Columbia. Shot himself under temporary insanity."[24]

From the *British Colonist*:

"Lamentable Suicide. —Yesterday, Mr. F. J. Barnard received a telegram from Yale, informing him that his agent at that town—Charles Evans—had committed suicide yesterday morning by shooting himself through the head with a revolver, causing instant death. Although no cause is assigned, it is thought that drink was the proximate cause of the terrible act. Deceased has been in Mr. Barnard's employ for nearly eight years, and was greatly liked. He leaves a widow and three children. The sad affair has caused great distress in the community where it occurred."[25]

The following is Evans's obituary:

"Charles Evans died suddenly at Yale, Colony of British Columbia, on March 14, 1871. Still a young man, he was in his thirty-second year. A magistrate and resident of Yale for eight years, Charles Evans had been in the employ of Mr. Francis J. Barnard (as manager for Barnard's Express) for most of that time. Mr. Evans had a special interest in colonial affairs; and was a delegate for Yale when the Confederation League held a convention there in May 1868. This was a time of considerable controversy as to whether or not the Colony of British Columbia should join with the other provinces of Canada. Mr. Evans was given a Methodist burial service. A well-known personality in the town of Yale and in the Chilliwack area; of Mr. Evans, it was said that he was generally liked and respected by all who knew him. Charles Evans was survived by his wife, Jane, and three young children, all of whom were born in Yale: John Allen, 1867; Charles Henry, 1868; and Sarah Ellen, 1869."[26]

British Columbia would become part of Canada four months later, on July 20, 1871. Evans's grave is marked by a wooden headstone placed in the cemetery in later years by members of his family.

Church, Robert

1839 - 1871

Church is listed in the 1871 British Columbia Directory as a miner. In the St. John's church burial book, he is also recorded as being a baker. He was born in Kingston, Ontario, at some time in 1837 or 1838, and died April 7, 1871, after a few days of illness. Interred by Reverend Holmes two days later, Church's was the sixteenth burial to take place in the Yale cemetery.

Peck, Maria

1831 - 1871

Maria Litherland was born in 1832 in Wigan, Lancashire, the same town in which her future husband had been born seven years earlier. Maria and Edwin Peck were married January 9, 1851, in Bolton and were living in Wigan the next year when daughter Annie was born. Sometime in the 1860s, the family relocated to Canada, settling in Yale, where Edwin was a carpenter and cabinetmaker. Maria passed away on May 28, 1871, of unknown causes. Her gravestone is remarkably well preserved in the Yale cemetery and can be visited today. Edwin passed away in Yale in 1882. Annie Peck, who was in her early teens when the family moved to Canada, married Samuel Moorhouse in 1872, and had had three children by 1877. Her husband died in Victoria in 1879 and she was remarried in Yale in 1881 to a William Jameson. Together, they had a son in 1886, but, sadly, Annie, too, passed away just two years later in Silverdale, British Columbia.

Dunbar, George

1829 - 1872

Dunbar came to Yale from Iowa. He was in the Fraser Canyon in the 1870s where records show he was a hotelkeeper and a miner. He was likely drawn to the area to try his hand at the kicked-over diggings on the Fraser in the years after the gold rush had turned quiet. The sandbars on the Fraser were still paying modestly for decades after the initial crush of miners had moved on. Dunbar died on December 1, 1872, of unknown causes. Yale's Dr. Foster "declines certifying the cause of death, not having seen deceased for fourteen days prior to and not at all after the event."[27] The informant on his death certificate is well-known Fort Hope merchant James Wardle. Dunbar's name is not listed in the church's burial book, and the location of his grave is no longer known.

Rombrot, Vincent

1824 - 1873

Yale resident Vincent Rombrot was a hotelkeeper and respected pioneer of the town, having moved there just after the excitement of the 1859 gold rush. He ran an establishment called the 16 Mile House, which served the travellers of the Cariboo Wagon Road. The native of France worked as a miner and prospector on the side.

"Death. —We regret to hear of the death of Monsieur Rombrot of the 16 Mile House from Yale. M. Rombrot was a pioneer settler of 1861 and was much respected. He had been suffering for some time. It is supposed the cause of death was inflammation of the mucous membrane."[28]

Also:

"Yale, Jan. 14 —Mr. Vincent Rombrot, an old pioneer of the colony and for the past eight years proprietor of the 16 Mile House, died yesterday morning. He had been unwell for some time."[29]

In the memoirs of W.H. Holmes, a railroad construction worker who came from Portland, Oregon, to work for Andrew Onderdonk, great detail is provided about the layout of the town of Yale, and some of the personalities that populated the place. In addition to his contract with Onderdonk, Holmes worked as a ferryman on the Fraser at various construction camps, providing material and equipment for blasting and other general freight. Holmes related a story of a wild ride down the river that ended at Rombrot's hotel:

"One Sunday Bishop Sillitoe drove up the road and signalled for the ferry; he was going to hold a service in the camp (Camp 13 at the Big Tunnel). It was high water at the time, and the boat's crew had to tow the boat by walking along the shore, and I stayed in it to steer. The men let the boat take a sheer, and the current was so strong that it dragged the rope out of their hands, and of course I was drifting down the Blue Canyon. This is the most wild part of the Fraser—there is no place to land until you get through it. All I had was the steering oar, and the last thing I saw was the bishop and his wife. They were running along the wagon road, with Mrs. Sillitoe in the lead. I could see an occasional man high up on the grade, shaking his hands goodbye, for no one thought a boat could go through the canyon. I used the oar all I could to keep the boat straight, but sometimes she was on end in a whirlpool. Near the end of the canyon, I noticed a large flat stretch of rock, about water level, and the boat was almost going to touch it; so I seized the end of the rope, and as soon as we came near enough, I jumped onto the rock; there was a tree close to, so I ran the rope around it, and snubbed up the boat and tied it. Then I began to look for a way to get up the face of the bluff; and when I reached the top I found I was just across the road from the Rombrough (sic) road-house. Rombrough had a garden, just where I came over the top, and happened to be out there gathering watercress; and when he looked up and saw me, he started to run to his house; but I hulloa'd out to him, and when he saw who it was, he stopped. I was all wet and muddy; but he took me into his house, and made me take off my clothes, and get into bed while he dried them. He also gave me a hot brandy, and cooked me a fine meal. In order to get back, I had to walk about four miles to the bridge, to cross over, and then up the river several miles to the camp and home. It was after dark when I got there, and I found the camp mourning me for dead; and when I opened the door, my wife was in hysterics, and some people, who were sure I was drowned, were trying to pacify her."[30]

A Roman Catholic, Rombrot's name is absent from the Church of England burial register housed at St. John the Divine; however, he was laid to rest in the Yale cemetery.

Oney, David

1833 - 1873

Forty-year-old David Oney was born in Huntingdon, Quebec, one of Asa and Mary Oney's eleven children. David was married to Elizabeth (Tait) and had two daughters, Ophelia (born 1858), and Harriet (1859). Both girls were born in their father's hometown, although it appears Ophelia did not survive infanthood as her name is absent from the family record in the 1861

Census of Canada. By that time, Oney was a blacksmith in Huntingdon. Sometime in the next decade, he came to the Fraser Canyon and settled in Yale, where his name appears in government documents applying for a license to supply water to the town and to lay pipes underneath its streets. Oney was also employed as a teamster on the Cariboo Road, and it looks as if he had left his wife and daughter behind in Quebec, because he was living on his own when he died in mid-January, 1873. A coroner's inquest was held to determine Oney's cause of death, and it's apparent that he was relatively unknown in Yale at the time, likely due to the itinerant nature of his work. News of Oney's death was carried in Barkerville's *Cariboo Sentinel* on January 18, the same day he was being laid to rest in Yale.

"Yale, Jan. 17 —At three o'clock yesterday afternoon a man named David Oney was found dead in his room by a man, who immediately gave the alarm. It is thought he had been dead some time when found. An inquest will be held this afternoon. Oney formerly owned an interest in the ferry at Quesnel."[31]

The coroner and Yale's Dr. Foster weren't sure of his place of birth, saying only that Oney was "said to be a Canadian." "David Oney," wrote the coroner, "was found dead in his own dwelling house in Yale on Jan. 16. An inquest was held, and a post-mortem by Doctor Foster, who certified to the cause of death as above, and the coroner's jury brought a verdict in accordance."[32] The inquest took place on January 17, 1873, at the McDonald Hotel in Yale, where jurors Benjamin Bailey, B. T. Muller of the California Hotel, William McDonnell, local merchant Peter Clair, shoemaker Daniel McQuarrie, and Thomas Dwyer heard witnesses describe Oney's last day. Thomas Graham, an acquaintance of Oney's gave his testimony:

"Thomas Graham, duly sworn, testifies: I am a labourer residing in the town of Yale. I know the deceased David Only. I met David Seater yesterday after mid-day, and he told me that a Klootchman (Indian woman) had told him that David Oney was dead. I and Mr. Belcher then went up to Oney's house. I went in first; we found him lying on the floor, dead. Mr. Belcher touched him and said 'he's cold; he's been dead some time. I went and repeated it to Mr. Evans, the Constable."[33]

Constable William Evans, who would pass away and be buried in the Yale cemetery ten years later, offered his version of events:

"William Evans, duly sworn, testifies: I am Constable and Gaoler for the town of Yale. I knew the deceased David Oney well. Yesterday about two in the afternoon, Mr. Thomas Graham came to me at the Gaol and reported that David Oney was lying dead in his house. I went to the house and found the body of Oney lying dead on the floor. His face was downwards and blood coming from his mouth. I turned the body over and examined his face carefully but found no marks of violence on it. Oney had been in failing health for a long time."[34]

The inquest also heard the statement of Reverend David Holmes of St. John the Divine:

"David Holmes, duly sworn testifies: I am a priest of the Anglican Church. I have been in the habit of visiting the deceased, David Oney, knowing him to be an invalid. I called at his house about six o'clock on Wednesday evening (January 15, 1873). I knocked at the door but no one answered. I open'd the door and just looked in but no one was there. I went back about quarter before seven and found him at home. We had some religious conversation. He seemed in good spirits as regarded his health, which he thought was improving and spoke of going to Sumas. After a while, we had some little conversation and I left. I saw his door open about twelve o'clock on Thursday morning, but I did not go to his house. I saw it from the church steps about a third past two. I was informed by Mr. Andrew that Oney was dead."

Oney's possessions included a sliver watch, six dollars, "a lot of old furniture, and two old blankets of small value." The cause of death was determined by Yale's Dr. Foster to be a ruptured blood vessel in the lung and an enlarged heart. The expressive hand of Reverend Holmes expanded on this finding, writing in the St. John the Divine register that Oney was "found dead in his house. He had been sick and was thought to be recovering."[35] Oney was interred at Yale on January 18, 1873.

Cline, William

1833 - 1873

Cline was born in Germany about 1833 (the note on his death certificate supposes he was about forty when he died). He was a gardener and general labourer while in Canada, but how he came to Yale remains a mystery. Cline's death certificate reads:

"Deceased was a naturalized British subject. He was attended in his illness by Dr. McInnes, the informant. Mr. McInnes practices as a doctor but admits that he has no diploma."[36]

Given that Cline died from "general debility," it can be assumed that he didn't have access to optimal medical care. In fact, Yale listed no doctor in its directory in the late 1870s. Cline was buried in Yale on January 24, 1873, with the burial rites read by Reverend David Holmes of St. John the Divine.

Reed (or Baxter), William

1828 - 1873

The Cariboo Wagon Road that connected the lower Fraser region with the gold fields of the interior of British Columbia was laid out through the Yale region under the supervision of John Trutch, beginning in 1871. The route through the Fraser Canyon was treacherous and required constant maintenance as washouts and rockslides could happen at any time of year. William Reed was an Irish labourer working on the upkeep of the road between Hope and Yale. On January 29, 1873, Reed and his crew were working on a section of road about ten miles south of Yale when he passed away.

"Deceased was in employment of Mr. T. Spence at the time of his death removing one of the "Sister Rocks" on the Fraser River and informed Mr. Spence that although generally known by the name of Baxter, his real name was William Reed."[37]

Also:

"A man named Baxter, formerly foreman under Mr. Spence on the upper road, died at the Sister Rocks yesterday from disease of the kidneys."[38]

The cause of death was confirmed to be "inflammation of kidneys" by Dr. Foster of Yale. Reed was buried in the Yale cemetery on January 31. A follow-up story on the exploits of Mr. Spence at Sister Rock was published in the *Daily British Colonist* on April 12, 1874:

"Mr. T. Spence has completed the work of removing the Port Sister Rock between Hope and Yale. Mr. Spence has performed a difficult task and we regret to hear that it has been done at a personal loss."[39]

Goercke, Henry

1821 - 1873

Goercke was a miner working the gold-bearing sandbars in the Yale area in the years after the frenzy of the 1858-59 rush. He was born in Hanover,

Germany, about 1821, and passed away on March 1, 1873, of tuberculosis, at the age of fifty-two, in Yale. His burial was not handled by St. John the Divine, as the conscientiously detailed records of Reverend Holmes make no mention of him in the church's official records. Goercke's gravesite has been lost.

Buie, Thomas Russell

1837 - 1873

Thomas Buie was born to James and Isabella in Garmouth, Morayshire, Elgin, Scotland. In 1851, when Thomas was fourteen, his father was listed as an innkeeper and blacksmith in Speymouth, Scotland. Thomas arrived in British Columbia in the early 1860s, as the Civil War was raging in the United States. He was married to Agnes Caroline Laumeister on April 1, 1866, at Victoria First United Church, and by the next year, was a telegraph operator at Lytton. The Buie family lived in Lytton for the next six years, when Buie, on his way to see a doctor in Victoria, passed away in Yale on April 20, 1873. Notification of the thirty-six-year-old's death was sent by telegram, likely to his own station in Lytton. The cause of his death is not listed, and his burial was overseen by Reverend David Holmes. Buie's grave remains in the Yale cemetery, an upright marker surrounded by an iron fence.

Foster, Robert

1839 - 1873

Born in 1839 in Picton, Ontario, Foster was a physician living in Yale in the early 1870s. He was found dead in his home on June 22, 1873. William Teague, acting as the district registrar for Yale wrote on Foster's death certificate:

"Inquest held, verdict returned, deceased died from causes unknown."[40]

Isaac Oppenheimer, a local merchant and the brother of future Vancouver mayor David Oppenheimer, signed as the informant on the record of Foster's death.

Diederichs, William

1828 - 1874

Born in Hanover, Germany, in 1828, William Diederichs was a trader in the Yale area in the years between the gold rush and the construction of the CPR. On August 27, 1874, heart disease claimed his life. He was about forty-six years old at the time of his death. He identified as a Catholic, so his name is not recorded in the St. John's records, but he was buried in the pioneer cemetery. Local government agent William Teague (buried in one of the most prominent plots in the cemetery) signed Diederichs's death certificate.

McIntee, Ann

1832 - 1876

No records remain of the McIntee family or their involvement in Yale, although there was a P. McIntee in the 1868 directory, and "McEntee" serving as Yale's butcher in 1874. They may have been an itinerant family, as Ann's death certificate doesn't indicate much connection to the town. She had no doctor and the signing informant, a James Fitzpatrick, was from New Westminster. What is known is that Mrs. McIntee was born in County Cavan in Ireland in about 1832, she was the wife of Patrick McIntee, and was forty-four years old and pregnant when she died in or near Yale on August 18, 1876. According to the death certificate, written in William Teague's hand, McIntee died of "inflammation of the womb while in a state of pregnancy."[41] Mrs. McIntee, a Roman Catholic, does not appear in the St. John's burial records.

Guiterez, Rosario

???? - 1877

Rosario Guiterez was a Mexican-born packer working on the Cariboo Wagon Road when he died of causes unknown, on March 27, 1877.

Jeffrey, Andrew

1827 - 1877

Jeffrey was a Scottish miner working in the Fraser Canyon in the years before construction began on the railway. He died on June 7, 1877, of unknown causes, at the age of fifty, and was buried in Yale by Reverend Ditcham.

Forsyth, Matthew

1830 - 1877

There is no death certificate available for the Scottish-born Forsyth. What is known is that he was a miner working near Yale in the years between the gold rush and the construction of the CPR. On October 22, 1877, he died unexpectedly, and was interred at the Yale cemetery four days later. The suddenness of his passing is noted by Reverend George Ditcham in the St. John's burial record. He notes, "Fell dead. Heart disease." Forsyth was forty-seven when he died.

Denny, Hugh

1838 - 1878

Denny was an Irish-born packer working in and around Yale and the Cariboo Wagon Road in the 1870s. He suffered from consumption (tuberculosis) and passed away from the disease on August 23, 1878, at the age of forty. Reverend Good's notation in the St. John's church records reads "died of consumption, weather very hot."[42] Denny was buried the same day he died, and the exact location of his gravesite is unknown.

Mayes, William C.

1832 - 1878

William Mayes was a native of Hall County, located in the northern part of the state of Georgia. His early years were spent farming in the American south, alternating between his birthplace and nearby Lumpkin County. While the gold rush was raging in Yale, Mayes was married to a woman named

Lucinda, and together the couple welcomed a daughter, Mary J. Mayes, in 1859. The year 1860 saw Mayes move, seemingly without his wife and infant, across the United States to Tuolumne, California, where he was employed as a "ditch tender," presumably helping out farmers in the area. His stay in California was short, however, and as the American Civil War raged, Mayes moved back to Georgia where he and Lucinda had a second daughter, Milley, in 1863. In 1870, the family was living in Polksville, Georgia, and although the circumstances around William's move north are not known, he acquired the Branch Saloon in Yale on April 3, 1873. At that time, the town was a stop on the Cariboo wagon road, and Mayes would have been a contemporary of Edwin Peck, Daniel MacQuarrie, William Teague, and the Oppenheimer brothers as businessmen of Yale. There are no mentions of Lucinda, Mary, or Milley during this time.

The Branch Saloon had been previously owned by a W. Sutton and Mayes bought it from the estate of the recently deceased George Dunbar. Photo evidence of the establishment is dated 1868, so it may have been able to survive the years of Yale's decline after the end of the gold rush. Mayes is one of only two saloon keepers listed in 1874, but if he had lived to see the commencement of railway construction and the subsequent boom in Yale a few years later, he would have had competition from the many drinking establishments that would once again spring up along Front Street. William was involved in an incident in 1873 that merited attention from the *Daily Colonist* in Victoria.

"Yale, Oct. 15 (1873) —Weather: Bright, clear and sharp. On Monday last, Mr. W. C. Mayes, proprietor of the Branch Saloon, received a severe wound and narrowly escaped death from the accidental discharge of a double-barrelled shotgun. Mr. Mayes was in the act of raising the gun from the floor when the hammers caught against the side of a safe and discharged both barrels, carrying away the end of his middle finger, passing through the fleshy part of the butt of his thumb on the left hand, grazing the left temple, and lodging both charges in the ceiling. The wounds, though painful, are not considered dangerous, and the sufferer commands the sympathy of all."[43]

On August 20, 1878, Mayes died of consumption and was buried in the cemetery above the river. He was attended to by Dr. John Sebastian Helmcken and Reverend Good. Helmcken was a key figure in bringing British Columbia into Confederation, and there are streets in Victoria and Vancouver that bear his name. The Reverend notes that Mayes was known as "Buck" by the locals. The monument to William Mayes' resting place has survived over 135 years and can still be seen in the Yale Pioneer cemetery.

> **"BRANCH" SALOON,**
> Front Street, Yale.
> NEWTON ASH, Proprietor.
>
> **BRANCH RESTAURANT,**
> Opposite Branch Saloon,
> JAMES COWLES,
> Proprietor.
>
> This Restaurant is now so favorably known that lengthy recommendation is unnecessary. Suffice it to say that the present building was erected for the purpose now used and we expect not only retaining old friends and patrons, but with our increased facilities be able to do better than ever and secure new customers. We have a Private Dining Room and give particular attention to getting up Ball Suppers, Evening Party entertainments, etc. The best of OYSTERS kept on hand.
> House open day and night.

> **W. H. SUTTON,**
> WHOLESALE AND RETAIL
> DEALER IN
> **WINES, LIQUORS AND CIGARS,**
> Coal Oil and Coal Oil Lamps, &c.
> SOLE AGENT FOR
> LYON & CO.'S CELEBRATED
> **CALIFORNIA ALE!**
> IN BBLS. AND HALF BBLS.
> Yale, April, 1866.

Neilson, George William

1853 - 1878

George Neilson was a native of Belleville, Ontario, born there around 1853. He was living in Yale in 1878, where he was employed as a clerk in the offices of Uriah Nelson. Nelson was a well-known businessman in town, operating a freight-shipping outfit along the Cariboo Wagon Road in the years before railroad construction, and a general store on Front Street during the boom times. Neilson, only twenty-five, committed suicide in Yale on September 3, 1878. The *Daily Colonist* in Victoria carried the news of his death:

"Suicide at Yale—Early on Tuesday morning last, a young Canadian named Neilson committed suicide at Yale by shooting himself through the temples with a five-shooter. Deceased was a native of Belleville, Ont., aged about twenty-five years, and came to this country a few months since, when he was engaged by Mr. Uriah Nelson to take charge of his store at Yale. During Mr. Nelson's absence in (the) Cariboo, it appears Neilson had some slight misunderstanding with a person connected with the firm, and that in consequence thereof, he voluntarily relinquished his position. On the return, however, of Mr. U. Nelson to Yale, Mr. Neilson again accepted charge of the store, and had been employed only a few days under his second engagement when he committed suicide. In the room where he died, he left a long letter to Mr. Goodenough, telegraph operator at Yale, the contents of which will be made public at the inquest and will probably explain the circumstances that induced the young man to kill himself."[44]

Neilson's body was found in Uriah Nelson's store. A lay minister of the church named Alex Shaw officiated the young man's burial service as Reverend Good was away at the time. He reveals that the coroner's jury determined Neilson was temporarily insane when he committed suicide. The coroner's inquest acted quickly and the *Daily Colonist* carried the results and the contents of the suicide note on September 8, 1878:

"About seven o'clock on Tuesday morning, the third of September, the inhabitants of Yale were saddened by the announcement that George Wm. Neilson, a young man of much respectability, late of Belleville, Ontario, who was in the employ of Mr. Uriah Nelson as a clerk, had shot himself with a pistol, and had been found lying on a bed in his bedroom adjoining the store. The ball had passed through his head, causing death almost immediately. Deceased was twenty-five years of age, and had resided there for about five months, during which period he had gained the esteem of all the leading inhabitants of the place, and was much respected for his unassuming and pleasant manner. The cause of this rash act has cast quite a gloom over the neighbourhood, and the following copy of the letter found on a chair by deceased's bedside is sufficient to explain the cause of the mysterious deed:

Yale, Sept. 3d, 1878.

Friend Goodenow—When you receive this the writer will have taken a short walk. You will please take my personal effects and whatever balance may be at my credit here and give me a half-decent burial, and don't believe me guilty of any dishonest things. The only thing, and I firmly believe that when —— has seen any **** to get into the safe through an omission of**

an entry in the cash book, or vice versa, he having the key, has availed himself of every opportunity during my absence and has now brought on my death; my blood be upon his head. I wish you to take what personal effects I may have; write to my mother, Mrs. Geo Neilson, Belleville, Ontario, of my death sending her whatever cash may be (if there is any) left after seeing me planted. Break the news as gently as possible, and try to evade the disease which took me off. Goodbye, old fellow, God bless you,

[Signed] George Wm. Neilson.

An inquiry was held over the body on the same day by B. Douglas, Esq., Coroner, when the jury returned a verdict that deceased came to his death from a pistol shot fired by his own hand."[45]

With names censored, Neilson's note tells the story. The twenty-five-year-old accountant seems to have been under suspicion of stealing from Nelson. And judging from the *Colonist*'s tribute to Neilson as a well-liked and respected young man, his reputation had taken, or was about to take, a major blow. In response, he was so distraught that he chose death. Neilson was buried in the Yale cemetery on September 4, 1878, and the and any visual evidence of whatever money his friend was able to spend to give him a "half-decent burial" has been wiped away by the years.

URIAH NELSON,

Front Street, Yale,

General Merchant, Dry Goods, Groceries, Liquors,

CLOTHING, BOOTS & SHOES, &c , &c.

Freighting by Mules and Ox Team to Cariboo and way places.

Lewis, John

1857 - 1878

One of only five to be buried in the Yale cemetery in 1878, John Lewis was a teamster hailing from London, Ontario. His work carried him over the relatively new Cariboo Wagon Road in the years before the Canadian Pacific altered the trade route through the Fraser Canyon. Lewis was only twenty-one when he was struck down by illness on September 14, 1878. According to Reverend John Good, Lewis died while undergoing treatment by Dr. Frickleton at Yale, and, although the young man was sick, his death was unexpected. "Died suddenly whilst under medical treatment,"[46] the Reverend recorded in the burial records. "Congestion of the lungs," [47]reads Lewis's death certificate in William Teague's hand. Lewis may have lived in Cache Creek, as his informant, a George Stuart, notes that he only remained in Yale while he was sick.

Geordique, Dominique

1818 - 1878

Geordique was a French-born farmer living in Yale in the years leading up to the construction of the CPR. He died on September 29, 1878, from "congestion of the lungs," according to Dr. Frickleton of Yale. Geordique's death certificate is signed by a Clarence Delahi, "proprietor of the Columbia Hotel, town of Yale, British Columbia, where deceased died."[48] There is no record of Geordique's death listed in the St. John's burial book.

Wheeler, John

1815 - 1889

John Wheeler was a miner, born in England, who likely came to the Fraser Canyon during the gold rush of 1858-59. He was found dead in his bed at the Boston Bar Hotel on July 7, 1889, by John Webb, whose son Peter (see Webb, Peter) would pass away only a few months later. The cause of death for Wheeler was given as old age, and he was buried in the cemetery at Yale.

McLinden, Arthur

1831 - 1879

A native of Peru, New York, Arthur McLinden was the father of James and grandfather of Ernest (see above). He lived in the northeastern New York state town for most of his early life, but by the time he was twenty, he had relocated to Orland, Illinois, with his father and nine siblings. How and when McLinden came to Yale is unclear, but it is documented that, by 1874, he was working as a teamster on the Cariboo Wagon Road in the years before the construction of the CPR obliterated it. In the 1870s, with rumours of impending railway construction swirling, the government began to neglect maintenance of the important route to Barkerville, and the impact was felt by those such as McLinden who depended on it for his livelihood. The area in question was known as Nicaragua Bluff, and it included the Alexandra Bridge, an engineering marvel of the 1860s that was also left to deteriorate. The town of Yale erupted in protest about the neglect of the road, but their outrage seemed to fall on deaf ears in Victoria.

"Yale, British Columbia, July 22, (1875)

Editor *Colonist*: —The road at Nicaragua Bluff, for a distance of seventy-five feet, is gone. It is a most dangerous place—something like a perpendicular fall of 100 feet into the river. There are several teams that will not be able to get beyond that place for some days. It is a serious matter where feed is scarce for horses and mules, and there is no grass for oxen near the break. This is the very time—dry weather—when the road should be good. The teamsters have sent a long dispatch to Beaven (Chief Commissioner of Land and Works). It may be treated like their dispatch of the 9th inst. ("My information is different from yours!") [Commissioner Beaven had responded to complaints about the road's condition by referencing a report from superintendent Neil Black, also buried in Yale, that the road was in serene condition. The *Daily Colonist* of July 25, 1875, notes that, 'Unfortunately for Mr. Beaven, dates are against him. The dispatch from the people of Yale was received by him on the *ninth* July; the road was split open like a melon on the *seventeenth* July.'[49]] The road, of course, will answer for packers, while stages and teamsters cannot move. There is not sufficient force on the road. The men employed are first-class, but the poor fellows are dancing about from one patch to another, which makes it all the more treacherous. There is intense feeling here on account of the cavalier treatment of the dispatch of the merchants and teamsters by Beaven."[50]

The merchants of Yale, including saloon owner W. C. Mayes and freight shipper Uriah Nelson, lent their voices to the chorus of discontent with the government regarding the road and its poor condition, which directly affected the town. Finally, the teamsters themselves appealed to Victoria, with McLinden among the signatories.

> ## The Wagon Road.
>
> ### The Teamsters Make a Second Appeal.
>
> #### They Ask to have More Men Put On!
>
> YALE, July 22nd, 1875.
>
> *To the Hon. Chief Commissioner of Lands and Works, Victoria.*
>
> We the undersigned teamsters are now in Yale with big teams loaded and loading for the upper country. We cannot proceed on our way till the road is repaired. We beg to state that the road is, and has been all spring, in very bad order and dangerous to travel on. There is now a break in the road that will take a week to repair. This news has just arrived, and we have it from reliable authority. We beg you will give the road superintendent authority to hire more men and have things fixed up so that we can travel without endangering our lives and property.
>
> (Signed.)
> RICHARD PHARE,
> J. H. GAY,
> R. CURNOW,
> JOSEPH DEROCHE.
> R. McLAREN.
> W. WALKER.
> I. WALKER.
> ARTHUR McLINDEN.
> JOHN SHATWA.

McLinden's wife was from Boothroyd, and she gave birth to James on June 29, 1879. However, James would never know his father, for exactly two months after he was born, Arthur passed away in Yale from tuberculosis. Bill Teague and Walter Gladwin signed his death certificate and the forty-nine-year-old McLinden was laid to rest in Yale. The location of his grave is unknown.

> **British Columbia**
>
> # MARKET,
>
> Corner Government & Yates sts., Victoria, and Corner Front & Regent sts., Yale.
>
> THE BEST QUALITY OF
>
> ## Beef, Pork and Mutton,
>
> Principally from our own Ranges on the Mainland, will be kept constantly on hand,
>
> VanVOLKENBURGH & Co.

McCormick (or McCormack), William

1824 - 1880

On July 27, 1880, at about two o'clock in the morning, a fire broke out in or near Thomas York's Oriental Hotel on Front Street in Yale. In minutes, the flames engulfed the establishment and the men who had filled every bed fled into the street. "None of the inmates," the *Daily Colonist* reported, "saved a particle of clothing and many were more or less burned about the face and head."[51] The fire struck so quickly and at such a late hour that the town was caught completely off guard, and the results were devastating. Property losses included Uriah Nelson's store and home, Dr. Hanington's office and dwelling, newly constructed railroad buildings, the schoolhouse, Douglas and Deighton's store, livestock, and much more. Losses were estimated at $74,000 (nearly $1.8 million, in 2015 dollars), and the town was struck a serious blow. There were fears that the entire town would burn because of a strong wind blowing up the river that night, "but at the time, the heat was most intense and the railway office in flames, the wind veered in puffs and blew directly across the river—from the south, in fact—so the adjoining blocks escaped."[52] After the flames had died down, everything from the Oriental Hotel on the lower end of Front Street to Albert Street was gone.

Many people were suffered burns, but only two men were badly hurt. "A Mr. McCormick, carpenter, from Nicola Valley, and a Mr. James McKee, from Mud Bay, near New Westminster, were slow in getting out and had to jump through the windows, getting badly burned and considerably cut by the glass. The last-named party belongs to the railway and was taken to the hospital, and the former to a private residence."[53] The *Colonist* elaborated on McKee's fate, saying that the "able-bodied young man was seen to jump from the second storey of the rear part of the building and, on regaining his feet, moaned most piteously. On being approached, he begged not to be touched, even to be assisted to the hospital of the railway contractors situated a short distance up the hill."[54] Dr. Hanington, leaving his wife at home even as their house caught fire, rushed to aid the wounded McKee and quickly realized that the burns covering the man's hands, arms, chest, face, and feet were too much to overcome. The *Sentinel* reported that young McKee died the next evening at about ten o'clock. His body was sent home to New Westminster aboard the steamer Western Slope.

The other victim of the fire was fifty-six-year-old William McCormick, and as badly as McKee was injured by the flames, Dr. Hanington thought that McCormick was in much worse shape. He had escaped the second floor of the Oriental from the front of the building and down a verandah post. His face was burned beyond recognition, "and from his neck down the skin of the body [had] been entirely consumed."[55] McCormick, not being a railway employee, was treated by Dr. McLean, who acknowledged McCormick's grave injuries, and yet described the carpenter as "exceedingly quiet and [appearing] not to suffer much."[56] McCormick did not survive the night. He was buried in the Yale cemetery the day after the fire, and the location of his grave is unknown.

Cartwright, Emma

1862 - 1880

Emma Cartwright, born in Walla Walla, Washington, in 1862, was living in Spences Bridge with her husband, William Jeshua Cartwright, in the late fall of 1880. William was a clerk and his eighteen-year-old wife Emma was pregnant with their first child. Their son William Nicola Cartwright was born in Spences Bridge on November 18, 1880. Tragically, his young mother died from complications arising from the birth the next day, with the official cause of death listed as "apoplexy after childbirth" by Dr. Alfred Sheldon of Lytton.

"Died —At Spences Bridge, Nov. 19, 1880, Emma, wife of Mr. W. J. Cartwright, CPR aged eighteen years. Friends of the deceased are invited to attend the funeral on this Thursday afternoon, from St. John's Church."[57]

In the census of 1881, Emma's husband William is listed as living in a boarding house with their five-and-a-half-month-old son while his wife lay in the Yale cemetery, where she remains to this day in an unmarked grave.

Laidlaw, William

1832 - 1881

William Laidlaw was a bartender in one of the many saloons that appeared in Yale during the boom of railway construction. He was born in Inverness, Scotland and by the 1850s was living in Ontario.

"Died. —In Yale, morning of the 5th (January 5, 1881), of inflammatory rheumatism, William Laidlaw, aged forty-nine years. Deceased was a native of Scotland, and arrived at Cariboo from Oxford, Ont., in 1862, coming to Yale last spring to join Mr. James McLellan in buying out the Maharra Saloon. Those who knew him deeply mourn his loss. His brother came up from Westminster yesterday and the funeral will be today at one."[58]

McLellan, who is described as the "bartender to the deceased," acted as the informant on Laidlaw's death certificate. The funeral was officiated by Reverend Blanchard and, more than 130 years later, his grave marker, although broken, still stands in Yale.

Blanchard, John Albert

1838 - 1881

Blanchard was born in the state of Maine, on January 9, 1838. In census documents from 1860, he is listed as a farmer in Kennebec, Maine, and the same occupation is listed on his death certificate twenty-one years later.

Blanchard came to British Columbia as a young man and settled in the Fraser Valley before relocating to Yale. John Blanchard suffered an aneurism and died April 26, 1881.

"Died —Here on the 26th inst., J. A. Blanchard, aged forty-seven years. Deceased was a native of Maine, but for many years a resident of Chilliwhack (sic). He had been ailing for some months. He leaves a family and many friends to mourn his premature death. Funeral today at 2 p.m. from his late residence on Emory Road."[59]

Edwards, David
1825 - 1881

Edwards was a speculator working in Yale during the early days of railway construction when he died in the summer of 1881. He was born about 1825 in Pittsburgh, Pennsylvania, and came to the canyon in search of gold in the years after the rush of 1858.

"At Yale [due to] illness of general debility, David Edwards, a native of Pittsburgh, Pennsylvania, aged fifty-five. Deceased was one of the early miners in this province, and for some time resided in this town. He had a large circle of acquaintances, and his remains were taken in charge by a number of pioneers here and respectfully buried. [Pittsburgh papers please copy.]"[60]

Reverend Good listed Edwards' cause of death as heart disease; however, his official death certificate cites liver problems.

Lane, George
1829 - 1882

In 1882, what was previously said to be impossible was accomplished. The Skuzzy, a sternwheeler commissioned by Andrew Onderdonk to move railway supplies along the river north of Yale, reached Boston Bar. To date, no vessel had ever negotiated the rapids at Hell's Gate and, with water levels in the Fraser at a forty-year high, odds were given at 100 to one against the boat reaching its destination. The Skuzzy sat below the rapids through the spring of 1882; it wasn't until September that the ship would beat the odds. Onderdonk ordered 125 Chinese railway workers to the banks above the river and, straining at the cables fed through bolts hammered into the rock face, the unsung heroes of the CPR guided the Skuzzy through the impassable whitewater and onto Boston Bar, two weeks later. The accomplishment was recorded in the *Inland Sentinel* with a few lines that seem out of proportion with the scale of the event.

"The little Skuzzy has succeeded in getting to Boston Bar after nearly two weeks' effort. Capt. Smith and assistants deserve credit for the pluck, perseverance, and skill. She is to ply between Boston Bar and Lytton."[61]

There were two small stories below the acknowledgment of the Skuzzy's successful voyage, but more lines were dedicated to the passing of George Lane, whose death took place not far from where the ship pierced the heart of the Fraser.

"Accident —Monday last George Lane, a Cornishman, known here for twenty-odd years, was passing near Rombrot's (17 miles above this place,) when he fell off the bridge and was killed. He first struck some fifty feet down and bounded over the rocks a further distance of about seventy feet. Deceased was aged about fifty years. He was known as a good miner, but addicted to the intoxicating cup. He was brought down Tuesday by Mr. Alway and buried the same evening."[62]

Lane does not appear in the St. John the Divine burial register, so his funeral was likely not conducted by the church. The Alway mentioned in the *Sentinel* piece is John Alway, a local farmer and businessman. Lane's grave marker is intact in the cemetery and can be seen to this day.

Peck, Edwin

1824 - 1882

Edwin Peck was laid to rest next to his wife in the Yale cemetery on October 23, 1882, by the Church of England's Bishop Sillitoe. His death came as railroad construction had transformed the town from a sleepy stopping point on the Cariboo Wagon Road into a boomtown, and Peck, a carpenter, was no doubt very gainfully employed. His wife, Maria, and daughter Annie had accompanied him from his native England to Canada, where before the birth of their daughter in Peck's hometown of Wigan in 1852, he had worked as an oil cloth manufacturer. The family was living in Ormskirk, Lancashire, in 1861, and the exact date of their immigration to Canada isn't known, but he was considered a pioneer by his fellow Yale residents. The *Inland Sentinel* carried two notifications of his death on October 21, 1882:

"We regret to announce the death of Mr. Edwin Peck, an old and respected resident of Yale. The deceased was ailing only a few days, and his demise was altogether unexpected. The funeral took place Monday afternoon, from his late residence, Douglas Street, and was attended by all the pioneers of this place."[63]

Followed in the next column by the more succinct:

"Death —In Yale, on the 21st inst., Edwin Peck, a native of Wigan, Lancashire, England, aged fifty-seven years.[64]

In Dr. Frickelton's unsteady hand, he notes that the cause of death was "drink, collapse of the heart."[65] Peck's exact address can be found in the 1882 Yale directory, which lists him living at the corner of Douglas and Albert Streets. Maria had died in Yale in 1871, and her gravestone can still be seen, but Edwin's is gone.

J. D. FRICKELTON, M. D.

Member of College of Physicians & Surgeons Ont., and Registered in B. C.

Office Front Street, YALE, B. C.,

Cures all chronic or diseases of long standing; all who have tried other Physicians without benefit, give him a trial. Particular attention paid to the eye and ear and all Female complaints.

— In all cases of Hydrophobia and Cancer the money will be returned if a cure is not effected—provided the parties have not submitted to mercury or the knife.

Squire, James

1827 - 1882

Fifty-five-year-old James Squire was a nomadic jack of all trades who was likely in the Fraser Canyon seeking work on a CPR construction gang. He was from Zurich, Hall County, Nebraska, but it appears he had not lived there for some time. During the late 1870s, he was a prolific letter writer, keeping his family informed as to his whereabouts, health, and current employment. The letters, each of which began with the same "Dear folks at home," were sent from places like Walla Walla, Washington, Portland, San Francisco, and Seattle. Left behind at home were Squire's wife, Jane (McCune), and daughters, Ida and Sarah. Their firstborn, Catherine, had died in 1856 at age three. In his letters, Squire doesn't mention why he was traveling for work, but he does go into great detail about the jobs he took. From a sheep ranch, he wrote, "I am going to try my luck shearing. I think I can make good wages if I can stand the work."[66] He harvested grain in Walla Walla in 1878 and sought work as a carpenter in Oregon. In the late autumn of 1882, Squire boarded the steamer "Gertrude," which carried passengers, freight, and mail between Hope and Yale.

"James Squire died suddenly on the 3rd inst., from disease of the heart, while returning from the steamer 'Gertrude,' after taking a portion of his baggage on board. He was taken charge of by the Government Agent, who at once telegraphed to his daughter, who resides at Zurich, Hall Co., Nebraska, and wrote to his wife by mail, acquainting her of the facts of the case. Deceased was aged about fifty-five years. There was found upon his person $461.25—of which $300 was in gold. The remains were respectfully buried on Sunday under direction of Govt. Officer Dewdney."[67]

It's not clear if Squire had already been working in the area, or was just arriving and passed away en route to Yale. Reverend Whiteway conducted the burial service along with Edgar Dewdney in the Yale cemetery on November 5, 1882.

> **SELLING OFF!**
> **SELLING OFF!**
> **'CHEAP FOR CASH!'**
> The Remaining Fall and Winter
> **STOCK OF**
> **Dry Goods,**
> **Boots and Shoes, etc.,**
> TO MAKE ROOM FOR A LARGE CON-
> SIGNMENT OF SPRING GOODS.
> **KWONG LEE & Co.,**
> YALE, B. C.
> Feb. 20, 1883.

Evans, William

1822 - 1883

William Evans was born around 1822 in Glamorganshire, a county in Wales, and moved to the Yale area early enough in its existence to be known as a pioneer. In fact, Reverend Horlock refers to Evans as such in the "occupation" column of the St. John's burial record book. In 1861, Evans had been appointed jailer and constable for Yale. He was also the tollgate keeper on the Cariboo Wagon Road at Yale between 1862 and 1866. In subsequent years, he was also a constable in Lillooet. His home base, however, was Yale.

"Another Pioneer Gone. —William Evans died at the 'Oriental Hotel,' where he has been stopping for some years, this (Friday) morning, after a long complaining and brief severe illness from general debility, his age stated to be about 60. We learn from Mr. Budlong, undertaker, that the funeral will take place at 3:30 p.m. tomorrow (Saturday), to Yale Cemetery. Deceased was a native of Wales, and came to this country at the time of the gold excitement twenty-odd years since. He has been off and on from here to Lillooet, Cassiar, etc., as a Government constable; but of late years has remained at Yale, occasionally occupied in taking prisoners to New Westminster. We understand he made a will—having had some property— in favour of a brother, whose whereabouts is not known here at present; he was last heard from in Australia. Messrs. Gladwin and Alway, old-time friends, are the Executors. A matter that worried deceased a good deal of late was the manner in which the D. Government ... took possession of his property—where the Railway machine shop is—without giving what was thought by the owners fair compensation."[68]

Evans died of heart disease on March 2, 1883. The location of William Evans's grave within the Yale cemetery is not known.

Rathburn, Phoebe

1807 - 1883

Then as now, Queen Victoria's birthday gave the citizens of the Dominion a reason to take a day off to celebrate. The difference in 1883 was that the queen was alive, celebrating her sixty-fourth birthday in the forty-sixth year of her reign. Queen Victoria died in 1901, and the holiday that marks her part in Canada's history has become increasingly distant from the reality of acknowledging the "Grandmother of Europe." Today, "Victoria Day" has become the "May long weekend." The run-up to May 24, 1883, however, was greatly anticipated in Yale, and great tribute was paid to the queen as the town celebrated her birth as it did every year by holding a festival highlighted by all types of athletic competition. In 1882, the 100-yard dash awarded a first-place prize of $15, while the winners of the nine-a-side tug-of-war were the proud recipients of a keg of beer.

"Although somewhat late at moving in the celebration of the coming twenty-fourth, a liberal spirit prevailed in subscribing and it is now expected a good programme will be presented in a few days. Sports such as canoe racing, running, jumping, greased pole, etc., will be presented and, no doubt, well-contested. The committee in charge will use their best endeavours to honour the queen's birthday and satisfy the people of Yale and vicinity."[69]

The day after the big celebration, however, was also the day that Phoebe Rathburn died. She was born in Pennsylvania in 1808 and was a widow. She was spending time visiting her daughter and son-in-law in Yale when she died of old age as the town cleaned up from the party and the winners counted their money.

"Died —In Yale, on the 25th inst., at the residence of her daughter, Mrs. A.E. Angel, Mrs. Phoebe Rathburn, aged seventy-five years, formerly of New York State."[70]

Phoebe's son-in-law had been a warehouse clerk for the CPR. Reverend Horlock officiated Mrs. Rathburn's burial service in the Yale cemetery the day after she died.

McGirr, Mary Jane

1853 - 1883

Mary Jane (Davis) McGirr was born in Ontario in 1853. On October 20, 1870, she married William McGirr, an Irish-born carpenter in Glenelg, Grey County, Ontario. The couple would remain in Ontario until 1876, when they left for British Columbia. By that time, they had added sons, William (born 1873), Howard (1874), and newborn daughter, Annie (1875). The family lived in Vancouver, where daughter Ellen was born in 1878, and in Esquimalt, where Maude was born in 1880. Mr. McGirr bought a share in the California Hotel on Front Street and served as a tobacconist to railway workers and locals alike. In 1881, Howard passed away in Yale of heart disease. Sadly, less than two years later, on August 28, 1883, Mary Jane McGirr passed away, her life claimed by tuberculosis. News of her death appeared in the *Inland Sentinel* two days later.

"Died—In Yale, 28th inst., of consumption, Mary Jane, the beloved wife of Mr. William McGirr, aged thirty-one years and four months. Deceased was a native of Durham, County Grey, Ontario, and came to British Columbia in May, '76. She bore her long suffering with Christian resignation and full hope of Heaven. Everything was done that a devoted husband, relatives, and numerous friends could possibly do to ease her gradual decline. She leaves a sorrowing partner, four children, and cousins Messrs. J. and D. Davis and M. Staples, and host of intimate acquaintances to mourn her premature end. The funeral took place yesterday at 3:30 p.m., Mr. Ridley, of St. John's Church, officiating. The coffin was covered with a beautiful floral cross and wreaths of choice flowers, tokens of affection from dear friends. The attendance was large, and under the direction of undertaker Budlong, everything was orderly. During the funeral, all places of business in town were closed."[71]

Mr. Ridley was a lay minister at the church, as Mrs. McGirr's funeral would have been conducted by Reverend Horlock, who was away at the time. By 1891, William McGirr had moved his family to New Westminster, and had remarried a woman named Alice who was eighteen years his junior and only a few years older than eldest son William.

Tingley, Alex
1860 - 1883

If one lived between Yale and the Cariboo between 1860 and the 1880s, there was an excellent chance that they knew the Tingley name. Stephen Tingley, a native of New Brunswick, arrived in Yale in the gold-rush years and was a largely unsuccessful prospector. His true calling was discovered in the just-as-lucrative shipping industry that developed as miners tramped north from Yale to the Cariboo gold fields. The Cariboo Wagon Road, built between 1862 and 1865, opened up the interior of the province to stagecoach lines like Billy Ballou's express company, which carried everything from letters to work boots and mining tools. Ballou sold his Yale-based company in 1861 to local businessmen George Dietz and Hugh Nelson, who ran Dietz and Nelson's British Columbia and Victoria Express until 1867, when they sold to Francis Barnard.

Barnard attained legendary status because of his humble beginnings in the shipping game: he transported mail from Yale to Barkerville on foot, a one-way journey of 380 miles. After completion of the Wagon Road, Barnard acquired stagecoaches and horses and expanded his successful business by hiring Stephen Tingley in 1864. Tingley quickly gained a reputation for being the best stagecoach driver on the Wagon Road, and he parlayed that success into a quarter share of the entire company, sold to him by Barnard. The company from that point until its demise in 1920 became known as the British Columbia Express, quickly shortened to the more well-known moniker, "The BX." Tingley personally carried everything from gold dust to royalty along the road, and on it he suffered his greatest loss: the death of his wife, Elizabeth.

"Yale, September 21. —Yesterday as Mr. Tingley and family were returning from a buggy ride, his horse took fright at a wheelbarrow standing on the road at the bluff just above town, and threw themselves over the bank, dragging the buggy and occupants after them. Mrs. Tingley was very badly hurt about the head and now lies in a very precarious condition. She has been insensible since the accident. Mr. Tingley and the boy escaped with some cuts about the head, but none of them are seriously injured to cause apprehension. Dr. McInnes was telegraphed for from New Westminster, and arrived by special steamer at 10:30 a.m. today. He pronounces Mrs. Tingley to be suffering from a fracture of the skull. One of the horses was killed and the buggy very much broken, and it was swept away by the river as soon as the fastenings to the dead animal were cut away. It is thought that had it not been for the death of one horse the whole party would have been swept off by the river."[72]

Followed by:

"Yale, September 22 —Mrs. Tingley died at 8:30 this morning."

By 1886, Tingley had become the sole owner of the BX, but not before suffering yet another personal tragedy. In 1878, Stephen Tingley's youngest brother, Alexander, came west to join the BX as a driver. Twenty-five years younger than Stephen, Alex had been born on April 10, 1860, in Pointe de Bute, New Brunswick, the son of Caleb Tingley and Deborah Tuttle. The younger Tingley spent his early years on the family farm, and came to Yale when he was eighteen to learn the shipping trade. Unfortunately, in his fifth year on the Wagon Road, Alexander was struck by typhoid fever, and while convalescing at Stephen's home in Yale, was overcome by the disease. News of his death was printed by the *Inland Sentinel:*

"Died —At the residence of S. Tingley, Esq., yesterday morning, after a few weeks' illness of typhoid fever, Alexander Tingley, aged twenty-three years, a native of Pointe de Bute, New Brunswick. Deceased came to this district about five years since and has been in the employ of the BC Express Company, of which his brother is Superintendent, and was well known all along the Cariboo Road especially. Few young men could be more regretted, for his mild manner, and unblemished character, together with strict attention to duty, made him a favourite along the line. The funeral will take place tomorrow (Friday) at 11 a.m., when, no doubt, a large attendance will do honour to the remains of the departed."[73]

The next week, the *Inland Sentinel* carried the description of Tingley's funeral:

"The funeral of the late Alexander Tingley was largely attended last Friday. The remains were placed in a metallic coffin (with the intention of removing them to the home of his parents, East, hereafter), and an outside shell provided, which presented a neat floral offering, cross, and wreaths. The Rev. Mr. Hall, of Sumas, officiated at the house and grave, and Sunday morning, preached an eloquent and feeling sermon for the occasion to a highly respectable congregation. He referred to the exemplary character of the deceased and had good reason to believe he had gone to his reward, where cares and troubles cease."[74]

It appears that the planned move of Tingley's remains to New Brunswick never took place and, today, the only remnant of the once-prominent Tingley name in Yale is Alexander's elaborate grave marker, which stands almost unblemished in the pioneer cemetery. Stephen Tingley ensured that his brother was honoured with the marker, which reads "He hath done all things well." Tingley's grave also allows a glimpse into the deterioration of the cemetery in the greater part of the twentieth century, as earlier photos show the marker awash in weeds, while today, thanks to the efforts of dedicated individuals attached to the Yale and District Historical Society, Alexander Tingley's burial plot can be easily visited.

Holmes, Lionel West

1814 - 1883

Lionel Holmes was born in early 1814 in Howsham, Lincolnshire, England, to Lawson and Anne Holmes. He was baptized by the Church of England on March 20, 1814, in Cadney and married Elizabeth Skipwith on January 13, 1847, in Cabourne, a village not far from his birthplace. In the following years, Holmes worked as a farm manager for his widowed sister-in-law in the same town. Holmes filed for bankruptcy in 1854 in Caistor, another nearby town. There is no record of his voyage to Canada; however, there is a Lionel West Holmes listed in *Henderson's British Columbia Gazetteer and Directory* of 1889 as a resident of Yale working as a night watchman presumably for the CPR. Strangely, this record was published six years after L. W. Holmes' death in 1883, suggesting either that the listed Holmes was his son or the directory was somewhat out of date.

"Sudden Death. —Mr. L. W. Holmes, of this place, has been complaining for some time past and Tuesday morning Messrs. Kirkup and Ridley found him sitting upon the floor in his cabin near the railway office, dead. As his body was warm when found, it appeared that he had not been long out of bed when discovered. Deceased was aged sixty-nine years, a native of England and an old resident of British Columbia; he has lived at Yale for the past three years, and lately employed in looking after the Reading Room. Of a quiet and obliging manner, he will be missed from the position he lately filled. We learn he has a son in London, and other relatives who have regularly corresponded with him. The funeral took place yesterday at 3 p.m., Rev. Mr. Horlock officiating."[75]

The death certificate for Lionel West Holmes records his date of death as September 18, 1883, when, at the height of CPR construction through the Fraser Canyon, the sixty-nine-year-old collapsed and died suddenly of heart disease. The grave of L.W. Holmes in the Yale cemetery is unmarked.

Powers, Emeline Almeda

1842 - 1883

Emeline McCoy was born in 1842 in Durham County, Ont., the daughter of Samuel and Jerusha. Samuel was an American-born storekeeper, and Emeline was their firstborn. She married local farmer James Powers on April 1, 1869, but the marriage lasted only just over a year as James passed away on July 24, 1870. The next year, on December 29, 1871, Emeline married James's brother Hartwell and they had a daughter, Eva, in 1873. Son Lucius George Powers followed in 1878. When Yale became the headquarters for construction of the Canadian Pacific Railway in 1880, the opportunity to establish a business in a booming economy lured people from all over the continent to the shores of the Fraser. Hartwell and Emeline relocated to Yale in 1881 where the family opened a general store called Powers Bros. on Front Street to cater to the expanding town. Sadly, on May 20, 1882, Emeline's four-year-old son Lucius passed away in Yale from scarlet fever, while Emeline herself was in poor health. Just before Christmas in 1883, she died of heart problems that had plagued her for several years.

"Died—On the 12th inst., Emeline, the beloved wife of H. A. Powers, of the firm Powers Bros., in her forty-second year. Deceased has been suffering for some time from dropsy, and early in October with her husband and little daughter spent a few weeks at Chilliwhack (sic) and came home apparently some better. But her sudden taking off argues how deep-seated was her ailing. She was a devoted wife and mother, and fixed Christian principles. Her death is deeply mourned by all who knew her. The funeral took place yesterday afternoon and was largely attended, Rev. Mr. Horlock officiating."[76]

H. A. Powers, after losing his son and wife in the space of nineteen months, remained in Yale for several years, eventually remarrying and having more children. He relocated to Victoria after the completion of the railway and the inevitable decline in business. In 1887, he moved to the United States, and lived out his years in Los Angeles. Emeline was laid to rest beside her son in the Yale cemetery with a ceremony officiated by Reverend Darrell Horlock. The double grave marker is still standing, and reads: "She was a kind and affectionate wife and mother and friend to all."

Berg, Andrew

1816 - 1884

Andrew Berg was sixty-eight when he passed away on February 21, 1884. He was buried the next day by Reverend Darrell Horlock.

Cassaliggio, Michail

1840 - 1884

Cassaliggio was an Italian miner working in and around Yale when he died of consumption, the term used at the time for tuberculosis, on July 3, 1884. He was attended to by Dr. Ernest Barron Hanington, the CPR company physician. His funeral was conducted by Reverend Darrell Horlock, and Cassaliggio's death certificate was signed by Francois Chapperon, who would pass away two years later and is also buried in the Yale cemetery. Cassaliggio was forty-four years old at the time of his death.

Campbell, Bridget

1831 - 1884

The only record of Bridget Campbell is that she died on September 26, 1884, at the age of fifty-seven, and that her husband was Patrick Campbell. Her grave marker remains in the cemetery, adding to the mystery of their connection to Yale.

Nickerson, John

1847 -1885

Nickerson and his brother George were merchants on Yale's Front Street during the construction of the Canadian Pacific Railway. They both served as barbers and druggists, and ran the Magnolia restaurant on the crowded thoroughfare, taking advantage of the town's booming railroad economy. John was born on March 7, 1847, in Gloucester, Massachusetts, to George and Jane Nickerson, younger than brother George by two years and older than sister Eliza by the same. George Nickerson Sr. was a fisherman in the coastal town, born there before the United States was even fifty years old. The family remained in the area for George's entire life, but the sons were gone to Nova Scotia by 1870, where they worked as fishermen in the town of Wood's Harbor. In the following years, they would come west; their names do not appear in Yale until 1885, the year of John's death. On April 4, the thirty-five-year-old passed away from tuberculosis ("consumption," on his death certificate). His friend Thomas Michell (see Michell, David) acted as the signing informant on Nickerson's death certificate. He was laid to rest in the pioneer cemetery that spring by Reverend Edwin Wright in a grave that is today unmarked.

Gill, ????

???? - 1885

The mysterious entry in the St. John's record of burial only lists the last name "Gill," someone who died on September 5, 1885, and was buried the next day by Reverend Wright.

Chapperon, Francois

1814 - 1886

Chapperon was born in Savoie, a small town in eastern France, seven years before the death of Napoleon. When he came to Canada and how he ended up in Yale remain a mystery, although his name does appear on a Kamloops district land claim register in 1880. During the railway construction boom in Yale, Chapperon was the proprietor of the French Bakery, located on Front Street. A Roman Catholic, Chapperon does not appear in the St. John the Divine burial records. He was most likely buried by the Catholic church, but in the Church of England cemetery. Chapperon was seventy-two years old at the time of his death from natural causes on September 12, 1886.

McKenzie, Margaret

1818 - 1886

Margaret McKenzie, like her husband, William (see above), was a native of Pictou, Nova Scotia. She lived with her husband, daughter Jessie Revsbech (proprietor of Yale's Borden Hotel), and other family members in Yale from about 1885, so she was not a resident for long. She passed away October 2, 1886, from causes unknown and was buried in the Yale cemetery. Her grave marker still exists today in the cemetery, and her casket plate is on display in the Yale Museum.

Oppenheim, Louis

1811 - 1890

Not to be confused with the Oppenheimer brothers, also of Yale, Louis Oppenheim was a well-known figure around town in the 1870s and '80s. Details of his early life are lost, but it is known that he was born in Poland (although some sources say Frankfurt, Germany), and that he arrived in the state of Missouri in 1844. His name appears again in the *First Victoria and British Columbia Directory* in 1867, where it states that Oppenheim operated a dry goods store on Front Street with neighbouring businesses, including the aforementioned Oppenheimer brothers' general store, Uriah Nelson's store, and Adam McLardy's bakery. His name is misspelled more than once as "Oppenheimer" in the directories.

Osamote, the Roman Catholic chief of Spuzzum, had a daughter, Nukwa, whose English name was Hannah. She married Louis Oppenheim in Yale and had several children who were confirmed in the Church of England, as Hannah herself had been. Louis Oppenheim was Jewish, but had no opportunity to attend a synagogue in Yale."[77] When they were married in 1870, Louis was sixty years old; Hannah just fourteen. Soon, they welcomed the first of their eight children, a son named Phillip, born in Yale in 1872. Daughter Rachel followed in 1874, followed by Esther (1876), Rose (1879), Helen (1881), Dorothea (1883), and David (1886). Louis became a father for the final time in 1889 at age seventy-nine when son Nathan was born, like all of his siblings, in Yale. Nathan would be just over a year old when his father passed away the next year.

Oppenheim left the retail trade in the early 1870s and his title in the local directories changed from "merchant" to a "gentleman," living on Albert Street, where the last two decades of his life were devoted to his wife and children. However, as the announcement of his death in the *Vancouver Daily World* reveals, those final years were not the best of Oppenheim's life:

"Yale News/Notes. —Death of an Old Pioneer—The Fraser Rising Percepty (sic)—Siwash and Queen. —On Tuesday morning last, April 29th, Mr. Louis Oppenheim, an old and respected pioneer, died at the age of seventy-nine years, after an illness of several weeks' duration. It was evident to his friends that he was 'sick unto death,' and he was aware of his approaching end, as he made known his desires respecting his funeral to Mr. Teague. The funeral took place on Thursday afternoon, May 1 (1890), when a large number of friends assembled at the residence of the deceased. A procession was formed, and the family and friends of the deceased followed his body to its last resting place, Yale Cemetery, where the Church of England burial service was read, the officiating clergyman being Reverend Mr. Croucher, of Vancouver.

"Our departed friend, having desired a Masonic burial, his brother Masons resolved to carry out his wishes. The bearers were Messrs. Teague, J. P., Dodd, Oliver, and Page, who wore Masonic dress. Mr. Oppenheim opened a store in Hope in 1858. At that time, Hope was head of navigation of the Fraser River. The inhabitants of Yale determined to make their own town the head of navigation, which they accomplished by building the steamer Yale in 1861. This steamer was blown up on the Easter Sunday of the same year about five o'clock in the evening.

"Mr. Oppenheim, with other merchants, removed to Yale, where he conducted a large and successful dry goods business, retiring with a competency about the year 1870. After quitting business, he visited relatives in California. Before returning home, he left with his friends $15,000 for investment, believing he could invest his money better in California than in British Columbia. In this, he was, however, unfortunately for himself and family, mistaken, for we are informed that those with whom he had deposited his fortune speculated with it during the Stock Exchange excitement in California and Nevada, and he was left dependent upon the kindness and beneficence of the friends he had made in this country. The respect which the elders of Yale entertained for Mr. Oppenheim was shown by the fact that at the time of his decease, he was a member of the Board of School Trustees, a position he had held for some twelve years. He always took a great interest in the public school, and his children were among the most punctual and regular attendants. He has left behind him a family of eight children, five of whom are under eleven years of age. Under the circumstances detailed above, they are totally unprovided for. Their case is one for the consideration of the benevolent, and we are sure Mr. Teague, who was so well acquainted with the deceased, will be pleased to furnish any particulars to inquirers."[78]

After his death, Oppenheim's older children would have likely been working to help with the family finances, but things would have been tight for them, especially because Yale had been left behind by the boom years of railway construction. At least three of the Oppenheim daughters attended All Hallows school in Yale, and Rose became a talented basketmaker following the traditions of her Nlaka'pamux ancestors. In 1896, Hannah married Eli Joseph Martel, a widower from Quebec who owned land in the

Spences Bridge area. The couple had at least three children and fourteen years together before Hannah passed away in 1910 and was buried in the Spences Bridge cemetery. As for Louis, his relative success in life would not be evident to someone if they just read his death certificate. The final words on a man who had amassed $15,000 to invest (an amount that would be at least $400,000 in 2016 dollars) would be written by the hand of his friend, William Dodd: "Died in destitute circumstances." Oppenheim was laid to rest by Reverend Charles Croucher. His grave marker has long been lost.

Fink, Peter

1836 - 1890

Peter Fink was born in Hanover, Germany, in 1836. He was a hotelier and storekeeper in North Bend, British Columbia, and also served as the town's postmaster from 1884 until his death. In 1881, he was a single father to Annie (born 1870), Henry (1872), and John (1875). Fink's name appeared in newspapers in 1882 as he fought the provincial government in the Supreme Court over his inability to secure a liquor license for his hotel, which he had constructed in the CPR town to take advantage of business brought by the railway. This seemed to be an ongoing problem for Fink, as he reappeared in the Victoria papers six years later, again appealing a decision by the government to disallow a liquor license for his business. On this occasion, the Member of Parliament who brought up Fink's case in the legislature was Charles Semlin, who would go on to become Premier of British Columbia in 1898. On July 18, 1890, the fifty-six-year-old Fink died after a three-month affliction of dropsy (today known as edema). He was succeeded as North Bend's postmaster by his son, Henry. Fink was interred at Yale a few days later. The family business again made the news eighteen months later:

"Peter Fink's hotel at North Bend, which had been in existence since the opening of the railroad, was totally destroyed by fire this morning."[79]

Morrow, Mary Jane

???? - 1891

All that is known about Mary Jane Morrow is that she was born in Edmonton and passed away in Yale on December 18, 1891. She was interred in Yale two days later.

Johnson, Joseph

1827 - 1892

Sixty-five-year-old Joseph Johnson, a miner originally from Virginia, was found drowned on March 22, 1892.

Lawrence, Jackson (John)

1828 - 1893

Lawrence was an Ohio-born butcher and farmer living in Yale in the post-railway construction years. He must have had a small farm between Douglas and Front Streets, as Lawrence is listed in the 1887 British Columbia directory as a dairyman. Yale's decline in the years after the construction crews moved on would have opened up land for such agricultural operations in a once-bustling area. Lawrence had at least one daughter, Lucie (Holmes), who was born in Yale in 1860. In 1893, at the age of sixty-five, Lawrence died what must have been a painful death from a strangulated hernia. His death certificate was signed by William Teague before he was buried at Yale by Reverend Croucher on March 1, 1893, four days after his death.

Lamb, James

1846 - 1893

"Found dead on railway track near North Bend having been killed by a passing train. (Not) known how or by what means he came to be on the tracks. No evidence ... appears to the jurors (of the coroner's inquest)"[80]

This is the way the life of James Lamb came to an end on September 6, 1893. The inquest held by the coroner could come up with no reason as to why Lamb, a blacksmith living in North Bend, was on the tracks, nor why he was struck. A story that ran in the September 13, *Winnipeg Tribune* offered no further insight:

"Killed in the West —James Lamb, a Brother of Conductor Lamb, the Victim of an Accident. —Conductor Lamb, of the CPR, has gone to British Columbia, being called west on a telegram announcing the death of his brother, James Lamb. No particulars were given further than that deceased had been killed in an accident. Deceased was a blacksmith, and was employed in the CPR shops at North Bend, British Columbia."[81]

From the *Vancouver Daily World*:

"On the morning of the 7th inst., the body of James Lamb was found three miles east of North Bend in a horribly mutilated condition. He had been struck by a westbound passenger train. The coroner's jury attached no blame to anyone."[82]

No follow-up stories were published, so while Lamb's cause of death was determined, the circumstances surrounding it are still a mystery. Reverend Croucher buried the forty-six-year-old on September 11, 1893, in the Yale cemetery.

Rowe, Charles

1844 - 1894

Another native of Cornwall, England (see George Rouse, above), Charles Rowe was a gold miner working in the Fraser Canyon who arrived after the gold rush and continued on through the railway construction years and beyond. He had been in the Yale area for almost thirty years, arriving in town in 1868. On September 24, 1894, Rowe was killed in accident at Siwash Creek when a mineshaft in which he was working collapsed. Death was instant, and no doctor attended him. His body was recovered and brought to the Yale cemetery for burial, but today, Rowe's grave is lost.

Smith, George

1865 - 1898

As the 1800s drew to a close, there was still great interest in the gold-bearing sandbars of what the miners called "Father Fraser." While the rush of 1858 had slowed to a trickle, gold seekers were using the most advanced technology of the day to extract the Fraser's treasure. Men still combed the shores of the river from Yale to the inland gold fields of the Cariboo, but instead of washing pans full of gravel, large-scale dredges were deployed along the river. "In 1899," wrote T.W. Paterson, "the Yale Dredge Company turned its attention to Hill's Bar with its newly built 80-foot-long dredge which, supposedly, was capable of lifting 100 yards of gravel per hour."[83] In 1896, the Ottawa Mining and Milling Company operated a successful dredging operation at Boston Bar, pulling $1,830 (approximately $50,000 in 2016 dollars) from the river. "A very good return, considering the disadvantages encountered," noted the yearly mining report for that year. "The company is fully satisfied with the richness of its ground."[84] Two years later, the *Victoria Daily Colonist* carried the news that "the Ottawa people at North Bend made a second clean up this season and I understand it was satisfactory. The dredge at Boston Bar seems to be quite a success also."[85]

For George Smith, however, the Boston Bar dredge was where he met his end, in October 1898. Smith was a thirty-three-year-old able seaman who served on the Canadian Pacific Steamship, "RMS Empress of China," which sailed between the Canadian West Coast and the Far East. Smith was from Liverpool, and, after serving for a few years on the ship that brought mail from Hong Kong to Britain via Canada, he took a job working on the Boston Bar dredge. On October 22, 1898, Smith fell overboard and was presumed drowned.

"Last week, Coroner William Teague held at Yale an inquest on the body of the late George Smith, thirty-three years of age, a native of Liverpool, England. He was formerly an able seaman on the Empress of China, and was drowned on Saturday, October 22, 1898, by the swamping of a scow, near Boston Bar, in the Fraser River. The body was picked up at Emory by an Indian, on April 29 (1899). Though the body was in the water over a period of six months before it was found, it was in a remarkable state of preservation when picked up. After the inquiry, and the verdict of the coroner's jury—"found drowned"—the remains were interred, the funeral services being conducted by the Rev. C. Croucher, of the Episcopal church. The body was carried by the strong current of the Fraser canyon for a distance of thirty-one miles."[86]

Smith's grave in the Yale cemetery is today unmarked.

Anderson, George Webster

c. 1805 - 1899

Born in Dublin, Ireland, Anderson was a miner, bartender/saloon keeper, and hotel manager in Yale. The son of a farmer, Anderson took up the same occupation in his early life in Ireland. He sailed across the Atlantic in the late 1830s, settling in Lac-Beauport, Quebec, where Anderson continued to farm. He was a widower when he landed in Canada, but remarried on May 23, 1842, to Catherine Berryman in Saint-Gabriel-de-Valcartier, near Quebec City. They lived in Stoneham, Quebec, for the rest of their married lives, until Catherine passed away on April 7, 1883. A widower for the second time at age seventy-eight, there is evidence that Anderson concluded whatever business he had in Quebec and set his sights on the West Coast almost immediately following his wife's passing. His name first appeared in Yale's directory in 1891; the eighty-six-year-old listed his profession as "miner;" however, he was conducting business in the by-then-booming town in 1883. Whatever the circumstances of his cross-country move, retirement, it seems, was not an option for Anderson. In addition to mining, Anderson had a stake in the Railroad House hotel, an establishment located across the railway tracks from the current location of the Yale Museum on Douglas Street. Under the ownership of prominent Victoria furrier and soap-maker Arthur Churton and the management of Churton's brother-in-law, Reuben Elley, the octogenarian Anderson was employed as the establishment's bartender. In competition with a number of other such businesses in Yale at the time, the Railroad House was struggling in the mid 1880s and Churton was eager to divest himself of the hotel. In a letter to Anderson dated October 1, 1883, he wrote:

"Mrs. Churton being very ill and the Railroad House Yale being a great source of anxiety to us having been the means of completing my ruin. Are you prepared to buy us out or have it sold? An early answer will oblige."[87]

In other correspondence between the two, Churton chastised Anderson for forwarding rent money to Victoria late and in the incorrect amount. The contentious partnership was dissolved by 1884, as Churton and Anderson decided to sell the business to Simon Kinmond, a Scottish-born baker and storekeeper whose name appears on later advertisements for the Railroad House in the *Inland Sentinel*. George lived the rest of his years in Yale, and died on February 5, 1899, at the age of ninety-four. News of his demise was carried in Victoria's *Daily Colonist*:

"News has been received from Yale of the death of Mr. Anderson, proprietor of the Railway Hotel at that place. The deceased was well up in years. The funeral will take place at Yale."[88]

The oldest person on record to be buried in the Yale Pioneer Cemetery, George Webster Anderson, was laid to rest on February 6, 1899, by Reverend Charles Croucher of St. John the Divine. He lies today in an unmarked grave.

Creighton, Mary Alice

1870 - 1900

Mary Alice Ward was the daughter of Yale gold rush pioneer William Henry Ward of Digby, Nova Scotia, and Alice Squalabia, a Sto:lo Tait woman from Yale. At the time of their marriage, William was sixty-three and Alice was thirty years his junior. William was a teamster and worked between Yale and Barkerville on the Cariboo Wagon Road. He and Alice had eight children, five of whom were born before their wedding day on October 25, 1886, in Yale. Four years later at the age of sixty-seven, William became the proud father of little Amy Annie. When her youngest sister was born, Mary Alice was already twenty years old and had been married for five years to David Creighton of Yale. Mary and David had five children (see Amy Lillian Creighton) together. Sadly, Mary passed away six days after son Moses's thirteenth birthday on January 28, 1900, and only two weeks after her mother Alice had died in Yale. Dr. Proctor attended Mary Alice, and the cause of death was listed as "puerperal septicaemia,"[89] indicating that she was likely pregnant when she died. She is buried with her husband in the Yale cemetery.

Ward, William Henry and Alice

William - 1823 - 1915
Alice - 1856 - 1900

William Henry Ward was born in Digby, Nova Scotia, about 1823, to Benjamin and Sarah Ward. He came west in 1858 to try his luck at prospecting for gold on the Fraser, but it appeared he soon abandoned this pursuit and took up freight packing along the trails leading north from Yale into Cariboo country. After the construction of the Cariboo Wagon Road in the 1860s, Ward, who went by the nickname "Johnny" for most of his life, made his living as a teamster, hauling freight and passengers over the route, but always calling Yale home. He fell in love with Alice Squalabia, a local Te-it (also spelled "Tait," a Salish word meaning "those up river") woman and, in 1868, they welcomed a son named Albert. Seven more children would follow over the years: Mary (born in 1870), George (1878), Elizabeth (1879), Louise (1881), Nellie (1883), Annie (1888), and Deallia (1892). Tragically for William and Alice, their firstborn, Albert, was killed in 1872 in a stagecoach accident. The Wards became hotelkeepers in Yale during the railroad-construction years after the shipping industry was largely taken over by the CPR, although he was still identified in the late 1880s as a shipper.

Ward ran the Station Hotel, located across the tracks from the church, and his family home was a few doors down. The original Ward house and barn were destroyed in the massive Yale fire of 1880, but the home was quickly rebuilt and remains today as a glimpse into the town's past. It is open to the public during the warmer months as the Ward Tea House, a restaurant and gathering place and a chance to view one of the few remaining 1880s-era buildings in Yale. In 1900, Johnny's beloved Alice passed away, leaving him a widower at the age of seventy-seven. He remained in Yale over the next decade, likely with his youngest daughter, before finally moving in with daughter Louise Sturdevant in Flood, where he passed away in 1915. In an interview with Ward's granddaughter Irma Teskey, she said, "I like to recall, too, Grandfather Ward living out his last days with us on the farm at Flood. He loved to tell about his sea voyage around Cape Horn back in 1858, and his tales of Barkerville were full of the adventure of freighting to the goldfields."[90]

Johnny Ward lived ninety-one eventful years and saw Yale grow and decline, yet remained faithful to the little town. He is buried in the Yale Pioneer Cemetery, but over the years, his grave marker has disappeared. Alice Ward was also buried at Yale after she died in January 1900. Unfortunately, her grave has also disappeared.

Castle, Maggie McLinden

1875 - 1904

Castle was born in 1875 to Arthur and Lilly McLinden. By 1891, at the age of sixteen, she was married to August Castle, son of Martin Castle Sr. The marriage took place in Yale, where their five children would be born. The first,

Frank, was born in 1890 when Maggie was fifteen, followed by Helen (1891), Herbert (1894), Arthur (1897), and Margaret (1902). Castle passed away when she was twenty-nine years old, on February 21, 1904, from gastritis, leaving her husband, August, to raise their five children. Her grave marker reads "Faithful to her trust even unto death." It remains in the Yale cemetery.

Jackson, Mary Anne
1848 - 1906

Mary Anne Jackson (née Beattie) was born on December 22, 1848, in Ireland. In 1906, she was living with her husband in a camp along the CPR line near North Bend, British Columbia, where she died in a rather shocking accident on May 2, 1906. According to the findings of a coroner's jury:

"We believe upon our oaths that the said Mary Anne Jackson came to her deathly acute alcoholic poisoning by drinking a crude alcohol and believe the (drink) was taken in ignorance owing to the bottle not being marked poison."[91]

Mrs. Jackson was interred at Yale on May 3, 1906, by Reverend Croucher in the pioneer cemetery.

Alway, John
1827 - 1908

John Alway was a prominent member of Yale society since the 1860s. He arrived in Yale during the gold rush not to find his fortune in the mining claims that covered the river's banks, but to set up a business to serve the miners that flooded the area. In the following years, most of the miners moved on to try their luck elsewhere, but Alway stayed in Yale. He was a teamster on the Cariboo Wagon Road, reflecting Yale's importance as a trans-shipment point for freight and people between the lower Fraser and the gold fields near Barkerville. His business was a shipping concern on Yale's Front Street with partner Benjamin Bailey from the early 1860s until the partnership was dissolved in 1868.

In 1869, Alway made news when an Indian guide tried to kill him. The *British Daily Colonist* of Victoria carried the news that "The Indian sentenced to death at the late Yale Assizes for attempting the life of John Alway, has had his sentence commuted to penal servitude for life."[92] In 1880, he was celebrated as one of the town's twenty-year residents. By this time, he was farming in the Fraser Canyon and was a contemporary of hotel owner Thomas York, government agent William Teague, and famous Cariboo road teamster Johnny Ward. Alway served on more than one grand jury in the Yale assize court, a group that regularly consisted of Yale's businessmen and who, in 1881, made the following plea:

"Prison Labor —We have frequently urged that some change be made in the practice of conveying prisoners from Yale to New Westminster. No good reason can be given for neglecting the streets of this town, while expense is created in shipping offenders against law and order down the river. Since the commencement of railway work, considerable police business has had to be looked after, and it is well known here that heavy expense has been saddled upon the province. Every person visiting Yale must witness the neglected appearance of Front and other streets; this could easily be remedied by causing prisoners to work here instead of using their strength where comparatively little need exists. There is plenty of room in the prison here for half a dozen prisoners, and one officer could guard the gang, while picks, shovels, and wheelbarrows are no great expense. This is a subject worthy of the attention of our government, and, no doubt, a grateful people would give due credit to whoever moves in the matter and secures the improvements sought after. Now, at the opening of the spring, is the proper time to repair streets, sidewalks, etc. A few weeks' work would make a great difference in the looks of our streets, and Yale would no longer be known as 'the neglected village.'"[93]

A Yale old-timer named Everett Cox reminisced about John Alway in an interview:

"The one that served the whole community in navigation time with vegetables and fruit was old John Alway. John Alway, when he first came to the country, was with Barnard's Express. He wasn't a miner, he was with the Express, with stagecoaches and horses. He bought this property originally from a man named Hicks. He came here originally with Barnard and Bailey Express. This property here that we're on—Father bought it—John Trutch bought it from Alway. When Alway got it, he got it from someone named Hicks. Who he was—whether he was a Hudson Bay man, or who—I don't know. When Trutch bought it from Alway, he sold it to my dad. He had it for about fourteen years before he sold it to Father."[94]

A monument still stands to John Alway in Yale: the Teague House. Alway acquired the land the house sits on at auction from the Colony of British Columbia in 1865. He constructed the house in 1866 and sold it three years later. Today, it is an active bed and breakfast on the grounds of Fraser River Raft Expeditions, with owners dedicated to the preservation of its colourful history. John Alway passed away on November 2, 1908, in New Westminster, at the age of eighty-one. While his burial is not recorded in the register kept by St. John the Divine, he did at one time have a grave marker in the Yale cemetery. Yale's greatest historian A. C. Milliken wrote in the *Hope Standard* in 1977 that of the Cariboo Wagon Road's stage-driving heroes, Alway was one of only three that had some kind of monument in Yale. "John Alway," he wrote, "who arrived in 1858, whose small tombstone is in the Yale cemetery."[95] Since 1977, however, Alway's grave marker has disappeared.

Black, Neil
1840 - 1909

Neil Black was born on the west coast of Scotland near Argylshire on April 9, 1840. Black was in the Fraser Canyon during the gold rush, beginning in 1858 and remaining in the area for the rest of his life. In the 1870s, he was a maintenance foreman for the Cariboo Wagon Road based in the area where today Highway 1 crosses the Fraser at Chapman's Bar near Spuzzum. He was also a railroad foreman in the 1880s, and became a storekeeper in his later life. On March 2, 1909, Black died, leaving behind his wife, Suzy. News of his death appeared in the *Chilliwack Progress:*

"Was an Old Timer —Neil Black, one of the best-known pioneers of the famous gold rush to the Fraser River fifty years ago, and who during the following years was engaged as foreman on the construction of the government wagon road to Cariboo, is dead. He was in charge of the building of that section of the road from Yale to Lytton, and the feat which he accomplished in building a road at all through the canyon of the Fraser River had been a wonder to engineers and travellers for several decades. Black lived a lonely life in a small cabin at Spuzzum in the canyon of the Fraser, preferring to remain close to where he had sought gold and worked so many years. The cause of his death is unknown at present, as he was found dead on the road near Spuzzum."[96]

From the coroner's report:

"Having heard the evidence we are of the opinion that Neil Black died from natural causes, most probably heart failure while walking along the railway back about (a half) mile west of Spuzzum and that he was about sixty-five years old."[97]

Black was buried at Yale and his grave is not marked.

Castle, Monica

1860 - 1910

Monica was the wife of Martin Castle (see above). Researching her life is difficult because of the many different spellings of her name. She is recorded as Monica, Monash, and Monique, with the surnames O'Riley, O'Reilly, and Silweltow. From the Castle family notes:

"Martin Castle Junior married Monica or Monique O'Reilly. Monique was the illegitimate daughter of Peter O'Reilly and his aboriginal housekeeper, Gertie Jennie. Gertie was probably a native of Vancouver Island.

"Monique was educated in the white man's ways and the English language. Gertie Jennie taught her the native tongue and culture; her father Peter O'Reilly introduced her as a court interpreter. She moved to the mainland from the Island."[98]

She died sometime in 1910 of unknown causes. Her grave marker is still visible in the Yale cemetery.

Ward, Charlotte Delia

1892 - 1910

Charlotte was the youngest child of Johnny and Alice Ward, long-time residents of Yale, where Johnny worked as a teamster and hotelkeeper. On the census form in 1901, her name is recorded as "Deallie,"[99] referred to as "Charlotte" in the St. John the Divine church burial register. Her father was almost seventy years old when she was born on November 19, 1892, in Yale. Her mother, Alice, passed away in 1900 when Charlotte was eight years old, and not much is known about her life after that date. She passed away in May 1910, after a battle with pneumonia, and was buried in the Yale Cemetery.

Mitchell, Earnest

1881 - 1911

Earnest Mitchell was a resident of North Bend, British Columbia. The thirty-year-old passed away on January 27, 1911, and was brought to Yale for burial by Reverend Croucher.

MacQuarrie, Jessie Milroy

1853 - 1911

The MacQuarrie Family

Jessie MacQuarrie (née Kellie) was a native of Southampton, Ont., the daughter of James and Jessie Kellie. Her father was a farmer in the small community on the shores of Lake Huron. In 1876, she married Daniel MacQuarrie, a Yale-based bootmaker in Southampton. By 1877, the newlyweds were living in Yale, where their daughter Margaret was born that same year. Jessie and Daniel would go on to have ten children, eight of whom were born in Yale, including William Yale MacQuarrie, delivered by his father in 1888. Daniel ran advertisements in the *Inland Sentinel* for his Front Street store, and the family maintained a farm west of town. The MacQuarries lost their business and home in the fire of August 18, 1881, blamed on a sleeping drunk on the second floor of the Caledonia Hotel. The resilient family rebuilt and flourished once again in Yale. Jessie was also a midwife, assisting in many births between 1885 and 1901. The family relocated for a time to New Westminster, where their last two children were born. On November 14, 1911, only five weeks after the death of her husband, Daniel, Jessie passed away in Yale. News of her death was carried by the *Victoria Daily Colonist:*

"Mrs. Jessie M. MacQuarrie, aged fifty-eight years, widow of the late Mr. Daniel MacQuarrie, who pre-deceased her by but five weeks, died at Yale, British Columbia, on November 14. Five daughters survive the deceased lady … and four sons…. Interment took place in Yale."[100]

Reverend Croucher noted that Jessie's death had been caused by a stroke, and she was buried in the Yale cemetery next to her husband on November 17. The grave markers of Jessie MacQuarrie and her husband, Daniel, still stand today in the Yale cemetery.

MacQuarrie, Daniel
1839 - 1911

> **Look Here!**
> D. MacQuarrie,
> BOOT AND SHOE MAKER,
> Front Street, Yale, B. C.
> Boots Made to Order. Repairing done neatly.
> Work sent any where in British Columbia, c. o. d.
> LADIES, GENTS & CHILDRENS
> Ready Made Boots, Shoes and Slippers kept in stock. Sold Cheap for Cash.
> General assortment of Leathers and Shoe Findings kept on hand.

Daniel MacDonald MacQuarrie was born on April 26, 1839, in Lanarkshire, Scotland. He was the son of John and Elizabeth MacQuarrie. MacQuarrie worked as a carter, delivering goods in a two-wheeled horse-drawn carriage throughout Glasgow. It's not known when he came to Canada, but his name is prominent in the Yale community directories beginning in 1874. He was the town's bookmaker and ran a shop for many years on Front Street, including during the boom years of railway construction. He was married in 1876 to Jessie Milroy Kellie (see above) in her hometown of Southampton, Ontario. The couple would reside in Yale where MacQuarrie sat on many committees, ran his business, and tended to his farm on Gordon Creek, west of town. Jessie was Yale's primary midwife for many years, delivering babies in Yale and Hope. The MacQuarries would have ten children—five sons and five daughters—most of whom were born in Yale, one delivered by Daniel himself. MacQuarrie passed away on October 8, 1911, in New Westminster, noted by Reverend Croucher in the church's burial records. It's unclear why Daniel was living in New Westminster while Jessie remained in Yale during those years, but the pair would be reunited in the Yale cemetery, as Jessie passed away a little over a month later, on November 14. Their graves are still intact.

Robertson, John

1840 - 1912

Robertson was an Englishman who passed away on February 9, 1912, and was buried in Yale the next day. The cause of death was given as "senility." He was interred by Reverend Croucher of St. John the Divine.

Neilson, Martin

1883 - 1913

Neilson was not from Yale, but was passing through the area when he suffered a grisly death just east of town while travelling on a westbound CPR passenger train. According to coroner L. A. Agassiz, Neilson was killed instantly when he fell from the train and was cut in half. The young man was about thirty years old and was thought to have lived near Kamloops; otherwise, all fields on his death certificate are labeled "unknown."

Strouse, Henry

1850 - 1913

Henry Strouse was a German-born farmer living in the Fraser Canyon near Yale in the early twentieth century. He had lived in the area for almost twenty years when he was found dead about six miles from town, on January 22, 1913. Strouse was never married and appears to have led a solitary lifestyle. He had been dead for several days when his body was found, and it appears he was overcome by the winter conditions in the Canyon. He was laid to rest in the Yale cemetery, where he lies today in an unmarked grave.

McKenzie, William

1815 - 1913

William McKenzie was the father of well-known and long-time Yale resident Jessie Revsbech. His wife, Margaret, passed away in Yale in 1886. Mrs. Revsbech was a hotelkeeper in Yale and ran a successful business even in the years after the CPR construction was complete and the town's population had shrunk from the thousands in the 1880s to less than a hundred a decade later. She first ran the Railroad House, which burned around 1911. Following that, she was proprietor of the Hotel Borden on Douglas Street, which gained a reputation for being one of the best hotels in the vicinity. In his later years, McKenzie, a farm labourer from Pictou, NS, relocated to Yale, where he lived the last three decades of his life as a labourer and farmer, likely helping his daughter as he was living at the Hotel Borden when he died on February 24, 1913. His passing was announced in a few short lines in the *Chilliwack Progress*:

"One of the oldest residents passed away last Saturday in the person of William McKenzie. Mr. McKenzie was born in the year and month of Waterloo (Napoleon's final battle in June 1815) and was therefore in his ninety-eighth year. For the last thirty-two years, he has resided in Yale with his daughter, Mrs. J. Revsbech. The funeral took place on Monday and was attended by nearly every resident."[101]

McKenzie's funeral was officiated by Reverend Harold Underhill, who had arrived in Yale in 1907 to serve as the chaplain at All Hallows and to assist Reverend Croucher with his many duties. William McKenzie's gravestone has survived the past century in very good shape and can still be visited today in the Yale cemetery.

Unknown
???? - 1914

Reverend Charles Croucher of St. John the Divine made a note in the church's burial registry of two unknown men who were "killed whilst stealing a ride on a freight train"[102] on March 31, 1914. One of the men was twenty-two years old; there is no mention of the other's age. The two were buried in a common grave in the Yale cemetery on April 2, 1914.

Haines, W. Annie
1867 - 1916

Annie (Beynon) Haines was born in Dowlais, Glamorganshire, Wales, on April 27, 1866, to Elias and Elizabeth. She was the eldest of the family's three children, the sister of Charles (born 1869) and Edmund (born 1874). Elias was a tobacconist in Christchurch, Wales, in 1881. Annie came to Canada around 1911 and was living with her husband, Charles, in North Bend, British Columbia, when she passed away from the flu on January 20, 1916. Annie and Charles had been married for nineteen years and she was forty-nine at the time of her death.

Teague, William
1835 - 1916

One of the most prominent names in Yale from the gold rush through construction of the CPR to the quiet years of the town's fade from glory was William Teague, local miner, landowner, and government agent. He was born on July 18, 1835, in the village of St. Day, Cornwall, England, and arrived in California during the gold rush of 1849. Following the news of the rich paydays on the sandbars of the Fraser, Teague came north to Hope and Yale, where, following a stint in the Cariboo prospecting for gold, he would remain for the rest of his life. Returning to St. Day in 1871, he married

Alice Michel and welcomed daughter Charlotte the following year. The young family returned to Yale and had six more children (see Alice Teague). Unfortunately, daughter Charlotte and son Cundy (a family name from William's mother's family) passed away in a scarlet fever epidemic in 1881 that robbed not only the Teagues, but several other families, of more than one child. As a government agent and part-time coroner, William's signature is on most official documents from those years in Yale, including a great number of death certificates of railway workers killed on the construction gangs of the CPR. Teague was also a landowner in and around Yale and continued his work as a prospector, his name being attached to the Queen's silver mine above Yale and various other mining claims in the district.

In addition, Teague, along with a few partners, operated a cattle ranch in the Chilliwack area, driving them to Yale and on to the Cariboo. The Teague family home, bought from Joseph Trutch, is still standing in excellent condition in Yale and can be visited as part of an outing with local rafting company Fraser River Rafting Expeditions, who have taken great care to maintain the home and offer it as a bed and breakfast. It, along with the Ward house and the Yale museum, give a fantastic look at what life was like in the time of Yale's almost surreal beginnings. In 1916, on a visit to his daughter in Seattle, William Teague passed away.

"Pioneer of Cariboo Dead —Came to British Columbia in Gold Rush Days. —Mr. William Teague, one of the best-known local residents and an old-timer known all over the province, died here last evening. He was born in Cornwall, England, in 1835. He left England in 1855 (though he is often referred to as a Forty-Niner) and came to America, travelling to California around the Isthmus of Panama. He was three months into the journey and was not yet twenty years old when he reached the gold fields of the western United States. He mined and prospected in California for three years and then, at the time of the general excitement over the gold discovery on the Fraser River, came toBritish Columbia, in 1858. Deceased was a passenger on the first boat that sailed from California for Victoria. From there, he pushed on to Hope and then to Cornish Bar and mined and prospected there in the vicinity of Yale until 1864. In that year, he staked claims in the Cariboo country, walking a distance of 600 miles to locate them, and these he developed until 1875, when he was appointed provincial government agent of revenue of Yale, an office he held for twelve years. In 1871, Mr. Teague was married to Miss Alice Mitchell, of Cornwall, England, and they became the parents of five children."[103]

Two weeks later the *Progress* gave more details of William's passing:

"Yale News —The death of William Teague, who was a resident here for fifty years took place in Seattle. The funeral was held here by Reverend C. Croucher, last Monday. The honorary pallbearers were William Dodd, Edward Stout, and D. J. Creighton of Yale, and Isaac and Henry Kipp of Chilliwack, and W. A. Blair of Vancouver. Many old friends from a distance came to pay their last respects. Of seven children, five daughters survive. All were present with their widowed mother at the funeral service. For many years, Mr. Teague has been one of the best-known figures in the Fraser Valley. In earlier years, he took a keen interest in political and other public questions. He was an Anglican in religion, a Liberal in politics. He retained his faculties unimpaired to the end and, as he had a retentive memory, he was a very interesting talker on the events and characters of pioneer days. His death leaves another gap in the rapidly dwindling company of the men of '58."[104]

William Teague's grave can be visited today in the Yale cemetery in the most prominent plot on the grounds.

William Teague

Flann, James Francis Miller

1889 - 1917

James Flann was born in November 1889, to Thomas and Jane Flann, both immigrants to Canada from England in the 1870s. Thomas had been previously married to Almeda (Irwin), but the union was short-lived and produced no children. Thomas was born in Alberta, the oldest of six children, the rest of whom were born in British Columbia. The family suffered many tragedies in the 1910s as their second-born, James's sisters, Florence (Paffard) and Susanna, and Florence's young son died in that decade (see Paffard). In 1911, Thomas was employed as a quarry foreman in the Boston Bar area, and James was working for the Canadian Pacific Railway as a watchman and brakeman, based in North Bend. Tragically, James drowned in the Fraser River on September 8, 1917.

"Body Found At Yale. —Agassiz, October 13. —The body of the late Mr. James Flann, a CPR brakeman, has been found floating in Deadman's Eddy in the Fraser River, about three miles above Yale. Mr. Flann was out fishing about three weeks ago when in some unaccountable manner he fell into the river, which runs swiftly at that point. Much sympathy is expressed for his widow and parents, who reside at North Bend."[105]

After his body was recovered, Flann was buried at Yale; his funeral was officiated by Reverend Yates. Unfortunately, his grave is unmarked, but it is probably in the vicinity of the other members of his family interred there.

Cox, Samuel

1875 - 1917

Samuel Cox

This was a man of many names. On his enlistment papers in 1916, he is officially known as Samuel Lemuel Andrew Winston Cox, and often went by the name "Sunset." Born on January 26, 1875, in Inverness, Megantic County, Quebec, Cox was the son of Thomas and Catharine. Sunset and his six siblings were living on their parents' Megantic farm in 1891. It is likely that the name Sunset was given to him in tribute to an American congressman with the same name, Samuel Sullivan "Sunset" Cox (1824-1889). In 1897, Sunset married Annie Winifred Foster in Inverness. They would spend some time in the United States, as their son Everett, also interred at Yale, was born in St. Johnsbury, Vermont, approximately 150 miles from their Megantic County hometown.

The family was living in Yale in 1911, when their son Arthur died tragically in the Fraser River. Four years later, the Cox family called Hope home. Sunset was a carpenter by trade, and he was living with his family in Hope in 1916, when he enlisted to fight and swore allegiance to King George V as a member of the 131st Battalion of the Canadian Expeditionary Force. He was forty-one years old when he signed up and, unfortunately, like Martin Castle, also buried in Yale, his enlistment would be cut short by illness. By March 1917, Cox was frequently in hospital, battling what would eventually claim his life, pulmonary tuberculosis. "Disease took the usual course," reads his Canadian war grave register form. He passed away on November 1, 1917, in Vancouver, at the age of forty-two, and was buried at Yale with a temporary wooden fence surrounding his plot. In the ensuing years, Cox's grave came to be marked by a First World War headstone from the Commonwealth War Graves Commission. His grave remains in excellent condition in the Yale cemetery.

Ward, Annie Amy

1888 - 1920

Annie Ward was the daughter of longtime Yale residents William Henry and Alice Ward. She was born in Yale on February 22, 1888, and was baptized at St. John the Divine in 1890. Her father, known locally as Johnny, had lived in Yale since the gold rush days. At the time of her birth, he was a failed prospector and successful teamster. Her mother was a Tait (or "Te-it," meaning "those up river") woman whose ancestors had lived in the Fraser Canyon for centuries. Annie was the fifth of six surviving children born to the couple, who didn't marry until 1886, after they already had four children. Annie moved to Vancouver when she was about sixteen years old, finding work as a housekeeper and living on Hastings Street in the eastern section of the city. Unfortunately, she became ill in late 1919, and passed away on January 6, 1920. She was returned to her hometown of Yale and was interred in the local cemetery. Today, however, the location of her grave is unknown.

Whitley, William and Susan

William - 1841 - 1921

Susan - 1850 - 1927

The Whitley family appears to have moved to Yale about 1903. There, William was a gardener and orchard keeper. He was born in 1841, in Linn County, Missouri, while Susan, born in 1850, hailed from Calhoun, about 120 miles south. The couple had a son, Archie, in 1872, and moved to the Yale area in 1903 when they were already grandparents, although it appears their son relocated with them as he lived in Lytton for many years. William passed away in Yale on March 2, 1921, at the age of 79, and Susan lived another six years, dying on August 25, 1927. Husband and wife were both interred in the Yale cemetery where their fading headstones can still be seen today.

Creighton, Elizabeth

1862 - 1922

Elizabeth Creighton was the second wife of Yale pioneer David James Creighton. She was born in Portsmouth, England, to Henry and Mary Dorey on February 20, 1862. Henry was a cordwainer (shoemaker) and Mary worked as a boot binder in Southsea, Hampshire. While her parents never left England, Elizabeth immigrated to Canada in 1901, when she was thirty-eight years old. She seems to have taken a job in Yale looking after the family of David Creighton, whose wife Mary Alice had passed away in 1900. Soon after, the two were married, he a widower and she a new bride at the age of forty-four. The marriage took place at the home of a friend in Agassiz, British Columbia, on August 15, 1906, and would endure for sixteen years. David and Elizabeth had no children together. She passed away from pneumonia brought on by influenza on November 17, 1922.

Castle, Flora (Florence)

1889 - 1923

Florence, also known as Flora, Castle was the daughter of Martin and Monica Castle, born in early 1889 and baptized at Yale the same year. She lived her entire life in Yale, at one point running a newsstand across from St.

John's Church. She published an advertisement in the *West Yale Review* selling cigars, fruit, and newspapers. Flora developed heart disease in her twenties and passed away on August 4, 1923, at the age of thirty-four. Her headstone remains in the Yale cemetery.

> **Miss Florence Castle**
>
> Fruits, Confectionery
> Cigars, Soft Drinks
>
> News Stand Opposite Church
> YALE, B.C.

Stout, Edward (Ned)

1824 - 1924

Perhaps the most well-known person buried in the Yale Pioneer Cemetery is Edward (Ned) Stout, a man who saw Yale during the gold rush of 1858, the construction of the CPR in 1880, and the years between and beyond. Many stories have been told of Stout's exploits, all portraying an adventurous life lived and eyes that saw firsthand some of the most important events in the infancy of the province of British Columbia.

Stout was born in Germany on September 26, 1824, in the province of Bavaria, and spent at least the first twenty years of his life there. After spending time working on Lake Michigan, Stout moved to California as word of the gold rush spread in "the days of old, the days of gold, the days of '49."[106] In 1858, he followed the same golden call north, arriving in Yale via Bellingham in boats he and his fellow miners built themselves. While based in Yale in those early days, Stout was a frontline participant in the Fraser Canyon War, a conflict waged between miners and the Nlaka'pamux who had inhabited the area for thousands of years. He was seriously wounded as he and a party of miners beat a retreat from their claims on the Thompson to the safety of Yale. "I was shot in the arm and breast and a number of our men were killed and wounded,"[107] Stout remembered, seeming to downplay the nine wounds he had received. After he recovered from his brush with death, Stout made his way to the Cariboo along with William "Dutch Bill" Dietz in search of gold, and Stout's success at the claim that would be called Stout's Gulch led to Billy Barker's strike and the founding of Barkerville itself.

In the following years, Ned Stout worked various jobs throughout the province. In 1873, he married Mary Thorpe and the couple would have three daughters: Mary Ellen, Daisy, and Margaret. Following his wife's untimely death in 1880, Stout moved with his family back to the familiar town of Yale. In the 1891 census, Stout is listed as living with his daughter Mary Ellen; the whereabouts of the other two girls unknown.

"I remember my grandfather quite well," said Judge C.E. Barry. "He lived to his hundredth year. He was born in 1824 and he died in January, 1924. He always reminded me a great deal of Col. William Cody of Wild West fame and, like him, he was a dead shot. Once, when our boys' gun club was shooting with traps, with shotguns, he took a rifle, and from his hip he made a better score than we did with the shotguns. He was about eighty-eight at the time when he did this; it was something marvellous. I think the gentleman in charge of the boys' club asked him if he acquired this, and he said, 'No, I was born with this capacity to shoot in such a marvellous way.' He also told a story about one time when he was in San Francisco about being in a theatre of some kind and there was a shooting match started, and he said he had a revolver with him—he named the kind of revolver, but I can't just remember what it was—[and] he said he shot the two lights out, and then he crawled on his stomach out through the door. He could see a very faint light. I've heard him tell that story quite often."

Calling Ned Stout in 1913 the "pioneer of pioneers," the *Times Colonist* wrote: "To British Columbia he came just one decade later (after the California Gold Rush) and he shares with Mr. James Moore alone, it is believed, the distinction of surviving the other members of the party credited with the discovery of gold in the Cariboo. More than this (for his life is o'ercrowded with adventures), although he frankly admits that he left his country originally to escape military service, he had scarce entered the then wilderness of British Columbia when he was actively and enthusiastically engaged in fighting hostile Indians, and is today the only one left of those few escaping the memorable massacre by the reds of Cariboo days. When hale and happy, Ned Stout—now eighty-seven years young—went first from what today is New Westminster to the site of Spuzzum, his present home, the trip by Siwash canoes consumed five wearisome days. It is now negotiated over the Canadian Northern Pacific in less than half as many hours.[108]

Politician and journalist David Higgins, a resident of Yale in 1858-59, had a chance meeting with Stout on Front Street in 1906. Remembering Stout's fame in connection with Barkerville, Higgins remarked, "Stout's Gulch was famous once." "Yes," Stout replied. "I made a good bit of money out of it, but I did not keep it. It all went somehow, and after many years, I have come back to Old Yale to live and die. It is the prettiest and best place on earth, anyhow." Higgins realized with shock that "in almost half a century it seems that (Stout) had not aged a day." Sharing stories on the once busy but now overgrown street, Higgins's "mind trailed back forty-six years, to the day when the men and women Stout now mentioned were living, breathing people; when Yale was in its glory; when the events they recalled were being enacted beside the Fraser. He was returned to the present by the painful thought that all but the three of them—Higgins, Stout and Bill Alway—were gone. Everything had changed; everything but the over-hanging mountains, the river, and Ned Stout."[109]

The *West Yale Review*, a newspaper published in Hope when the town was alive with the construction of three railways, gave an update on Stout in 1911:

"'General' Edward Stout —The men who came to the Fraser River in 1857 when gold was first found on Hill's Bar have nearly all crossed the Great Divide. But in many parts of British Columbia there may be found lone survivors of that period and of the next chapter in British Columbia's history, the 'rush' to the Cariboo. Among all the veterans there is none more hale and vigorous than 'General' Ned Stout of 'Old Texas's band of twenty men who led the advance up the Fraser from Yale in the spring of '58, and lost fifteen of their party in Indian fights. None escaped injury and Mr. Stout still wears many scars. He was born in Bavaria in 1824. In 1846, when he attained manhood, he declined military service in time of peace, and made his way to Hamburg and thence to New York. He joined the rush to California in '49, crossing the plains and the mountains. Though he did fairly well, he did not make a 'stake.' But he contracted the gold-mining habit and word of the finding of gold on the Fraser was enough to turn his face to the north. His stories of the journey by way of Bellingham and the Lower Fraser would fill a volume. The Indians had already shown ill-will and individuals and small parties had been murdered.

"The Squamish Indians used to ascend the North Arm of the Fraser in war canoes and lie in wait at the head of Lulu Island. They were all armed with muskets purchased from the Hudson's Bay Company. The most desperate fighting came in the spring of 1858. 'Old Texas,' a veteran of the Mexican wars, undertook to go up the river. His party numbered twenty. For a while, they were not molested. Then an Indian woman warned one of the party named McLennan that murder was intended. The first fight occurred at a place known afterward as Slaughter Flats. The Indians were beaten and never afterward came hand to hand. But retreat was forced. Finally, five survivors were found by 'Captain' Snyder who went up from Hope with a party, including 'Dad' Yates. 'Captain' Snyder fought the Indians up the river as far as Lytton, when they gladly made a treaty of peace. Mr. Stout shows little sign of his age and looks good for many years yet. He resides at Yale."[110]

Judge Barry shared a story about his grandfather's adventures in mining in his later years: "My grandfather had a dredge at one time just below Yale from which he took out $1,000 the first day, $900 the second day; I just forget the record but something like that for three or four days and then he went to Victoria to refinance or something, and unfortunately the dredge turned over and went away. In those days there was no such thing as insurance so it was a matter of an entire loss. I'm sure if it had been me I would have been at my wit's end but the old man came back and said 'Well, we'll start all over again.'"[111]

Stout remained in Yale until his last day. He passed away months shy of his 100th birthday and was buried in the Yale cemetery on January 18, 1924 by Reverend Yates of St. John the Divine.

"Ned Stout is Dead at Yale —Almost on the century mark, 'Ned' Stout, the oldest pioneer of Yale, died on Tuesday of last week. He would have reached his hundredth birthday on February 7 next (though his death certificate gives his date of birth as September 26, 1824.) Ned was one of those congenial spirits with a love of nature who make the true pioneer. Of an affectionate nature, a quiet, unassuming disposition, and an ever-ready smile, he was beloved by all.

"In the early days, he was an employee of the CPR on construction work. He was one of those who made the hard journey to California to make his pile in the gold rush of '49. Then, attracted by the news of gold finds in the '70s, he came to Canada, ultimately settling at Yale, where he lived until called by death. It is stated that the only time he came to Vancouver during the last half century was when the Hudson's Bay pageant was given some years ago, the company bringing him to Vancouver to take part in it as one of the early miners. During the last fifteen years, he enjoyed what he termed his second sight. Prior to that, he had worn glasses to read, but his eyes becoming stronger, he was then able to discard the glasses. He was a single man and lived in a shack at Yale."[112]

Ned and Mary Stout

The *Vancouver Daily World* broke the news of Stout's death even more eloquently, on January 19, 1924:

"Another Argonaut Gone —One of the Last of the Thinning Band of Old Cariboo Men Crosses the Great Divide —Now and again, the death of some real pioneer gives us pause in the rush of modern life in this province. In the cities, at any rate, despite our mechanical up-to-date-ness, we are thus brought to a realization of the nearness of time of British Columbia's white beginnings. The day must soon arrive when the last survivor of the Cariboo Gold Rush will cross the Great Divide. Then, and only then, will that notable episode in our provincial annals become part of the historic past. The thought is prompted by the death at the remarkable age of ninety-nine of Mr. Ned Stout, one of the best-known miners of the Cariboo days and one of the most delightfully entertaining of old-time characters. To Mr. Stout, even the days of Sir William Van Horne appeared recent. Like the late Thomas Earl of Lytton, he was a 'Forty-Niner'—almost certainly the last survivor on this side the line of that famous Californian Gold Rush. The news of the passing of this grand old man of the wilds, whose striking appearance was as unusual as his longevity, may perhaps cause a few of us to pause in our mad rush after the movies, mah jongg, or the latest bunny hug, and give a thought to the strenuous type of life which has made the enjoyment of those high-grade products of civilization possible."[113]

Richardson, Eaton B.

1877 - 1924

It was not a good week for Fraser Canyon merchants in early October 1924. Just two days prior to the passing of storekeeper Hubert Reynolds's wife, Kate (see above), North Bend merchant Eaton B. Richardson died of liver disease at his home. Richardson was a native of Salinas, California, born there on May 9, 1877, to Abner and Harriet. Abner was from Vermont; Harriet from England. By 1880, Abner had passed away, leaving Harriet a single mother to Eaton and his older brother Arthur (born 1875). Harriet worked as a milliner, or hatmaker, to support her family. Eaton came to Canada in 1888 and, three years later, was working in the Yukon as a clerk for an unnamed company, likely a general store, earning about $100 per month. In 1907, he was living across the river from Boston Bar in North Bend, a CPR division point, running his own general store. He married Annie Flann in Yale at St. John the Divine on April 5, 1909, and they had a son named Arthur the next year. Frederick followed in 1912, along with Evelyn (1915), Eleanor (1917), and George (1919). Richardson ran his store in North Bend for close to seventeen years, but the 1920s were marred by a series of health problems for him. He passed away on the evening of September 30, 1924. A funeral service was held in North Bend, after which he was brought to Yale and interred in the cemetery. Like Kate Reynolds, his funeral was officiated by Reverend Yates, and his grave today is similarly unmarked.

Reynolds, Kate
1871 - 1924

Kate and Hubert Reynolds, along with their son Fred, came to Canada in 1905. In the years prior, the family owned a hotel in North Berwick, Scotland. In the 1901 Scotland Census, the family included Hubert, Kate, and sons, Hubert (born 1895) and Harry (1896). Fred appears to have been born about 1903 and was still living with his parents in 1921 when they were settled in Spuzzum, unlike his older brothers, who had moved on by that time. Between 1915 and 1919, the family farmed, retiring from that to run a general store in Spuzzum, in May 1919. On October 1, 1924, fifty-three-year-old Kate passed away from complications of hepatitis. Her funeral service was conducted by Reverend C. F. Yates at St John the Divine, and Reynolds was buried in Yale, the closest active Church of England cemetery to Spuzzum. Her grave is no longer marked.

Barry, Charles
1862 - 1928

Charles Barry was born in Ontario on August 8, 1862. He moved to British Columbia and married Mary Ellen Stout, daughter of Ned and Mary, on December 28, 1904, in Yale. Charles and Mary Ellen had one son, Charles Edward Barry. The elder Barry was, at different times in his life, a carpenter, a railway watchman, and Yale's postmaster. "My father Charles Barry," remembers Judge C. E. Barry, "came west with the building of the Canadian Pacific Railway in 1884. He was a bridge man and worked on several of the bridges—I believe Pitt River, Coquitlam River, White's Creek, and Illecillewaet Canyon. Now these were the old wooden bridges, and afterward when he was working, he was always designated as a carpenter, but he always said, 'Now, listen here. That's not my occupation, I'm a bridge man.'"[114] He died of cancer on July 19, 1928, and is buried with his wife in the Yale cemetery.

Teague, Alice

1847 - 1929

Born Alice Michell in Cornwall, England, on February 17, 1847, Mrs. Teague was a longtime resident of Yale whose family is associated with the town to this day. On April 19, 1871, Alice married Forty-Niner and Cariboo Gold Rush veteran William Teague in the Village of St. Day, Cornwall, England. There, the family remained as they welcomed daughter Charlotte in 1872. The rest of the Teague children were born in Yale: Alice (1876), only son Cundy (1877), Nannie (1880), Minnie (1883), Elizabeth (1886), and Gladys (1889). The summer of 1881 was tragic for the Teague family, as Alice and William suffered the loss of two of their children to scarlet fever. Nine-year-old Charlotte succumbed to the disease on July 27, 1881, and son Cundy passed away only a week later, on August 4. Nannie, only about a year old. Another of the Teague children was stricken by scarlet fever at the same time, but recovered.

Alice and William bought a house in Yale from Joseph Trutch, a politician and surveyor who had laid out the Cariboo Wagon Road through the canyon and constructed the Alexandra Bridge. The Teague house can still be visited today as one of the best-preserved buildings from Yale's past, today kept in excellent condition by the Baerg family of Fraser River Rafting Expeditions. The family also owned other plots of land around Yale, and William continued his work as a successful prospector. William died in 1916, and Alice remained in town until her own passing, at the age of eighty-three, in December 1928. News of her passing was carried in the *Chilliwack Progress*:

"Mrs. Alice Teague, who has been associated with historic Yale almost since its establishment and was well known to old-timers throughout the Fraser Valley, died on Thursday morning at the home of her son-in-law and daughter, Mr. and Mrs. R. L. Chrane, of Agassiz. She had come down from Yale to spend Christmas with her relatives when she was taken ill with a severe cold. Being eighty-three years of age and not very strong, she was unable to resist the subsequent developments. The last gathering of pioneers which Mrs. Teague attended was in Stanley Park a year or two ago when the guests of honour were pioneers who had been in the province more than fifty years.

"The late Henry J. Cambie, pioneer railway builder and explorer, and Judge F. W. Howay, were among Mrs. Teague's friends, and it was not surprising that, when the cairn in memory of the historic happenings in Yale was erected a few years ago, she should be invited to perform the unveiling ceremony. The late Mrs. Teague is survived by four daughters, Mrs. W. W. Bailey, Mrs. W. A. Nunan of Tacoma, Mrs. E. C. Johnston of Seattle, and Mrs. Chrane of Agassiz. Another daughter, Mrs. F. W. Mackenrot, died last year. She is also survived by ten grandchildren. All the daughters except one were born in Yale and went to school at the beautiful All Hallows, the Church of England school.

"Mrs. Teague's husband, the late William Teague, a Forty-Niner in the California Gold Rush, came to British Columbia in the early days of the Cariboo, returning home to the little Cornish village of St. Day, to marry his fiancéee, bringing her out with him to Yale. The voyage on the sailing ship lasted for fifty-three days. Later, Mr. Teague occupied most of the chief posts in the government of Yale, including those of justice of the peace, Indian agent, and clerk of the court. The funeral took place at 2:30 on Saturday afternoon at the cemetery at Yale, where the remains of her husband are resting."[115]

Alice Teague's grave can be viewed today in the Yale Pioneer Cemetery in the family plot.

Alice Teague

Creighton, David James

1857 - 1930

David Creighton was born on April 5, 1857, in County Fermanagh, Northern Ireland, to parents David and Jane (Dundas). He came to Canada with his family in 1869, first to Ontario, then to British Columbia. By 1885, Creighton was in Yale, the owner of various plots of land in town and one or two businesses, including the Oriental Hotel, which had been reduced to ashes in the fire of 1880. His establishment took full advantage of its liquor license the very next day, as he served alcohol to the shocked and weary town, protected from the elements by only a tent and four poles.

David married Mary Alice Ward on October 29, 1885, in Yale. She was a local girl, born in town in 1870, a decade before the construction of the CPR would sweep through the canyon. The Creightons had five children: Moses, Francis, Alice, and Amy, all born in Yale, and a stillborn child in 1890. The family house is the current home of the Yale museum, overlooking the railway tracks and Douglas Street. David and Mary's son, Francis, married Margaret Castle in 1920 (see above), thus joining the Creighton and Castle families and helping to create an interesting and somewhat convoluted family tree that even living family members today have a hard time sorting out. Mary Creighton died in 1900, and in the next year's census, David shows up as a forty-four-year-old widower with three children at home. By 1921, he had remarried, to Elizabeth (born in England about 1868), and was Yale's postmaster. On September 12, 1930, at the age of seventy-three, David was found drowned in Yale.

"David James Creighton, aged seventy-three, one of the most widely known of the old-timers, was found drowned in Yale Creek at Yale on Friday night. He had been missing from early in the afternoon, and the body was found by a search party conducted by provincial police. An inquest was held by coroner A. K. Stuart of Hope and a verdict of found drowned was returned. No evidence was available to show how [the] deceased came to meet his death in the creek. The deceased pioneer came to Yale about fifty years ago from Ireland and carried on the business of general merchant, from which he retired some years ago. The deceased was a widower and lived with his son, F. Creighton, and his wife, who have the post office and general store business in Yale. The funeral took place on Monday afternoon, interment being made at Yale."[116]

Holmes, Richard Henry

1864 - 1930

Holmes was born in England about 1864 and emigrated to Canada in the early 1882. By 1891, he was living with his wife, Sarah, and their young daughter, Mabel, in Vancouver, where Holmes worked as a carpenter. In the following years, Holmes made his way to Yale where, in 1921, he was listed as an unemployed carpenter. By then, sadly, his wife, Sarah, had passed away. There is no information on Sarah's death or what became of Mabel, or if in fact they had more children. When Holmes died on July 3, 1930, he was a hotelkeeper in Yale. His funeral and burial were presided over by Reverend Yates, who noted in the church record book that Holmes was "about sixty-eight" and had been "a resident of Canada for over forty years."[117]

Angus, Felix

1883 - 1930

Father of Donald Angus, Felix is listed as "Canadian Scotch." Born at North Bend, British Columbia, in 1883, Felix was the son of a Scottish father and a Thompson Indian mother named Matilda. He lived most, if not all, of his life in North Bend, where he spent his working years as a watchman for the Canadian Pacific Railway. Angus and wife Sarah were parents of seven children, born between 1907 and 1921. As an employee of the CPR, he claimed an income of $800 per year in the 1921 Canadian census. Felix Angus passed away on September 11, 1930, at the age of forty-seven and was buried at Yale; however, his grave is today unmarked.

Fagervik, Helga

1886 - 1931

Helga was born in Harstad, Norway, on November 22, 1886, to Wilhelm and Anna Bringsrud. Like her husband, Ludwig, Helga crossed the Atlantic

Creighton's elaborate and remarkable gravesite is one of the more well-preserved in the cemetery.

at least three times in her early life. She married Ludwig on December 15, 1907, at St. Luke's Church in Minneapolis, Minnesota. They returned to Norway the next year, where first son Wilhelm was born, on October 26, 1908. Ludwig came to Canada in 1909, and Helga and eighteen-month-old Wilhelm followed the next year on the S.S. Victorian. In Canada, Helga gave birth to Mildred (1911), Anna (1912), Erling (1915), and Leif (1920). The family farmed in the area known today as Vulcan, Alberta, before moving to Yale in the late 1920s, where Ludwig worked as a patrolman for the CPR. Helga, like her son Wilhelm, suffered from tuberculosis; she endured it for close to seven years, and it took her life on April 12, 1931. Frank Creighton of Yale signed as the undertaker on Mrs. Fagervik's death certificate. Helga's headstone still marks her grave in the pioneer cemetery.

McLinden, Ernest

1906 - 1934

The son of Emma and James, McLinden suffered from epilepsy throughout his life. He was born in Yale in 1906, although his birth year varies from source to source. The 1911 census lists him as a four-year-old living in Yale. By 1921, his parents had separated, James had remarried Janet (Little), and the family was living in Lytton. Fourteen-year-old Ernest remained with his father and became part of the rapid expansion of the McLinden family, which would grow to include Lilly (1916), Mary (1918), Billy (1922), Arthur (1924), Esther (1926), Rita (1929), and Clifford (1933). McLinden worked as a labourer, but his illness became a major issue for him, especially in the last twelve years of his life. He spent his last year living in the Provincial Mental Hospital (later known as Riverview Hospital) in Coquitlam, and passed away on September 16, 1934, at the age of twenty-five. He was brought home to Yale and interred in the pioneer cemetery two days later.

Urquhart, William

1857 - 1934

William Urquhart was the son of Allan and Jane (Steedsman) Urquhart, born on October 1, 1857, in Inverarity, Forfarshire, Scotland. Urquhart came to Canada in 1883, where he eventually found work on the CPR, becoming a watchman in the following years. In 1911, he was based at Saddle Rock and, in 1913, married Rhoda Dominic, a Nlaka'pamux woman from nearby Spuzzum. When they were married just prior to World War I, William was fifty-four; Rhoda thirty-five, and son Arthur was two. "Rhoda gave birth to Arthur in Spuzzum," writes Irene Bjerky, "and times being as they were, did not actually marry Arthur's father until 1913, perhaps due to the grieving period, perhaps due to the availability of the priest, it is unknown. Because of the fact that Rhoda's previous husband was of Chinese descent, many people mistakenly thought that Arthur was also Chinese, though in truth he was born more than a year after Kimm died."[118]

Urquhart retired from the railway in 1924 and lived his remaining years in Spuzzum with his wife. He passed away on November 5, 1934, and was buried in the Yale cemetery. Rhoda died just over sixteen years later, and was laid to rest beside her husband. Their graves have survived the years and can still be seen in the cemetery to this day.

Green, Frederick

1877 - 1937

The son of a farmer, Frederick Green was a resident of North Bend, British Columbia. Green learned the art of farming from his father and grandfather in England, and transferred his skills from Albion to the Fraser Canyon around 1916. Green also served as the local butcher. He was born to John and Emma (Rouse) Green in Seal, Kent, England, in late 1877. A lifelong bachelor, Green was living with his sister Edith at the time of his death from a heart condition on June 2, 1937. He was attended to in death by Allan K. Stuart, the coroner from Hope, who has his own connection to Yale in the early part of the twentieth century as his daughter Marjorie was a student at All Hallows boarding school. Green's grave is no longer marked.

Castle, Martin

1860 - 1938

One of the many members of the Castle family who called Yale home, Martin was the son of Martin Castle Sr. and his wife, Mary. He was born February 25, 1860, in Victoria, where his father owned at least two bakeries, one located on Johnson Street, and the other at the Craigflower Manor Farm. In the years after his parents died in 1871, Castle moved with two of his brothers to Yale, seeking work. He married Monica (or Monash or Monique) Silweltow (or O'Reilly) on July 24, 1885, and by 1900, had five children. The youngest, Herbert, died in 1902 at two years old. By 1891, Martin was working as a section foreman for the CPR. His wife passed away in 1910 and was buried in the Yale cemetery. By the time World War I broke out in 1914, Castle was a logger still living in Yale. The fifty-six-year-old widower enlisted in August of 1916, joining the 242nd Battalion of the Canadian Expeditionary Forces. Strangely, his enlistment form gives his birth date as December 25, 1870, nearly ten years after his actual birth, and the enlisting officers estimated his age at anywhere between thirty-five and forty-five years old. The five-foot-five-inch Castle was declared fit for duty, but he almost immediately ended up in the hospital. From his medical files:

"Has been treated in hospital since enlisting for varicose ulcers of the left leg. I consider him unfit for service for fear of aggravation of the above conditions. He is also over age; being fifty-six years old (more liable to disease or death.)"[119]

On October 19, 1916, two months after enlisting, Castle was discharged from the CEF, with his conduct as a soldier being listed as "good."[120] He returned to Yale and, later in life, was stricken with stomach cancer. Castle passed away on June 16, 1938, on a CPR train bound for Vancouver and St. Paul's Hospital. He was interred at Yale, where his grave marker stands to this day.

MacKenzie, Joseph

1858 - 1938

MacKenzie was a longtime resident of Yale and a retired employee of the CPR when he passed away on July 15, 1938, at the age of eighty. He was born in Nova Scotia on November 9, 1858, the son of William MacKenzie of Scotland and Margaret MacLeod of the same province. By the time he was thirty, MacKenzie was living in Yale, working as a conductor for the railway in its early years, riding the rails that were less than five years old. Following his retirement and in his early sixties, MacKenzie tried his hand at gold mining in the area[121] He would remain in Yale until his dying day in 1938. By then eighty years old, MacKenzie was discovered dead of natural causes in his home by his niece Margaret Pearson. He may have been dead for quite some time when he was found, but the date was recorded as July 15, 1938, and he was interred three days later in the Yale cemetery.

Mansell-Clare, Catherine Annie

1902 - 1938

Mrs. Mansell-Clare was born Catherine Annie Clare, the daughter of long-time Yale residents William and Clara (Dominic) Clare. Catherine was the firstborn of their five children. Miss Clare studied nursing and graduated in 1927, about a year before her marriage to Geoffrey Mansell, in Naniamo. Catherine worked in nursing until early 1932, when she left the profession. Unfortunately, she was afflicted by tuberculosis, which ultimately claimed her life, on October 17, 1938, only three days before her thirty-sixth birthday. The news of her death was carried in the *Chilliwack Progress*.

> **MRS. C. A. MANSELL**
>
> Mrs. C. A. Mansell, Yale, passed away in the Vancouver General hospital Monday. Formerly Miss Catherine Annie Clare, she graduated from the Royal Columbian hospital in 1927. Surviving are her parents, Mr. and Mrs. Clare, Yale; two brothers, Leonard Clare and Sidney Clare, and two sisters, Mrs. A. Algie, and Mrs. W. Talbot, Yale.
>
> Funeral services were held at St. James' church, Vancouver, at 9 a.m. today, and the remains were forwarded to Yale for burial.

Catherine Mansell-Clare's grave can still be visited in the cemetery.

Berry, Ellen

1861 - 1938

Ellen Berry is connected to the Castle family, though whether she was a relative or family friend is not known. She called herself an "Indian" on the 1901 census of Canada while living in the Burrard district of Vancouver. At that time, she and her husband John had Martin Castle, son of August Castle, staying with them. It's possible that Ellen was from Yale or the surrounding area. She was born July 4, 1861, and passed away November 30, 1938. She was interred in the Yale Cemetery.

Johnson, Edward (aka Adolf Fridstrom)

1880 - 1938

Adolf Fridstrom, a Swede with the unexplained alias Edward Johnson, had been in Canada nearly thirty years when he passed away in Yale in 1938. He had spent the previous six years living in Yale, working as a miner and general labourer. On December 27, his life was claimed by a chronic heart condition that, according to the coroner at Hope, was brought on by years of heavy drinking. Johnson was laid to rest in Yale two days before the calendar turned to 1939.

Wolfe, Cameron

1868 - 1939

Cameron Wolfe was a farmer who lived in the small farming community of Rosedale, just outside Chilliwack, British Columbia. Wolfe was born in Williamsport, Pennsylvania, in 1868, and came to the Fraser Valley in about 1927. His only apparent connection to Yale was his daughter, Mabel Martin, whose husband worked for the CPR. After the seventy-year-old Wolfe passed away on January 6, 1939, his remains were brought to Yale for burial.

Skynner, William Jarvis

1861 - 1939

William Skynner was a lifelong prospector and explorer who lived the last fifteen years of his life in Yale running a mining outfit. He was born in Springfield (now part of Mississauga), Ontario, in 1861, to Henry Skynner and his wife, Mary Jarvis, the last of their five children. Sadly, Mary passed away on February 27, 1861, when William was not yet a week old. Henry Skynner found himself a widower with five children aged newborn to nine years old. But he was soon back at work as a deputy sheriff in Toronto and there is no indication he ever remarried.

Skynner's name appears again in 1884 when, at twenty-three years old, he was part of an expedition to explore Hudson's Bay and to determine whether or not it could be utilized as a reliable option to ship Canadian grain to Europe, even in the winter months when it was believed the shipping lane was frozen solid. As the true potential of the vast Canadian prairies was being realized, the shortest route for getting the grain to England involved shipping it via the CPR from Winnipeg to Montreal, a journey of some 1,700 miles. Grain was then loaded onto ships that sailed through the St. Lawrence, then across the Atlantic. However, farmers were outraged at the exorbitant freight rates charged by the railway, and they had little choice but to pay. If Hudson's Bay was found to be a viable alternative, the distance over land could be cut in half, as a rail link from Winnipeg to York Factory on the bay would be about 700 miles. The objective of the voyage was to establish six observation stations at different locations around the bay, and to leave three men at each remote outpost to record the conditions year round. For his efforts as lead observer of the expedition, Skynner had a cove named after him, which housed the last of the six observation posts.

"There remained now but one station to establish," wrote William Anderson in *Science* in 1885, "which had been intended for Resolution Island or the lower Savage Islands. On both trips, this neighbourhood was carefully examined, but no harbour could be found; and the station was consequently fixed at Skynner's Cove, on the north side of the entrance to Navchak Bay."[122]

For William Skynner, this was perhaps the most successful aspect of the trip, as the official recommendation of the 1884 expedition was that more expeditions needed to be undertaken. In New Brunswick in 1890, Skynner married Sarah Gilbert, but the marriage lasted only three years as Sarah passed away in 1893. William never remarried, but became a prospector around Ontario, an occupation that would eventually lead him to the worked-over goldfields of the Fraser. He arrived in Yale around 1925 and prospected for a few years before becoming manager of the Hardrock Hydraulic Mining Company with partner, L. A. Gibbs. The company operated on the shore opposite Hill's Bar for many years as the river continued to pay well even in the years after the '58 gold rush. William Skynner was found unconscious near the railroad tracks near his property at Gordon Creek on March 29, 1939. He was rushed from Yale to Chilliwack, but was pronounced dead at the age of seventy-eight. He was brought back to his adopted hometown and laid to rest in the pioneer cemetery where he lies today in an unmarked grave.

Forsberg, Uno Ragnvald (John)

1905 - 1939

Forsberg was born on May 1, 1905 to Nils and Katarina in Forsnäs, Västerbotten, in northern Sweden. He worked as a woodsman in his early life. Forsberg came to Canada in 1923 via Bergen, Norway, and England. On September 5, 1939, four days after Germany invaded Poland instigating World War II, Forsberg was found dead in his shack by his own hand on the Canadian National Railway side of the Fraser near Yale. At the time, he was working for the CNR as a section hand. Forsberg was buried at Yale two days later on September 7.

Fagervik, Wilhelm

1908 - 1940

The son of Ludwig and Helga, Fagervik was born October 26, 1908, in Trondheim, Norway. He arrived in Canada on May 20, 1910, with his mother, aboard the S.S. Victorian, landing at Quebec City. They soon joined his father, Ludwig, in Alberta, where he was farming. Fagervik became a teacher later in life, working in the public system in Port Alberni, British Columbia. On July 4, 1931, he married Muriel McLean in Beaver Cove, located on Northern Vancouver Island. Wilhelm was afflicted with peritonitis, an inflammation in the abdominal wall, and spent time at the Tranquille Tuberculosis Sanatorium near Kamloops. He returned to Yale in 1940 and had been in town for only about two weeks when he passed away, on August 1, just shy of his thirty-second birthday. He was buried near his mother, Helga, in the Yale cemetery, where his grave can be seen to this day.

Creighton, Margaret Pearl

1902 - 1944

The cemetery at Yale is home to a number of those who died in tragic circumstances, but there is perhaps none as shocking as the story of Margaret Pearl Creighton. She was born in Yale on January 24, 1902, the daughter of August Castle and Maggie McLinden Castle. In 1920, Margaret married Francis Creighton, a local boy and Great War veteran who had served with the No. 2 section of the Skilled Railway Employees in the Canadian Expeditionary Force. Frank was a merchant, perhaps inheriting the family business from his Irish-born father. They would have five children in Yale, by then long past its glory years as a booming railroad construction centre. The Creighton children would all grow up in and move on from Yale, save for Thelma, who lies forever six years old near her mother in the cemetery. By 1944, the family was living in the Ward house, which had belonged to her mother-in-law's family, a house that still stands across from the Yale Museum on Douglas Street. On December 13, 1944, young Frank Creighton's thirteenth birthday, his mother was shot and killed in his presence in their home.

"Woman Dead in Yale Shooting —Mrs. Margaret Creighton of Yale is dead and Constantine Cucubinac (sic) is at death's door following a double shooting at the canyon town earlier today. Report is that Cucubinac shot the woman, then turned the death weapon on himself. Mrs. Creighton is the wife of Frank Creighton, toll gate attendant at Yale, and Cucubinac is a railway section worker. Sergt. W. J. Thomson of BC police is in charge of investigation of the case."[123]

A jury returned a verdict of murder-suicide in the case. Margaret Creighton's grave can still be seen today in the Yale Cemetery.

Jensen, Hans Leding

1907 - 1944

Jensen was born on July 6, 1906, in Denmark. In 1928, he arrived in Halifax on the passenger ship Arabic from Southampton. A gardener and farmer, Jensen came across Canada, stopping to stay with an uncle in Port Arthur, Ontario, along the way. While living in Spuzzum and working as a logger Jensen married Irene Castle on August 21, 1937, in St. John the Divine at Yale. Irene was the daughter of August and Annette Castle. Unfortunately, in their seventh year of marriage, Hans was severely injured in a logging accident on May 17, 1944. At the time, he was living in a logging camp while Irene remained in Yale. The medical examiner determined that Jensen suffered "intense injuries" after being struck by a log. He was taken to the Chilliwack hospital where he passed away nine days later on May 26. He was thirty-seven at the time of his death, and was buried in Yale, likely by Reverend Scudamore.

McLinden, Emma Annette

1885 - 1948

McLinden was born in or around Yale on October 15, 1885, to Charlie and Annie McMillan. Why the family was in the area is a mystery, as they don't appear in any of the local directories of the day. By the time she married Yale-born James Arthur McLinden in 1906, the couple already had two daughters: Jeanette, born in Spuzzum in 1898, and Winnie (1902). She was pregnant with their third child, a son named Ernest (1909), who would be born three months after the wedding. McLinden would have one more child with James, a son named Fredrick, in 1912.

By 1914, James and Emma had divorced, and Emma had married Yale pioneer August Castle, with whom she would have at least two more daughters. Emma's new husband had previously been married to her first husband James's sister Maggie (See Maggie McLinden Castle), and August's numerous marriages (at least four) contribute to a fair amount of confusion even to members of their family who try to make sense of their somewhat convoluted family tree. Sixty-three-year-old Emma passed away on January 18, 1948, in Chilliwack, and at the time of her death, she had reverted to using her former McLinden surname. According to one long-time resident,

McLinden was the last burial in the Yale Pioneer Cemetery prior to the massive Fraser River flood of 1948.

> **Mrs. Emma McLinden**
> Funeral services were conducted at Yale Anglican church today at 2 p.m., Rev. H. B. Scudamore officiating, for Mrs. Emma McLinden, 63, who passed away at Chilliwack hospital Sunday. Interment will be in Yale cemetery.

Clare, William Frank

1868 - 1948

William Clare was born on October 2, 1868, in Crowmarsh Gifford, Oxfordshire, England, the youngest of William and Elizabeth Clare's eight children. William Sr. was an innkeeper in Wallingford, England, and in 1871, was living apart from the family, perhaps because his business was in a different town. Young William was living with his grandmother, mother, and six siblings that same year. The details of Clare's arrival in Canada are not known, but in his own words, he jumped "ship off an old tub from overseas"[124] in 1887. He was a carpenter and a track watchman, performing both jobs for the CPR. In 1902, he married Spuzzum-born Clara Kesutetko Dominic (1881-1974) in Yale; she would take the name Clara Clare as a result. William and Clara would have five children and live in Yale for many years. In 1963, Clara gave an interview to the CBC's Imbert Orchard, which provides fascinating insight into what life in Yale was like during her lifetime. William would pass away from heart disease at Chilliwack General Hospital on January 16, 1948. His grave is still visible today in the Yale cemetery. Clara, one of Yale's pioneers, was not buried in the cemetery. Her remains were cremated, and her ashes were spread at Frozen Lake, located in the mountains above Yale.

Urquhart, Rhoda

1878 - 1951

Rhoda Urquhart was the daughter of well-known mule train packer Jean Jacques "Cataline" Caux and Amelia York, a Nlaka'pamux woman from the Spuzzum area. She was born in 1876 in Spuzzum and would remain in the area for most of her life. Caux, born in France, came to try his luck in the Fraser River Gold Rush of 1858, and soon found employment and fame as a pack train driver on the Cariboo Wagon Road. He allegedly fathered many children with women up and down the road, and so was the absentee father of Rhoda and her brother William. Unlike their nomadic father, however, Rhoda and William remained in Spuzzum for most of their lives, although they did receive periodical visits from him. Rhoda's niece Annie York, herself a lifelong resident of Spuzzum, detailed what a visit from Cataline looked like:

"Those pack trains had little bells, and they would go ding, ding, ding, ding. And Cataline would come along, and my father (Rhoda's brother, William) would be watching by the fence, and Cataline would say to the packtrain to keep going, and he would come down and give money to my father, but my father wouldn't take it because he didn't know his father. And every time he came, he would buy clothes for his children. They say that Cataline was the most generous man. But my father couldn't use that name, Caux, because my grandmother wasn't married to him."[125]

Also known by her native name "Ji-ji-wat-ko," Rhoda undoubtedly had the same type of strange relationship with her father. "When Nlaka'pamux women who had married European men stayed in the community," writes historian Andrea Laforet, "it was hard to escape the fact that half the relatives of the child were either missing or did not participate in the Nlaka'pamux systems of economic support. The children lost the benefit of connection with their father's relatives, and sometimes they had uncertain relationships with their fathers."[126] Rhoda was a student at All Hallows in the West, the Anglican school founded at Yale in 1884; based in Andrew Onderdonk's former residence. She would marry twice, first to William James Kimm, who was born in Spuzzum and was of Chinese descent. Kimm died in 1910 at the age of forty after spending two years in the Provincial Hospital for the Insane, and Rhoda found herself a widow. Three years later, she was remarried in a wedding ceremony in Spuzzum on March 15, 1913, to fifty-four-year-old William Urquhart, a Scottish-born watchman on the

CPR. The ceremony was performed in the house of William's brother by the Archdeacon of Yale. Before they were married, Rhoda and William had a son named Arthur, who would become a British Columbia policeman and Nlaka'pamux elder. William passed away in 1934 and was buried in Yale. Rhoda lived until 1951, passing away on May 7 of that year. She was interred in Yale next to her husband, and her grave can still be seen today.

Fagervik, Ludwig
1880 - 1958

Ludwig Fagervik was born on April 26, 1880, and left his native Norway for the United States sometime in the early 1900s. He married Helga Bringsrud in Minneapolis, Minnesota, on December 15, 1907, and, sometime in the next year, the couple returned to Fagervik's homeland. On October 26, 1908, the couple welcomed a son, Wilhelm, while living in Trondheim, Norway. The next year, Fagervik sailed for Canada, bound for Winnipeg via Liverpool and Quebec City. Helga and Wilhelm joined him in Canada in 1910, where he was working as a farm labourer. It appears the family was living in Yale in 1912, as records show that daughter Anna was born there on January 2 of that year. By 1921, Fagervik was working his own farmland near present-day Vulcan, Alberta. In the years since their emigration from Europe, the family had four more children: Mildred, Anna, Erling, and Leif.

Fagervik, who would also be known as Louis, was living back in Yale by 1931 where he worked as a patrolman for the Canadian Pacific Railway. He retired in 1945, fourteen years after the death of his wife, Helga, in Yale in 1931. Son Wilhelm also predeceased his father, dying also at Yale in 1940. The youngest Fagervik, Leif, born on May 17, 1920, would serve as a private in the Seaforth Highlanders of Canada during the Second World War. He was killed in action on October 17, 1943, in the months leading up to the Battle of Ortona, and is buried in the Moro River Canadian War Cemetery in Italy. Mount Fagervik was named in his honour. The mountain peak is located west of Yale, near the Old Settler. Ludwig Fagervik passed away on December 6, 1957, at St. Vincent's Hospital in Vancouver, and his cremated remains were buried in Yale soon after.

Railway Workers

These are the stories of the men who died during the construction of the Canadian Pacific (1880-1884) and the Canadian Northern (1912-1914) through Yale and the Fraser Canyon.

Canadian Pacific

strange
how in this cold rational country
it seems reasonable
to love or hate
a railway
-Jim McLean

Flynn, William

1838 - 1880

Flynn was an early casualty of the dangerous tunnelling work going on just north of Yale at the onset of construction on the CPR. Just as Yale was preparing the annual celebration of Queen Victoria's birth, Flynn was killed at number one tunnel.

"Accident at No. 1 Tunnel! —The accident at the east header of Tunnel No. 1, Thursday evening, although not so bad as first reported, proved a very serious one. It seems that three shots were fired almost simultaneously, and the fifty-odd men who were at work at this end of the tunnel, all state that they heard the three reports and all started back on the work, and just as three of the men reached the header another explosion occurred, seriously injuring one man named Wm. Flynn, and slightly injuring two others. It is feared that the unfortunate man Gwinn can hardly survive. Mr. Bray was promptly on the scene with Dr. Ellis, and everything is being done for his care and comfort. From all the information we can glean no blame should attach to anyone, and the accident seems to be one of those unfortunate occurrences that no one can foresee. P.S. We learn poor Flynn died last evening. We have no further information."[127]

Accidents like the one that claimed the life of William Flynn were an all-too-familiar occurrence for the CPR, especially in the early days of construction in the perilous Fraser Canyon. A few months after Flynn was laid to rest, Michael Hagan described the dangerous nature of railway construction work in Yale's *Inland Sentinel:*

"Railway Accidents. —Since our last issue, considerable excitement has prevailed at and near Yale, owing to some accidents up the line a short distance. Rumours are always wild, and, we are happy to say, in the present case, greatly exaggerated. It would appear that while Mr. Duncan Macbeth was tamping a blast about two-and-a-half miles above Yale, he caused a premature explosion, receiving part of the powder back in his face, while his hands were badly burned and two fingers shattered. A man named Galway had his thigh badly crushed, but is, like Mr. Macbeth, now in a fair way for recovery.

"Both are in the hospital, receiving proper attention. Monday, about four miles up the line, a blast was let off at the side hill cutting, which caused a great shaking up of rock that tumbled into the road, blocking up the highway. A number of men proceeded to remove the obstruction, when the earth and rocks from the side of the hill near where the blasting had been done commenced rushing down upon the workmen, and before part of them could get out of the way they were caught and partly buried in the falling earth, stones, etc. Efforts were immediately made to free the unfortunate men from their perilous position. It was found that none had been killed, although some of them seriously injured. They were removed to the hospital and are being attended to. We learn the names of the injured men are: Mr. Cavillie, blow on the back, fracturing the ribs and causing internal injuries; Mr. Jenkins, a comminuted fracture of the leg; Mr. Fink, two fingers broken and ankle dislocated; Mr. McLean, shoulder blade broken; Mr. Kelly, severe bruises on the back of the shoulder. Beside these severe injuries each of the men have smaller wounds in various parts of the body. No deaths have occurred since June 15 (1880), except the one after the fire, and while it is to be regretted that the hospital accommodation is too limited at present, we are glad to be able to say that the Yale hospital will be immediately enlarged to accommodate thirty beds, and another hospital is to be erected at Spences Bridge, and an assistant doctor stationed there. We have reason to believe that the headmen of the railway desire to take every precaution against accidents, and we believe if the men themselves were more cautious, less injuries would have to be reported. Far better to take time and move with caution."[128]

Hagan's notion that the CPR "take time and move with caution" was his idea alone; under Andrew Onderdonk's leadership, slow and steady was not standard operating procedure. Many men died in easily preventable accidents, especially when explosives, solid granite walls, and tight deadlines were involved. Nowhere was this more evident than in the number of Chinese coolies that were killed in Canyon, which, even by Onderdonk's conservative estimates, work out to four dead per mile. Enlarging the hospital at Yale and building a new one at Spences Bridge seem to be a concession from the CPR that these types of accidents were both inevitable and unavoidable. According to William Flynn's death certificate, he was employed as a driller by the CPR. And while Hagan was careful not to assign blame to anyone for his death, it appears Flynn died because of a lapse in his own judgment. Dr. Ellis states that Flynn died instantly while examining an unexploded charge in the rock of tunnel No. 1.[129] The accident took place on May 28, 1880, and Flynn was interred three days later.

Tunnel Number One Just Above Yale

Lincicum, Nathan

1847 - 1880

Nathan Lincicum was born in 1846 in Delaware County, Indiana, to Caleb and Nancy (Archer) Lincicum. He was one of seven sons and three daughters. In his early life, the family moved between his home state and Iowa, eventually settling in Jackson, Indiana, where the family farmed. Lincicum was an American Civil War veteran who enlisted as a seventeen-year-old on March 18, 1864, in Wabash, Indiana, joining the 47th Indiana Infantry Regiment. During the war, Lincicum and his regiment would see action in several battles in the American South, including the Red River Campaign, the Battle of Sabine Crossroads, and the Campaign against Mobile, Alabama. Nathan was discharged on May 5, 1865, a little less than a month after the surrender of Robert E. Lee's Confederate army, and three weeks after President Abraham Lincoln's assassination.[130]

After the war, Lincicum returned to Indiana, where he settled for a time. When and under what circumstances he came to British Columbia are not known, but it is probable he came to seek work on the Canadian Pacific. While in the province, he suffered from what his attending physician Dr. Donald McLean called "phthisis," more commonly known as pulmonary tuberculosis. Seeking treatment for his ailment, the thirty-three-year-old Lincicum relocated to Nicola, British Columbia, believing that the drier climate would alleviate his symptoms. However, death found him in Yale. William Teague wrote that Nathan "arrived at Yale from Nicola on the evening before, where it appears the deceased had been visiting that district for the benefit of his health."[131] Lincicum died on July 25, 1880, and was buried the same day in the Yale cemetery by an A. W. of New Westminster, as it appears Reverend John Good was not in town at the time.

O'Reilly, John
1836 - 1880

John O'Reilly was buried in the Yale cemetery on October 21, 1880, by Reverend John Good. O'Reilly had been killed two days prior while working on the railway when a log he was attempting to lift slipped and crushed him. The forty-four-year-old Irishman was a general labourer and derrick man for Andrew Onderdonk, clearing the right of way and moving obstacles to track laying. He was attended by CPR surgeon Dr. Ernest Hanington, who noted that the deceased suffered from internal haemorrhaging and shock for about fourteen hours before he passed away. Any stone that marked his grave has disappeared over the years.

McCarthy, Thomas
???? - 1880

By autumn of 1880, residents of Yale had become accustomed to the near round-the-clock blasting as tunnels 1 and 2 were drilled through the solid granite walls just north of town. The *Inland Sentinel* reported in its October 28, 1880, edition that the number 2 tunnel was "doing well," and that "recently, new men have been added to the force so that now day and night the work continues."[132] The next column, however, demonstrates the human cost of the dangerous work of tunnel boring, and the sacrifices made to push the rails through the Fraser Canyon.

"Another Accident! —At 10 o'clock to-day, while the workmen were busy at tunnel No.2, a portion of the roof fell in and killed (Thomas) McCarthy, (a man who lately came from [the] Cariboo) and recently commenced tunnel work, and severely injured a man named McGillivray upon the head and back. Also, a man named Dupee had his arm broken. We are told the place where the accident occurred was to have been timbered, but unfortunately was deferred too long. It certainly looks as if more precaution should be taken by the foremen in charge, both for their own sakes as well as the men under them. No doubt this case will be inquired into."[133]

McCarthy's death highlights the extreme danger of railroad work, and by modern standards, the antiquated construction methods that were at Onderdonk's disposal in the 1880s. Stories of careless handling of blasting implements in the tunnels were common around Yale, and the manner in which the work was conducted resulted in numerous accidents in which some men died, and many more were seriously wounded. Walton Holmes, who ran a lumber and iron supply yard for Andrew Onderdonk, describes in his memoirs the Yale of 1880 in great detail, and tells of the ignorance of workplace safety that today seems unbelievable.

"A blacksmith who was there (tunnel No. 1) said he could put a detonator on his anvil and that it would not be powerful enough to lift the hammer out of his hands. But when he tried it, he didn't know what became of that hammer."[134]

He goes on to describe an incident where he missed death by minutes because of the mishandling of blasting equipment:

"And a few days afterward, when I was myself up there (tunnel No. 1), I found a man with some kind of oven, thawing out giant powder. After talking to him for a while, I noticed the melted glycerine running down the front of the oven, and called his attention to it. He said there was no danger—there were only three sticks in there. I told him I was going to get out, and he said he would walk with me as far as the toll gate. But we were not halfway there before the powder blew up; and if we had stayed two minutes longer we would have gone with it."[135]

Only months earlier, perhaps with a naive sense of excitement about the tunnelling work that was about to begin and in a bid to reassure the public that the invasive work was going to be carried out properly, Yale's *Inland Sentinel* ran a short article detailing the great care and attention being paid to workplace safety and a workforce that was dedicated to the safe handling of explosives in the blasting of Tunnels 1 and 2. :

"The work fairly commenced by Mr. Bray firing the first shot at No. 1 tunnel, at 9 a.m., May 15 (1880). The location is just out of Yale, adjoining the gorge turn in the wagon road; each working day enlarges the tunnel entrance; while the mountain is being pierced at one end a force is, also, busy at the other end of the first tunnel, and thus will work be regularly prosecuted until daylight is let through what is at present a formidable obstruction. yet engineering skill overcomes all such difficulties. Operations have, also, commenced upon No. 2 tunnel, both ends, and as 'a constant shock will split a nation, or indent a rock,' we expect to be able to report good progress from week to week. The greatest care is being taken to guard against accidents, and a hope entertained that few will occur upon this contract. Of course, explosives, giant powder, etc., are freely used in the blasting, but great care is exhibited in the handling, only sober, reliable men in charge of the magazine, and with the powder in use."[136]

Unfortunately, any notion of care and attention to detail was discarded almost from the first day, and it is not surprising, taking all of this into account, that Tom McCarthy's death would have likely been prevented if the tunnel had been properly reinforced, and safety guidelines followed. He died less than six months after a similar incident took the life of William Flynn at tunnel No. 1 (see "Flynn") It is not known how old McCarthy was when he died. He was buried on October 30, 1880, in the Yale cemetery, but it's no longer known where his grave lies.

Habrois, C.B.

1810 - 1881

Habrois was a labourer for the CPR during its construction. He was an anomaly for victims of the rugged Fraser Canyon because of his age. Where most of the men killed by rock slides, premature blasts, etc., were young men in their early to mid-twenties, Habrois was seventy-one years old when he died at his pickaxe. According to Dr. Hanington of Yale, Habrois was killed by "fracture of ribs and perforation of lungs by the falling of a rock."[137] From the *Inland Sentinel*:

"Last Saturday, 8th inst., while some men were working at Camp 13, Tunnel 11, a man named C. B. Habrois was killed and another named James Stuart had his leg broken. It appears a piece of rock fell from the roof and caused the accident by which one man lost his life and another received serious injury. Deceased was aged seventy-one years, and came here from Portland, Oregon. His remains were buried in Yale Cemetery. Mr. Stuart is in the hospital."[138]

The notation in the St. John's burial book claims that Habrois was from France, so he may have been in Oregon working for a different railway before coming to Yale to help build the CPR.

Kennedey, Daniel

1830 - 1880

Kennedey was a railway labourer who passed away on November 21, 1880. He was born in Ireland in 1830 and came to the United States, settling in Neponset, Illinois, where he likely worked for the Chicago, Burlington and Quincy railroad. Daniel and his wife Mary had 4 children: James (born 1858), Patrick (1860), Catherine (1862) and Eliza (1864). After work dried up in the US, Kennedey moved on to the next railway construction project, the Canadian Pacific Railway, where he was based in Yale from the very beginning stages of work in the area. It is not known if his family followed him to Canada. After his death from what Dr. Hanington called "disease of the heart,"[139] the 50 year old Kennedey was buried in the Yale Cemetery. Today, however, his grave cannot be found.

Eberts, Melchior

1845 - 1881

While most death notices in the *Inland Sentinel* were short and to the point, considerable space is dedicated to the announcement of the passing of Melchior Eberts on a cold January day in 1881. He was born in 1845 in Upper Canada, likely in Chatham. His father William was born in the same area, just before the War of 1812. Eberts's mother came to Canada from Scotland where she and William would raise seven children. In 1861 at the age of sixteen, Melchior and his older brother Herman were working as cashiers for his merchant father. In 1871, Eberts, about twenty-six at the time, is listed simply as a captain. At some point over the next decade, Eberts studied engineering and came west to work for the CPR. He wouldn't live to see much of the railway constructed through Yale, as documented in the January 20, 1881, edition of the *Sentinel*:

"Sad Accident —The melancholy and terrible death of Mr. D. M. Eberts of the Canadian Pacific Engineering staff has shocked our community, as it will doubtless shock his numerous friends throughout Canada, when the sad news shall have reached them. On Saturday last (January 14) Mr. Eberts was crossing Alexandria Bluff, near the Alexandria Bridge, in the performance of his duties, when, by some means, he lost his footing and fell a distance of over 200 feet, until he was thrown against some stumps, which alone prevented his being plunged into the river, from which his body would in all probability never have been recovered. When found, about an hour after the accident, Mr. Eberts was unconscious, in which state he remained until about 9 a.m. Sunday morning, when he died. The deceased gentleman appears to have been thrown upon his head, as no bones were broken, death having been caused by effusion of blood on the brain.

"Mr. Eberts was very enthusiastic in his profession and was possessed of more than ordinary nerve, which doubtless tempted him to take risks such as most men would avoid. To this is probably due that he essayed Alexandria Bluff on Saturday last, a bluff dangerous enough in summer, but especially dangerous when covered with ice and snow as at present. The deceased gentleman was about thirty years of age and leaves a young wife and child to mourn him. To these, our community offers the deepest sympathy, which is little in the face of an affliction such as deceased's family and relatives now experience.

"Mr. Eberts was very popular with the engineering corps, and had, we understand, many friends in and about Ottawa and throughout western Ontario, whence he came. He had been long connected with the Pacific Railway surveys and we doubt not, stared the grim messenger many a time before his final terrible plunge. His brother is a practising barrister in Victoria, and his brother-in-law is A. Rocke Robertson, Esq., who has just been elevated to the Bench. The inquest was held on Sunday last, by Mr. R. Deighton at the Suspension Bridge, and a verdict of accidental death returned. The funeral will take place today (Friday, January 21) at 1 o'clock, from St. John's Church." [140]

The Eberts family was well connected in Ontario and their influence was spreading in British Columbia. The A. Rocke Robertson mentioned in the *Sentinel* is Alexander Rocke Robertson, who came to British Columbia in 1864. Robertson married his cousin Maggie in Chatham, Ontario, in 1868; thus, Robertson and Melchior Eberts were both cousins and brothers-in-law. Alexander Robertson was a lawyer, would eventually become mayor of Victoria, was a member of the first provincial cabinet under Premier McCreight, and was a Supreme Court Judge. It's from Aleck that young Melchior received prodding to become an engineer.

"On May 14, Aleck was back at the steamer terminal, this time to welcome Maggie's younger brother Melchior Eberts, who was visiting Victoria for the first time. Aleck was fond of Melchior, as was almost everyone who knew the personable young man, whose nickname was 'Buz.' Now twenty-five years old, Melchior had left school to travel extensively in eastern Canada and the United States. Recently, while living in Denver, he had almost gone into a mining venture in New Mexico. However, his mother Mary Bell Eberts had sent him several forceful letter telling him that it was a very bad idea. He would be better off going to British Columbia, which was much more stable and had lots of mining going on. He had been persuaded, and here he was ready to seek his fortune. With Melchior there Aleck's social life inevitably became more active. In response to Buz's questions about work opportunities, Aleck convinced him that he should study engineering, and take advantage of the jobs available on the survey work for the railway. He also introduced Buz to the survey officials."[141]

From the *Daily Colonist* (Victoria):

"The remains of the late Melchior Eberts were interred at Yale. The funeral procession was very large and the expressions of sympathy were universal."[142]

Just after Eberts fell to his death, his daughter was born in Victoria. There is no record of the mother's name, or if she and Melchior were married. Sadly, in 1882, the baby passed away.

"Sudden Death —It will be remembered that shortly after the lamented death by accident on the CPR of Mr. Melchior Eberts, about two years ago, a daughter was born to him in this city. The child died very suddenly a few days ago in Ontario."[143]

Walker, Isaac
1825 - 1881

The *Inland Sentinel,* Yale's local newspaper during the early 1880s, carried the news of the death of yet another European labourer in its issue on March 31, 1881:

"Died —At the 'Cascade House,' 29th inst., of congestion of the lungs, Isaac Walker, a native of Kent, England, aged 56 years. Deceased came to this province from Australia and was a Foreman at No. 2 Tunnel (the second tunnel north of Yale); he caught cold and a short time since had to stop work. He had no family in this country. His funeral took place yesterday at 3 p.m."[144]

Walker was attended by CPR doctor Ernest Hanington, but he was unable to overcome his sickness and passed away in a local boarding house. Reverend Blanchard performed Walker's funeral and burial services on March 30, 1881, in the Yale cemetery, where today the Englishman lies in an unmarked grave.

Ramsay, Allan
1855 - 1881

Ramsay was a British railroad labourer who was killed during construction of the Canadian Pacific near Yale. He came from Middlesex, near London, but his stay in the Fraser Canyon was short, as he was killed by an explosion near Camp 5 on May 6, 1881.

"Fatal Accident at Yale —Special dispatch to *The Colonist* —A fatal accident occurred this morning four miles up the road whereby Allan Ramsay, a foreman, was so badly injured that he died soon after being brought into the hospital. One other man was slightly hurt. It appears that they had just sprung a hole with giant powder and Ramsay was in the act of pouring in a keg of black powder so as to finish the blast when it exploded, shattering his head and hands. It is supposed either that the rock was still too hot from the first charge, or that a piece of smouldering fire remained in the hole."[145]

Although the labour was done for Ramsay, "railway works," *The Colonist* goes on to note, "are being pushed ahead with great rapidity." The twenty-six-year-old was laid to rest in the Yale cemetery the next day by Reverend Charles Blanchard in a grave that can no longer be found.

Jones, Ezra
1857 - 1881

Hailing from Maine, Ezra Jones was one of the many young American men labouring for the Canadian Pacific Railway, and like so many of his compatriots, he passed away not long after arriving in Yale. Jones wasn't killed on the job, however. He died in the CPR hospital in Yale, treated there by Dr. Frickelton for cerebrospinal meningitis. Jones was twenty-four when he died on May 13, 1881, one of the six funerals conducted that month by Reverend Charles Blanshard.

Daig, George
1853 - 1881

George Daig came to Yale via San Francisco, probably around the same time as George Cunningham (see above). He was born in Germany in 1853 and left in 1869, sailing from Bremen and landing at Baltimore, Maryland, on June 4, 1869, on the steamship Ohio. On May 21, 1870, Daig enlisted in the US Army at Fort McHenry (the fort where, fifty-six years earlier in 1814, a Washington lawyer named Francis Scott Key composed a poem called "Defence of Fort M'Henry" after heavy bombardment of the fort by the British. The poem would eventually be renamed "the Star-Spangled Banner"). Daig deserted the army in October of the same year and was apprehended four years later, on August 29, 1874.[146] He was dishonourably discharged the next month. Sometime between 1874 and 1879, Daig moved across the United States to San Francisco, where he was able to re-enlist in the army on September 14, 1879; however, he deserted again on Tuesday, May 10, 1881, seven days before he died. He arrived at Yale on the following Sunday, May 15, to work with a CPR blasting crew. Like some of his fellow immigrants from California, he arrived seemingly unprepared for life and work blasting, grading, and digging through the granite walls of the Fraser Canyon. In fact, all of Daig's military paperwork says he was trained as a baker. Like Cunningham and W. E. Bailey, Daig would not see San Francisco again.

"Another Sad Accident —While Geo. Daig and seven others were in a boat three miles above the Big Tunnel landing powder, a blast was let off, in a cut some forty feet above the party, and a rock of about ten pounds struck Daig in the head and killed him instantly, throwing his body half over the boat side. The other seven men escaped uninjured—notwithstanding rocks dropped around them. Deceased was a German, aged about thirty years. A baker by trade, he was married five months ago in San Francisco, where his wife resides. He only arrived here last Sunday. Mr. Harry St. Clair brought the body down last night and the funeral takes place today. No doubt, as the unfortunate man is well known in this province, his many friends will learn his sad fate with deep sorrow."[147]

George Daig was about thirty when he died; the location of his grave within the Yale cemetery is not known.

McLean, Daniel

1823 - 1881

Fifty-eight-year-old Daniel McLean came to Yale via New Westminster where he had worked as a ship carpenter for a number of years. Originally from Scotland, he had arrived in Yale to work as one of Andrew Onderdonk's men pushing the railway through the Fraser Canyon. On May 26, 1881, he passed away in the CPR hospital located just behind the church. Dr. Ernest Hanington had been treating McLean for about a week as he suffered from seizures which eventually left the Scotsman paralyzed.

"A man named Daniel McLean, a ship carpenter by trade, aged about fifty years, died in the hospital here today. We learn deceased formerly lived in New Westminster. He had worked upon the railway."[148]

His death occurred just a week after the accident at the Big Tunnel killed David McKay and John Corsen. McLean, the forty-eighth person buried in the Yale cemetery, was interred the next day by Reverend Charles Blanchard.

Cunningham, George

1854 - 1881

Cunningham was a San Francisco-born blacksmith working for the CPR when he died suddenly on May 27, 1881. The cause of death given by Dr. Hanington was heart disease. It's not clear if Cunningham is buried in the Yale cemetery, as his name does not appear in the St. John's Church burial book. It's likely that his body was sent home, or that his burial was overseen by the Catholic Church.

Kerr, Charles

1836 - 1881

Forty-five-year-old Charles Kerr, a CPR construction foreman, was killed at work along the line near Spences Bridge on May 29, 1881. The Scot made a fatal mistake while engaged in blasting work meant to clear the right of way in the town north of Boston Bar. News of his death was featured in the *Inland Sentinel*:

"Another Sad Accident. —While a man named Charles Kerr was bossing a Chinaman gang near Spences Bridge last Saturday, he received an injury from which he died the next day. We are informed deceased thought the charge had exploded, and on advice of his men went forward, when one of the shots went off, the pieces of rock flying into his face and knocking him senseless, and he did not return to consciousness. Thus have we another case similar to that of poor Ramsay (Allan Ramsay, died May 6, 1881), and all the cautions do not seem to make men more guarded."[149]

Kerr's death certificate elaborates:

"Death caused by wounds on the head resulting from discharge of a blast in a boulder which deceased thought had not exploded, and was in the act of examining the fuse at time of explosion. His men state that he had not waited sufficient time to allow the fuse to explode the powder and one of them endeavoured forcibly to prevent deceased. Death ensued twenty-four hours after the accident occurred."[150]

Interestingly, even though Kerr identified as a Protestant and was buried by Reverend Good in the Yale cemetery, his name doesn't appear in the St. John the Divine register.

At the time of Kerr's death, CPR rails were about to reach the town of Yale. Hagan reports in the same edition of the *Sentinel:*

"Track laying progressing favourably; expected to reach Yale from Emory Saturday evening (June 4, 1881), or soon after. 'Look out for the engine when the bell rings.'"[151]

McKay, David
1843 - 1881

The Big Tunnel was a large-scale project for the Canadian Pacific construction workers located just upriver from Spuzzum, about fifteen miles north of Yale. It is mentioned several times in the pages of the *Inland Sentinel* because of the large camp required to house the workers. Known as Tunnel City, it was at times a toxic mixture of white and Chinese workers, stranded in a remote place with escape only available by rail. Illegal liquor sales were a regular event at Tunnel City and the camp was the site of a major sting in 1882, leading to multiple convictions against mainly Chinese offenders. The steamer Skuzzy was constructed near Tunnel City before its famous journey through the rapids at Hell's Gate. Unfortunately for David McKay (also called Donald McKay on his death certificate), it was also the place he would lose his life, like so many others, in a rock fall accident.

McKay, a Scotsman, was a farmer from Chilliwack (his property in 1880 was near Adams and Hopedale Road), and a foreman for the CPR. John Corsen, a Frenchman also known as Rocky Mountain Jack, was also killed in the slide. From the June 4, 1881, (Victoria) *Daily Colonist*:

"Yale, June 3rd. —This evening at the upper end of the Big Tunnel, Donald McKay, of Chilliwhack (sic), foreman, and a hand named Bustel (John Corsen's name was incorrectly written as 'Bustel' in the Victoria paper) met their death from a slide of rock as they were labouring in the tunnel."[152]

Michael Hagan carried the story in much greater detail in the *Inland Sentinel*:

"The Big Tunnel Accident —Editor *Sentinel*. —A very sad accident occurred at the Big Tunnel this morning a few minutes past six o'clock a.m., wherein two men were instantly killed by a large rock falling from the roof of the tunnel upon them. David McKay, one of the victims, had his head almost bruised to a jelly and turned to one side, but strange to say that the flesh was not cut; he was a native of Edinburgh, Scotland, and possessed a farm somewhere near Chilliwhack (sic), British Columbia, and was unmarried. John Corsen ... had his head cut, body badly bruised and both legs crushed. He was an old pioneer of the Rocky Mountains for nearly thirty years; also unmarried. Both men were very quiet, steady, and industrious.

"No blame can be attached to any of the persons in charge of the work in the tunnel; the instructions of the overseer to his foreman ... no rock that presents the slightest danger; pick the roof well that no accident ... instructions the foremen have endeavoured to carry out most rigidly and caution their men from time to time, to take no risks that might possibly be the cause of death. Unfortunately a bad seam crosses the tunnel at the place where the rock fell from, and it was the full determination of the day-shift foreman on resuming his work that morning to remove the rock (which fell upon the poor, unfortunate men), should he even be compelled to do it by blasting it down, as he had a mental prejudice against its appearance; but two hours too late, as his time for resuming work did not commence until seven o'clock a.m. Another man had the back of his skull slightly fractured by a small piece of the fallen rock from the same place the large rock fell. Half an hour previous to the sad occurrence, one man was slightly wounded in the mouth and chin by the falling of a large piece of rock. This accident cast a sad melancholy gloom over the place for the time being."[153]

A week after McKay's death, the *Daily Colonist* officially placed the blame for the accident on the deceased men, saying "the men had disregarded instructions of the overseer."[154] Both men were buried in the Yale cemetery the next day, June 4, by Reverend Blanchard. McKay was thirty-eight years old at the time of his death.

Corsen, John

???? - 1881

Corsen was born in France but had lived in Canada for at least three decades before his death on June 3, 1881, at the Big Tunnel, fifteen miles upriver of Yale. He was a miner and was at work that morning excavating the tunnel when, against the orders of his supervisor, he and fellow worker David McKay attempted to dislodge a large rock from the ceiling which, in turn, fell on the men, killing McKay instantly and mortally wounding Corsen. The man also known as "Rocky Mountain Jack" from his years homesteading in the rugged terrain "had his head cut, body badly bruised, and both legs crushed; he was an old pioneer of the Rocky Mountains for nearly thirty years (and was) unmarried."[155] His injuries being great and the extremely remote location of the accident meant that Rocky Mountain Jack had no hope of reaching the CPR hospital at Yale alive, and he passed away later in the day. John Corsen was buried the next day in the Yale cemetery; his funeral officiated by Reverend Blanchard of St. John the Divine. Today, the location of his grave is not known.

Corbitt, Michael
1850 - 1881

Corbitt was an Irish immigrant labourer working on a tunnel-blasting crew when he was fatally injured on the job on June 13, 1881. According to Dr. Hanington of Yale, "death was caused by a scale off round falling from the roof of the tunnel near the fifteen-mile post, striking deceased on the head."[156] Corbitt lingered in hospital for ten days, passing away on June 23. His burial seems to have come at a time when Yale was between resident reverends, as the Bishop of New Westminster signed the burial book, just after Reverend Blanshard had left town, and a month before the arrival of Reverend Good. The location of Corbitt's grave has long been lost.

Galloway, Peter
1841 - 1881

Galloway came to Canada from Ireland to help build the CPR. On the night of July 14, 1881, he was killed while at work. Dr. Hanington wrote on Galloway's death certificate that he died accidentally, and that "the accident was due to his [accidentally walking] under a dump during his work at night."[157] While the doctor's penmanship has obscured forever the exact cause of death, it can be deciphered that Galloway was simply in the wrong place at the wrong time, and it cost him his life. His funeral was officiated by the authority of the Bishop of New Westminster and Galloway was buried on July 18, 1881, in Yale.

Powell, Amos

1816 - 1881

Amos Powell was a railroad labourer born in New York state in 1816. At age sixty-five, he was an old-timer by comparison to most of his fellow workers on Onderdonk's construction crews. In 1850, he was living in Brooklyn where he worked as a stagecoach driver. During this time, he also had a fairly serious brush with the law:

"In the case of Amos Powell, who was charged with selling liquor without license, on his premises in Fulton Street, near the Fulton ferry, the jury found a verdict of guilty. There was also an indictment against him for keeping a disorderly and gaming house. On this count, however, he was acquitted."[158]

Powell seems to have had a slew of legal troubles in the run up to the Civil War, as his name appears weekly in the *Brooklyn Daily Eagle* in the "Legal Notices" sections. He was fined several times for different infractions. His name doesn't surface again until he died in Yale on July 31, 1881; his whereabouts during the Civil War are unknown. He died of natural causes and what Dr. MacLean of Yale termed "old age" (sixty-five years old being considered as such in 1881). His grave is unmarked.

Gillen, Henry

1839 - 1881

Gillen was a labourer killed by a blow to the head and skull fracture in the early days of CPR construction through the Fraser Canyon on August 4, 1881. It's not known where Gillen came from, but it is recorded that the itinerant labourer was about forty-two years old when he died. Attended by Dr. Tunstall, Gillen died the same day as Cundy Teague, the young son of local government official William Teague. It is easy to assume that his death on the railway would have been overshadowed by the tragic passing of the young boy. Mr. Gillen was interred at Yale two days after his death.

Thompson, William

1848 - 1881

William Thompson was a Danish-born CPR labourer who was killed in a violent explosion while helping to construct the transcontinental line through the Fraser Canyon. The accident occurred on August 9, 1881, during the exceptionally dangerous blasting work that took place to push the rails through the solid granite walls north of Yale. Thompson was working at Tunnel No. 7 that day when he and a fellow worker made a fatal mistake.

"Another Fatal Accident —A blast was let off Tuesday at No. 7 tunnel, and some of the men went in too soon. Wm. Thompson, a Dane aged thirty-three years, was struck by a falling rock and instantly killed. A man named Chas. Wilkinson, a native of England, aged about forty, was seriously injured and died yesterday morning. The company's officers notified Mr. Dewdney and he proceeded up to the place of the accident and held a coroner's inquest. James H. Wade acted as foreman of the jury and, after hearing the evidence, a verdict of an unforeseen accident was rendered. Both the unfortunate men had some means saved up and are well spoken of by their fellow workmen."[159]

Thompson's funeral and interment were performed by Reverend John Good on August 11, 1881, in the Yale cemetery.

Wilkinson, Charles

1851 - 1881

Shock from a blast took the life of Charles Wilkinson on August 9, 1881, north of Yale on the CPR.

"Another Fatal Accident —A blast was let off Tuesday at No. 7 tunnel, and some of the men went in too soon. Wm. Thompson, a Dane aged thirty-three years, was struck by a falling rock and instantly killed. A man named Chas. Wilkinson, a native of England, aged about forty, was seriously injured and died yesterday morning. The company's officers notified Mr. Dewdney and he proceeded up to the place of the accident and held a coroner's inquest. James H. Wade acted as foreman of the jury and, after hearing the evidence, a verdict of an unforeseen accident was rendered. Both the unfortunate men had some means saved up and are well spoken of by their fellow workmen."[160]

According to church records, Wilkinson was from England and was thirty-five when he died, although the *Sentinel* suggests he was "about forty" and his death certificate claims he was thirty. Also killed in the blast was William Thompson (see Thompson) and the two men were buried by Reverend Good on the same day in the Yale cemetery.

Moore, John
1828 - 1881

John Moore was killed while working on the railroad north of Yale on Monday, September 19, 1881. While little is known of Moore, save for he was about 52 and from Ireland, the notice of his death in the *Inland Sentinel* sheds at least some light on the CPR hospital in Yale, and some of the services Dr. Hanington provided to the white railway construction workers.

"Died —At Yale Hospital, on 19th inst., John Moore, aged fifty-two years. Deceased was a native of Ireland, and spent some years in California; he came to the Railway work some time since. He was injured up the line and brought to the Hospital Sept 6. One of his legs was amputated on the 15th, and the other on the 18th and death put an end to his suffering the next day. Of his history, very little is known here; the grave adds another to the number resulting from following railroading in this country."[161]

While the direct cause of Moore's death isn't recorded, Hagan implies it would have been better for him to die much sooner. While Hanington was widely regarded as an excellent doctor, those entering the hospital in Yale with serious injuries faced an uphill battle. The town was still relatively remote and a man staring down a double amputation could not simply be moved to the next big town with a better hospital. Using bone saws and chloroform as an anaesthetic, Dr. Hanington did his best to save Moore, but his injuries were too great.

Dr. Ernest Hanington

Graham, Joseph

1821 - 1881

Graham was a sixty-year-old CPR general labourer from England. He fell ill and passed away due to complications from pneumonia on September 30, 1881, and he was buried in Yale two days later.

O'Brien, Patrick

???? - 1881

O'Brien was an Irish railway hand based at Camp 13 near the Big Tunnel. His death came early in the railway construction years and highlights the living conditions at these remote camps, not unlike Peter Johnson and John Corsen (see Johnson and Corsen above). The news of the day when O'Brien died in October of 1881 was the crackdown on bootlegging carried out by (but likely not limited to) Chinese coolies working in the same area. The story preceding the news of O'Brien's death in the *Inland Sentinel* of October 27, 1881, details efforts to curb the flow of illegal liquor:

"Squire Deighton, having convicted Ah John of selling 'Chinese Gin' whereby he was find (sic) $100 and cost, Mr. Gibbs appealed the case to the County Court and was before Judge Crease Monday and Tuesday, Messrs Gibbs and Edmonds appearing for the Chinaman, and Mr. Leamy for the prosecution. After a long trial, the judge reserved his judgment."[162]

Mentioned again a few spaces lower:

"Saturday, a railway man named Michael Welch, at Camp No. 6, went out of his mind from the use of 'Chinese brandy' and rushed into the river and was drowned."[163]

And again:

"We are credibly informed that large quantities of the vile stuff called 'Chinese brandy' are being disposed of all along the line. It is about time some active steps were taken to check this poison traffic."[164]

The newspaper attributes O'Brien's death to the same affliction:

"Last week, a man named Patrick O'Brien died in great agony at Camp 13, believed to be from the effects of drinking 'Chinese brandy.'"[165]

Officially, O'Brien was "said to have died October 23, 1881,"[166] by the CPR's Dr. Hanington, while Reverend Whiteway at St. John the Divine lists his cause of death as "heart disease,"[167] the truth likely being somewhere in the middle. Nowhere is his age mentioned; he had likely not been in the area long, yet another victim of the railway construction buried in the Yale cemetery.

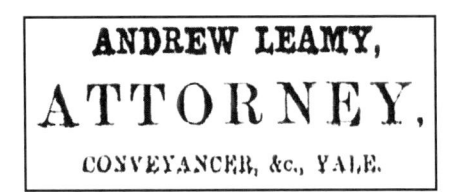

> **ANDREW LEAMY,**
> **ATTORNEY,**
> CONVEYANCER, &c., YALE.

Salani, Antony

1848 - 1881

Another railroad casualty, Antony (or Antonio) Salani was killed on November 24, 1881 not far from Yale. The Italian immigrant labourer was buried by falling rock from the roof of a tunnel. "Killed by explosion," wrote Reverend Whiteway. The *Inland Sentinel* carried the news of Salani's death:

"Another Blow Up! —Loss of life. Monday afternoon while a gang of men were working at the opening of Tunnel No. 6, Camp 13, another sad occurrence took place. A Swede named Irwin Olsen was tamping for a blast; the foreman O. R. Leonard urged him to hurry up, which not being done to suit, the latter caught up a bar of iron, or steel, and commenced pounding in the powder, when the blow up took place, killing an Italian named Antonio Salani, and severely wounding Leonard himself, as well as slightly injuring Olsen, who with the Italian was trying to escape when the saw the foreman's rash act. The body of the dead man was brought to Yale for internment, and the wounded men are in the hospital here (Yale), the foreman Leonard is in a precarious position having one eye out and the other badly cut, while severe injuries are upon his body."[168]

Salani's death is another example of the ignorance of many of the workers along the line in their handling of explosive material, and as a result, another construction worker was laid to rest thousands of miles from his home. Salani's grave is unmarked.

Kelley, Patrick

c1855 - 1881

Patrick Kelley's death warranted extensive coverage in the *Inland Sentinel* in the winter of 1881, a time when St. John the Divine was busy with the numerous burials taking place due to the harsh working conditions along the railway. Kelley, however, was not buried by the church but by the government, and the coroner's inquest discovered some mystery surrounding his death.

"The Late Patrick Kelley. —Mr. Dewdney having received notice of a mysterious death at Camp No. 7, Friday evening, next day held an Inquest, W. E. Blacket, foreman. George Wilson, being duly sworn states as follows. I was going to work on the morning of the 18th inst. I found the deceased Patrick Kelley lying on the ground; with the help of some of the men we brought him into Camp No. 7. His bundle was picked up about forty or fifty yards from where he was lying. We found him with his face toward the ground, insensible. We discovered no marks of violence about his body, probably he was in liquor and fell down, and not being able to get up, was exposed to the severe frost, which I imagine was the cause of his death. To my knowledge he never came to his senses after being found.

"James Sheppard, being duly sworn, states as follows: On the morning of the 18th inst., the deceased was brought to No. 7 Boarding House, by three of the witnesses whose testimony has been taken. The deceased, when brought into the house, was unconscious but still alive. We then applied all the remedies known to us in regard to frost bites. We applied the remedies best known to us for four hours but no improvement was made in the case of deceased. The remedy we used was ice water, and by its application and well rubbing, we drew the frost from his frozen parts, but the patient never rallied nor came to his senses. Dr. Hanington called about 12:30 o'clock, examined the deceased, gave him some medicine to revive him without any success whatever.

"The deceased expired at twenty-five minutes past five in the evening. His Time Cheque was made out in the name Patrick Kelley, but a stranger in Camp 7. I am informed the deceased was a temperate man. John Rabyor, after being duly sworn, states as follows: On the morning of the 18th inst. about eight o'clock a.m., in a senseless condition, deceased was brought to the Boarding House, Camp No. 7; he was then taken in by a couple of men who gave him all the attendance they could. Dr. Hanington called to see him and gave him some medicine, such as could be got down him. I don't think that the man had been drinking; there was no signs of liquor on him or about him. He never spoke after he was brought in, and died about five o'clock in the evening. I immediately reported the circumstance to headquarters at Yale. He had some money in his possession, a Time Cheque and a bank receipt amounting to $20. The cash was paid for doctor fees, and men looking after him amounting to $23.

The jury found that Patrick Kelley, deceased, came to his death, in their opinion, from exposure in lying out all night, (or a portion,) of the night of the 17th inst. Deceased was aged about fifty-five or sixty, and had formerly worked for the railway company, but, it is said, was out of work of late. The government had to take charge of his remains, and he found 'a pauper's grave.'

It is said he leaves a wife and children in San Francisco. Those who worked with deceased ... near Yale last winter and along the railway during the summer, speak of his temperate habits and general good nature. A good deal of talk has been had, especially among railway employees, and some feeling exists, growing out of a circumstance connected with this case. We are creditably informed that out of the money found upon poor Kelley's person, Dr. Hanington insisted upon $15 for his pay, and two men received

$4 each for trifling service on such an occasion. The steward, not knowing the law of this country to be for the government to take charge of all valuables and settle all fair claims, holding the balance of money, if any, to be paid over to relatives or those entitled to it, he handed over doctor's fees, etc. A trifle is now in the hands of the govt. agent and he reports the whole circumstance to the government, so that such ... action may not occur in the ... future."[169]

Maltby, Thomas

1841 - 1881

Maltby was involved in an accident while working on the CPR a week before Christmas, 1881. According to Dr. Hanington, the Englishman was caught up and killed in a collapse incident, in which he suffered a serious leg injury. This is confirmed by the church, which note that on December 17 of that year, Maltby was "killed by the fall of a stone."[170]

"Accident at Camp 13. —Last week a young man named Thos. Maltby, well known in Victoria, while working at Camp 13 had a piece of rock slide down and cut his leg severely. While he was being brought to hospital, he died at Camp 6. His body was brought down and buried last Monday."[171]

Maltby was buried by the visiting Reverend R. C. Whiteway, whom Bishop Sillitoe had stationed permanently in Lytton. Whiteway served the Indian communities strung out along the Fraser Canyon in tandem with Reverend Horlock, and Maltby's interment capped a grim year for the reverends that served the area. The year 1881 saw twenty-eight burials in the Yale cemetery, the "busiest" year in its history.

Johnson, Peter

1837 - 1882

Irish-born Peter Johnson was a tunnel labourer for the CPR during its construction in the 1880s. While at work in the winter of 1882, he collapsed and died while at work near Camp 13. The *Inland Sentinel* carried the news of his death in its February 23 edition:

"Another Death —Toward the close of last week, a man named Peter Johnson was found dead in a tunnel near Camp 13. He had been engaged in carrying tools from the blacksmith shop to the men at work. Deceased was aged, we learn, about thirty years, and arrived here upon the railway works over a year since, coming direct from San Francisco. It is thought heart disease was the cause of death. His habits are stated to have been good. It is not known where his friends reside."[172]

The description of Johnson's "habits" is interesting to note, as Onderdonk and the government were engaged in an almost constant battle with the issue of illegal liquor consumption at the remote work camps that dotted the canyon. Intoxication was the cause of death of more than one man along the line, especially during the winter months when there was little else to do when one wasn't working, and the harsh weather drove men to find a way to cope. Two weeks after the original story detailing Johnson's death, the *Sentinel* ran, under the title "Law Breakers," a summary of a trial that took place at the Yale courthouse in which Ah Coon, a Chinese railway labourer, was charged with "selling spirituous liquor without a licence, etc."[173] "For some time past," Hagan wrote, "it has been generally known that liquor selling has been going on extensively along the line, and the authorities found it difficult to procure satisfactory evidence to convict."[174]

In a follow-up article in the next week's newspaper, more information came to light in the story of the death of Peter Johnson.

"We are in receipt of two letters, one dated Camp 13, giving an account of the disgraceful manner in which the body of poor Peter Johnson was hawked about as a scarecrow, and the other from above Tunnel City relative to the disposal of another unfortunate man's leg—said to have been ordered by the "superintendent" to be "pitched into the Fraser."

We can hardly credit that the inhumanity charged in these letters could be done by any "white man" in this province. We purpose inquiring into the matter as soon as time will permit. It is also believed to be the duty of our government officials to institute an inquiry as to charges made. If the statements are true, no wonder the workmen are leaving the locality and speak hard of some, at least, placed in authority."[175]

The story of Peter Johnson's death paints an interesting picture of the conditions the workers faced as they pushed the rails east, and Michael Hagan's mistrust and open disdain for the system in place, and those in authority seems to tell the real story. There is no record of the location of Johnson's gravesite as his name is not listed in the burial registry.

Lennihan, David

1859 - 1882

The young Irish Catholic David Lennihan lost his life just as Yale was about to celebrate Easter in the spring of 1882.

"Camp 13. —Another life lost, said to be the eleventh at Camp 13. The accident occurred Saturday night. This time it was a man named David Lennihan, aged twenty-three years, two years out from Ireland, and up from San Francisco about two weeks. The alarm was given for a blast, and before he could get out of the way a piece of rock struck him in the back of the neck and almost instantly killed him. We learn he was working under a Mr. Carroll, foreman. The attempt of the div. supt. to make a graveyard near Camp 13 caused great dissatisfaction, and the remains were brought to Yale for burial."[176]

Lennihan was examined by Dr. Ernest Hanington, who determined that his death was indeed instant, adding "deceased was found dead 200 feet from the mouth of tunnel 13 after a shot had been fired."[177] The location of Lennihan's grave is unknown.

Foley, Michael

1827 - 1882

Foley died during construction of the Canadian Pacific Railway on April 30, 1882.

"A middling-aged man named Michael Foley died Sunday evening at Camp 16, from bronchitis. His remains were brought down to Yale for burial."[178]

Foley's name is absent in the St. John's burial book, which leaves some doubt to the exact location of his remains.

Hyland, Patrick

1824 - 1882

Hyland was a railway labourer for Andrew Onderdonk who met his death on May 24, 1882, in Yale. There is no record of his death in the St. John's records, as Hyland identified as a Catholic. His name does appear in the September 2, 1880, edition of the *Inland Sentinel*, where he is said to be a foreman, a rank he seems to have held from the beginning of construction activities in the Fraser Canyon. This particular article details how Hyland set events in motion that led to a traffic jam on the Cariboo wagon road:

"September 1, about two miles above Yale, Foreman Hyland put off a little shot—about 10 lbs of powder—and pretty soon after a boulder of over 50 tons might have been seen making good time down a side-hill and landed in the wagon road, travel was stopped for a couple of hours, while Overseer Myers broke up the 'pebble' and hove it into the Fraser. Almost every time, the heavy shots are fired off at the tunnels the rocks and stones are loosened along the mountain side and sometimes do damage, as was the case the other day when a 'young boulder' went through the roof of the engine house, No. 1 tunnel, somewhat injuring a couple of men and making others 'lave that.' Too much care cannot be exercised by the employees of the railway company."[179]

Hyland, according to Yale's Dr. Hanington, passed away after suffering from haemoptysis (coughing up blood) due to an unknown ailment for about a week. He was fifty-eight years old.

Connill, Paul

1847 - 1882

The record of Paul Connill's death in 1882 raises some questions as to whether he is actually buried in the Yale cemetery. He is not listed in the St. John's burial records, yet he died suddenly at the age of thirty-two on May 25 that year. He was not attended by a doctor and there is little to no vital information on his death certificate, which suggests that he died in a remote area of somewhere along the railway and was buried nearby.

Kelly, Michael

1832 - 1882

Kelly was a labourer for the CPR. According to Dr. Hanington, he passed away on July 6, 1882, in Yale of natural causes. Reverend Darrell Horlock would provide the cause of death as heart disease. The fifty-year-old Kelly was buried in a quick funeral at the Yale cemetery the same days as his death.

Gillian, James

1842 - 1882

Gillian was an Irish immigrant working for the CPR in the construction years of the early 1880's. The forty-year-old when he was killed while at work on August 1, 1882. He suffered a fatal blow to the head from a derrick winch, a tool that would have been used to help lift heavy materials.

"We learn from Camp 16, that James Gillian, aged about forty years, a native of County Longford, Ireland, formerly of Cassiar, while working on Tuesday at a derrick, the crank struck him, causing death. His remains were brought in town last evening and interred today, Reverend Father Horris officiating."

Gillian was buried in the Yale cemetery under the authority of the local Catholic Church.

Farrell, Thomas

1854 - 1882

Thomas Farrell was a native of what is today Kingston, Ontario. He was born to James and Jane Farrell about 1854 and when he was old enough, became a carpenter. Farrell married Anne Isabella Richardson on Christmas Day, 1879 in Kingston. They had at least one child. Thomas left his family in Ontario and came west to use his carpentry skills on one of Andrew Onderdonk's CPR construction crews.

"Fatal Accident —A young man named Thomas Farrell, fell from a bridge at Camp 13 last Thursday morning, and was killed instantly. The body was conveyed to town for interment. He was about twenty-six years of age, and leaves a wife and child to mourn his untimely end. We believe his family resides in one of the Eastern provinces."[180]

Farrell's grave is unmarked in the Yale cemetery.

Ashworth, Lawrence

1847 - 1882

Born in Rhode Island in 1847, Lawrence Ashworth was working at the CPR Acid Works at the time of his death.

"Sad Accident. —As we go to press we hear of the body of a man picked up under the bridge in front of Mr. Onderdonk's residence, supposed to have fallen off the bridge last night. His name is Lawrence Ashworth, (brother to the superintendent of the Acid Works.) Deceased came from California. We believe he was a single man. No further particulars at present."[181]

Ashworth is buried in an unmarked grave.

Shea, Michael
1855 - 1883

An Irish railroad labourer, Michael Shea, died near the Big Tunnel close to Spuzzum in the winter of 1883. From the *Inland Sentinel*:

"Found Dead —A young man named Michael Shea, well-known here, was found dead near the Big Tunnel Wednesday morning (January 3, 1883). He was, of late, given to strong drink and it is thought 'whisky did it.' He was an American by birth, and formerly served in the US Army, and was about twenty-three years of age. Squire Dewdney has gone up the line to enquire into the case."[182]

Dewdney determined that an inquest was to be held, the details of which were recorded in the January 11 edition of the *Sentinel*:

"The Coroner's Inquest. —We stated in our last that Govt. Officer Dewdney went up to Big Tunnel to hold an inquest on the body of Michael Shea. The following jury acted: W. J. Thompson, foreman; E. E. Austin; J. McLennan; Jas. Olwell; Martin Angel; Edward Bradshaw, and Wm. Kane. The evidence disclosed that deceased Michael Shea, J. T. Davis and Jas. Moore had left Yale together. They had a bottle of brandy each. Drink had been indulged in as the party proceeded up the line and soon, as admitted by Moore, both he and deceased were drunk. The following was the verdict: 'Michael Shea came to his death from injuries received in falling from the top of a bluff situated about 325 yards from East end of Tunnel No. 6 (Big Tunnel) on the night of the January 2, 1883, cause accidental'."[183]

According to his military records, Shea was born in Tipperary, Ireland, and was twenty-two years old when he enlisted in the US Army on September 14, 1880.[184] He was stationed during peacetime in Fort Thomas, Kentucky, with the 6th Infantry, but Shea didn't last long in the army. The red-haired, blue eyed Irishman deserted the Army on September 22, 1881, and his whereabouts were unknown. Like fellow army deserter George Daig (see Daig), he made his way north to the blasting and grading work taking place in the Fraser Canyon. Coping with the cold, wet weather (the same week the Chinese coolies working near Hope had refused to work in the conditions) and the remote location of his work, Shea, like so many of his fellow workers, took solace in alcohol and, as such, became one of the many casualties of mixing brandy and the rugged terrain of the canyon. Shea's body was returned to Yale and interred in the cemetery about a week after he died.

Bailey, W. E.

1853 - 1883

W. E. Bailey came to the Fraser Canyon from California to work on a CPR construction gang. He would have come to Yale at a time when debate was raging across Canada about the use of Chinese workers in railway construction. Pierre Berton writes:

"When Andrew Onderdonk arrived in British Columbia there were perhaps 35,000 white citizens in the province. Since he would need at least 10,000 able-bodied men to build his part of the railway—and actually many more, because of the turnover—it was clear that he would have to look elsewhere for much of his labour force."[185]

The only place any kind of surplus white labour could be found was San Francisco, and Onderdonk knew that even this source wouldn't provide him with enough men to complete his portion of the railway. Speaking in the House of Commons, Canadian Prime Minister Sir John A. Macdonald said:

"When Mr. Onderdonk was here in the beginning of the Session, he told me he employed every white man he could get, and that he tried to get every white labourer from Canada that he needed."[186]

Also:

"Mr. Onderdonk said also that he expected at one time to be able to get sufficient white labour from the United States; but such was the extent to which the construction of new railroads was proceeding in the United States this year that he could really get no satisfactory labour, but only the culls and refuse, persons who could get no employment at San Francisco, to work on the British Columbia Railway."[187]

Enter W. E. Bailey, arriving at Yale in 1883. Descriptions of his work ethic have been lost to history, but thanks to the February 1, 1883, edition of the *Inland Sentinel,* we know that Bailey was, like many of his colleagues from California, ill-suited to such hard labour, especially in a Fraser Canyon winter.

"A middle-aged man named W. E. Bailey, formerly of California, but recently of the railway work, through exposure from intemperate habits, got his feet frozen, and was brought down the line. Squire Dewdney, being notified that the unfortunate man was destitute, had him placed in the jail apartments. It is now feared that both feet will have to be amputated."[188]

The following week's *Sentinel* published a follow up story:

"The man W. E. Bailey, alluded to in our last as having frozen his feet while laying out up the railway line under the influence of liquor, died at the jail here last Saturday, and was buried at government expense."

Reverend Darrell Horlock from St. John the Divine oversaw Bailey's funeral and burial services, which took place on February 4, 1883. Today, the American's grave is unmarked.

Fraser, Thomas Alexander

1849 - 1883

T. A. Fraser was a native of Pugwash, Nova Scotia, born there in 1849 to Simon and Isabella. The circumstances surrounding his death while working on the Canadian Pacific Railway support the idea that Andrew Onderdonk faced a shortage of skilled labour. In the 1881 census, Fraser, staying at a boarding house in Yale, recorded "plasterer" in the occupation column on the form; however, two years later, he was working as a bridge carpenter, perhaps learning on the job. Fraser's accidental death occurred on March 27, 1883, as noted in the *Inland Sentinel*:

"Sad Accident. —Last Monday while T. A. Fraser, a bridge carpenter, was working at American Bar upon railway work, and while placing a stick of timber upon a bridge he lost his balance and fell, breaking his back. He was brought to the hospital here the same evening; he made his will, and died Tuesday. Deceased was about thirty-four years, and came from Nova Scotia three years since; he has a brother in California. Mr. Budlong has charge of the funeral."[189]

Further, Fraser's death certificate, administered by Dr. Hanington in Yale, notes that Fraser suffered for over thirty hours with "pressure on spinal cord from fracture of vertebra."[190] The Mr. Budlong mentioned in the *Sentinel* is

Frank Budlong, an upholsterer in Yale at the time. Fraser was a Presbyterian, and not listed in the St. John's Church burial book, but he was interred in the cemetery a few days after his death.

Carr, John
1856 - 1883

Carr was born in Cornwall, England, and came to Canada to work for the CPR. He was killed on April 29, 1883, in a rock slide near the Number 14 tunnel. From the *Inland Sentinel*:

"Killed. —A middle-aged man named John Carr was killed last Sunday morning at Camp 14, by the falling of some rock. He was badly mashed up; the remains were brought to Yale and buried Tuesday. We have not been able to learn particulars as to where the deceased came from, or the length of time employed."[191]

Carr was twenty-seven at the time of his death, which the *Sentinel* seems to insinuate was "middle-aged," a sobering commentary on the life expectancy of Onderdonk's lambs.

Rouse, George
1817 - 1883

Englishman George Rouse was a blacksmith in the employ of the CPR. One of the army of skilled tradesmen employed up and down the line, Rouse would have earned between $3 and $3.50 per day working for the CPR. He also was responsible for obtaining his own food and lodging, although he could have lived in one of the company boarding houses that were strung out along the right of way at a cost of $4 per week. Onderdonk paid his men once per month, on the tenth day, meaning labourers like Rouse would have had to watch their money carefully. His daily pay placed him at the upper end of Onderdonk's wage scale, ahead of a general labourer earning $1.75 per day, but behind the various foremen, who would bring in up to $4 for a day's work.

At age sixty-six, Rouse would have been considered elderly among his colleagues. He was involved in an unnamed traumatic incident that severely injured him in the early spring of 1883 that took a toll on him. He suffered in the CPR hospital for about six weeks before passing away on May 10 of that year. The native of Cornwall, England, was laid to rest in the Yale cemetery after a funeral service performed by Reverend Darrell Horlock the next day. He has a wooden grave marker that can be visited in the cemetery (although his date of death is incorrectly given as May 10. It reads "Erected to the memory of a kind father from his affectionate son." The day of Rouse's funeral and burial was almost a disastrous one for the town, as a major fire was put out just in time to prevent another conflagration in Yale's streets.

"Yale —Friday (May 11, 1883), about 11 a.m., a car with some score of sacks of nitre (saltpeter) and oil was discovered on fire while passing along Douglas Street. The barrels of oil were soon rolled off and the burning car disconnected from the engine near the fireman's hall. no sooner was the discovery made than some firemen and others were on the spot, and soon water was taken from a tank nearby and applied to the fire, which had the effect of checking it, when the prompt action taken from the house to the tank, hose connected and tram of water drowned out the fire. Probably half the sacks were destroyed and the car somewhat injured. Loss about $150. This is the second time this same kind of article for the chemical works has caused a fire alarm in our town."[192]

Connolly, Patrick

1838 - 1883

Connolly was born in Ireland about 1838, and at some point in his youth, made the trip across the Atlantic Ocean, first to New York, then on to San Francisco. From there, he and many of his fellow Californians came north to Yale to work for Andrew Onderdonk on the construction of the Canadian Pacific Railway. On June 12, 1883, Connolly was killed while at work. Stationed at one of the many remote CPR work camps, he fell from a bridge into the Fraser River. From the June 14, 1883, edition of the *Inland Sentinel*:

"Tuesday (June 12, 1883) about 4 p.m., while Patrick Connolly was employed in carrying scrap iron from the grade to the steamboat landing he accidentally fell into the river and the swift current carried him away and he was drowned. The body was recovered in about twenty minutes, but life had departed. His remains were brought down on the cars by Messrs. Thos. Hoye (who is listed as the informant on Connolly's death certificate) and Jeremiah Murphy to be buried at Yale. Deceased was a native of Ireland, a resident of San Francisco, Cal., for some time, and was aged about forty-five years. He was a temperate man, and was well liked by his fellow workmen and all who knew him."

Connolly, a Roman Catholic, was attended to by the Church of England's Darrell Horlock, the reverend who ministered to the railway builders and, sadly for him, buried more than a dozen of them in 1883 alone.

Larson, A. C.
1836-1883

A. C. Larson, a Swede working on a Canadian Pacific construction crew, fell to his death from a trestle on June 26, 1883.

"The Bridge Accident —Last Friday afternoon, a telegram was received at Yale by Bridge Sup't Keogh, who had arrived in town, giving a startling account of the falling apart of the bridge at Camp 23, about thirty-three miles up the railway. The first report would have it that eight men were killed and ten wounded. Fortunately, it has not been so bad as first stated— although bad enough it is true. It would appear that while the men were at work lining up the bridge, a bent gave way from the breakage of a rope, and the men and timbers fell some seventy-odd feet. This was witnessed from the opposite side of the river, and from the number of men and their appearance upon the ground, the report reached the telegraph office and was forwarded.

The same evening, Mr. Keogh went up by the pony engine and the seriously injured parties were forwarded to the hospital here (Yale). A. C. Larson, a native of Sweden, aged forty-seven years, severe fracture of leg and general contusion, died twenty-sixth inst. Thomas Hughes, Birmingham, England, aged twenty-six, compound fracture of thigh and leg broken below the knee, with severe concussion of the brain, still senseless. Antoine Jansen, from Norway, aged twenty-nine, broken arm and much bruised. In addition to the above named parties a few others complain of slight injury; one man jumped, said to be seventy-four feet, and lighting upon his feet in a sand bed, does not complain of injury. Of course there is a good deal said about where the blame rests for the accident—some of the men holding the foreman in charge responsible. But in the absence of the facts in the case, we forbear comments."[193]

Hughes, Thomas

1853 - 1883

Born in England around 1853, Hughes was a carpenter working on one of the many wooden trestles required to carry the CPR through the Fraser Canyon. On Friday, June 22, 1883, Hughes fell from one of these bridges and suffered severe, crippling injuries. He was involved in the same accident as A.C. Larson (see above) and suffered the same fate. However, he was not afforded the same quick death as Larson, as Hughes lingered for nearly two months in the hospital at Yale with multiple broken bones, in unbearable pain, and almost constant delirium. He passed away on Monday, August 20, 1883. Hagan, again in the *Inland Sentinel*:

"Our readers will recollect the bridge accident, June 22, when three men got injured. Two have died in hospital; the last one, Thos. Hughes, on Monday, after long suffering, during the greater part of the time he has been out of his mind. His funeral took place the same afternoon, Reverend Mr. Horlock officiating. Deceased was a native of England, and aged about thirty; he leaves some means now in the hands of the government officer here. Mr. Johnson, the other of the three injured as stated, is a young man from Norway, and was discharged from the hospital; he had his left arm broke, which is now stiff, and the elbow bone appears to be his present difficulty. He purposes visiting Victoria to see what medical aid there can do for him. His health generally appears to be pretty good."[194]

Dr. Hanington notes that Hughes was paralyzed from the fall, and that he did indeed suffer for about sixty days. The location of his grave site in the Yale cemetery is unknown.

Johnson, A.

1864 - 1883

Possibly H. Johnson, but listed in the church register as A. Johnson, Reverend Darrell Horlock's notation in the St. John the Divine's burial records and a brief mention in the *Inland Sentinel* give the only clue to the identity of this man. He was from Manitoba and was a nineteen-year-old logger clearing the right-of-way for the CPR when he was killed by a falling tree on June 28, 1883.

"We learn that a tree fell upon a young man named H. Johnson, lately from Winnipeg, while he was working upon the railway near Hope Station yesterday, and killed him instantly. The body was brought to town last night for burial."[195]

Kelly, Frank

1856 - 1883

In his great book, *The Last Spike*, Pierre Berton describes the multicultural profile of Yale during the period of railway construction. The crush of humanity that had descended on the town was from nearly every corner of the world. "The Irish," he writes, "were everywhere. There were five local characters named Kelly, all unrelated. Big Mouth Kelly had the contract for burying dead Chinese. Kelly the Rake was a professional gambler who seemed to have been sent out by a casting office: he dressed totally in black, from his wide sombrero and knotted silk tie to his leather leggings and narrow boots. Silent Kelly was so called because he played solitaire day after day. Molly Kelly ran a bawdy house. Long Kelly worked for her."[196]

Born in Oregon, Frank Kelly was about twenty-six years old when he was killed while working on a CPR construction crew. On August 16, 1883, while working near Boston Bar, an accident occurred:

"Thursday evening, Frank Kelly, while working upon the gravel train, near Boston Bar, was struck by the wire cable, the snatch block having given way; as the blow was a severe one upon the head he was instantly killed and his body found down the bank nearly 200 feet, close to the edge of the river. His remains were brought to Yale next day, and, Saturday, undertaker Budlong buried them. Deceased was a man of about twenty-six years of age and recently from Oregon. We learn he has left some means."[197]

Reverend Horlock officiated the funeral on August 18, 1883.

Haley, John

1859 - 1883

On September 13, 1883, Irish Catholic John Haley was working on one of Andrew Onderdonk's construction crews when he was caught in a rockslide and killed instantly. He was twenty-four years old when he died.

Kennedy, John

1827 - 1883

The Irish-born Kennedy was a fifty-six-year-old labourer for the CPR at the time of his death on September 23, 1883. The official cause of death determined by Dr. Hanington was delirium, although the *Inland Sentinel* put it in different terms:

"Accident. —Sunday morning at Camp 8, John Kennedy was thawing out some giant powder for blasting, when it exploded and fractured one of his legs. He is in hospital."[200]

Another layer was added to the story the following week, which added confusion as to the exact cause of this man's death:

"The man Kennedy referred to last week as under sentence for violating the liquor law, died in jail Saturday night from the effects of strong drink. It was not deemed necessary to hold an inquest; buried by authority of the gov't agent. Deceased was aged about sixty years, came to this place from the States some years since and worked upon the railway. He was addicted to heavy drinking, which brought him to jail and a dishonourable death at last."[201]

It seems part of the story is missing, and from Michael Hagan's description of Kennedy's mishap in the *Inland Sentinel,* only assumptions can be made about the sequence of events leading to Kennedy's death. The problem of liquor consumption along the line plagued the CPR during the construction years. When the labourers were not working, they had little else to do in the remote camps.

"Liquor Along the Line. —Complaints are frequently made that selling liquor along the line on the sly is on the increase. While the officers of the law are willing to do all in their power to prevent the free traffic in intoxicating drinks, it must be admitted it is difficult to find evidence to convict. Mr. Onderdonk and a few of those under him are anxious to put down the practice of beating the law; but it is thought that far too many of those who should be zealous to keep order along the line have a 'a weakness for the cup' and wink at the selling to others while they themselves receive free drinks. The Public Works Act that is in force in Manitoba and at other points East along the Canadian Pacific Railway should be put in operation in this country, where it is much wanted at present, and would have good effect. Especially the Indians employed by the railway Ccompany are being victimized. Now that Sir Charles Tupper will soon be here, his attention should be drawn to the subject. The law is all ready—it only requires a proclamation to put it in full force. Certainly this province requires wholesome restraint as well as more eastern locations of the Dominion."[202]

The above piece appeared in the *Inland Sentinel* in 1881, and Kennedy's death occurred two years later. Illicit liquor smuggling and consumption was impossible to regulate, must less eliminate. William Houston, a New Westminster police officer who worked in Manitoba during the construction of the CPR in that province put to rest the idea that there was no liquor problem on the prairies. In 1894, Houston reflected on his years as a constable in Manitoba during the construction years to Judge McDonald of the Royal Commission of the Liquor Traffic:

> "McDonald: Was (liquor) under prohibition provided by the Public Works Act?
>
> Houston: Yes.
>
> McDonald: Were you an officer?
>
> Houston: Yes.
>
> McDonald: Were you able to enforce the Act?
>
> Houston: No, it was impossible.
>
> McDonald: What was the difficulty?
>
> Houston: Smuggling.
>
> McDonald. What class of people did the smuggling?
>
> Houston: Railway men did a great deal of it, and men who made a business of it.
>
> McDonald: What kind of liquor did they bring in?
>
> Houston Liquor of very poor quality.
>
> McDonald: In what kind of vessels was it brought?
>
> Houston - In barrels, with meal packed all round. Sometimes, it was in barrels carried in front of the engine, and these would be dropped off at different points.

McDonald: From your experience and knowledge of this country (British Columbia), do you believe a prohibitory law could be effectually enforced and carried out?

Houston: Not if they had such a law as there was in Manitoba or the Northwest Territories. It would be easy to bring it from the United States."[203]

Liquor was a widespread issue for the CPR, and its abuse was the direct cause of death for several men in the Fraser Canyon, including John Kennedy. Patrick McTiernen, an Indian agent in the 1880s, described British Columbia as a place that held sobriety and orderly conduct in high regard, "except during one or two years, during railway construction in this province; then it was terrible."[204] He claimed that the social evil was brought to the province by a "new class of people" and acknowledged that the province never did introduce any kind of restrictions on the unconstrained flow of strangers invading the land. When asked about this, McTiernen stated "no, they let them fight away."[205] Kennedy was injured on September 16, 1883, and died in hospital on September 23. What happened to him during the week he spent in the CPR hospital at Yale will forever be a mystery. It is not a stretch to infer that the Irishman was intoxicated while working with blasting powder which led to an explosion, significant injury, and his eventual death from the "effects of strong drink." Kennedy is one of the few who identified as Roman Catholic to have his name appear in the St. John the Divine burial register. Church of England Reverend Darrell Horlock officiated Kennedy's burial service in Yale, where today he lies in an unmarked grave.

Roody, Edwin
1838 - 1883

Another Onderdonk man, Roody was a general labourer for the railroad during its construction in the early 1880s. In November 1883, Roody had a run-in with the law, and was in the local lockup when he died suddenly on the thirteenth. "This man," wrote the coroner, "died in jail between the hours of 2 and 8 a.m. Post-mortem held and finding of the jury was that the deceased came to his death from apoplexy."[206]

"Coroner's Inquest —A prisoner named Edwin Roody, a blacksmith, formerly employed upon Lower Section of the railway, died in jail, 13th inst. Coroner Dewdney summoned a jury and held an inquest. The evidence: William Insley being sworn stated as follows: The deceased, Edwin Roody, has been stopping at my house for the past two or three days; I have seen but little of him; I do not know whether he took any meal there; he drank very little on the premises.

"Last night, he was creating a disturbance in his room and in the hall. He acted as though he was crazy. So I sent Geo. Palmer for the constable, who took him in charge. This occurred about half-past two or three in the morning. He signed his name in the register as Roody.

"Emile Derdinger being sworn stated: I first knew the deceased at Harrison River where he was working for Mr. Ferguson; he came to Yale about four or five days ago and worked for me one day; he was a blacksmith by trade; his name was Roody.

"By the foreman: 'Was he sane when working for you?'

"'Yes, he was sane.'

"By the coroner: 'When he started to work for you, did he appear as if he had been drinking lately?'

"'Yes, he did. And from what he told me, he must have been drinking heavily.

"E. B. C. Hanington, MD, being sworn stated as follows: 'I examined the body of Edwin Roody. His face was very much congested, of a deep purple colour. No marks of violence on any part of his body. The eyeballs were very much congested; foam was running from his mouth, he had all the appearances of a man having died suddenly in a fit; there were no signs of any disease in any of the organs excepting the heart, the valves of which were not healthy. The liver was enlarged, the bowels were empty, the stomach had about a half a pint of fluid in it, the gullet was full of the same fluid as was in the stomach. The brain was congested thro'out and had a large clot of blood in the left ventricle. Death, in my opinion, was caused by the rupture of a blood vessel in the substance of the brain, causing apoplexy.

"Verdict: Edwin Roody came to his death, according to the evidence adduced by Dr. Hanington, by a fit of apoplexy on the morning of the November 13, 1883. Signed, Wm. McGirr —Foreman."[207]

Reverend Horlock of St. John the Divine buried Roody on November, 14, 1883.

Slater, Thomas

1858 - 1883

Slater, a twenty-fiveyear-old Ontarian, died at the CPR hospital located behind St. John the Divine in Yale on December 2, 1883.

"Accident and Death. —Recently, a railway hand named Thomas Slater received an injury while working up line that caused his leg to be amputated in the hospital here. He died on Monday and was buried by Undertaker Budlong. We learn deceased came from Toronto, Ontario, age about twenty-five years."[208]

Reverend Wright at St. John the Divine noted that Slater was originally from England. He was buried in the Yale cemetery the day after his death in a grave that has long since grown over.

Leslie, John

1858 - 1883

Twenty-five-year-old John Leslie died of typhoid fever on Sunday, December 16, 1883. He was a native of Ontario and a railway hand on one of Onderdonk's crews. According to Dr. Hanington, Leslie became ill about 8 days before his death. His burial, like that of so many other railway workers, was attended to by Reverend Darrell Horlock, who laid him to rest one week before Christmas, 1883.

Lindemuth, Theodore

1831 - 1884

Lindemuth was an American, born in 1831 in Lancaster, Pennsylvania. He worked as a railroad labourer in the United States before coming to work on the Canadian Pacific. The year 1870 saw him living in Snohomish, Washington Territory, likely working for the Northern Pacific. He arrived during the early days of construction of the CPR and took up residence at the Palace Hotel run by Newton Ash, who was also the proprietor of the Branch Saloon. Lindemuth appears to have lived at this establishment for at least a year, before following the work up the line to Boston Bar. Michael Hagan's *Inland Sentinel* carried the news of Lindemuth's death in 1884:

"Died —At the Palace Hotel, 9th inst., Theodore [Lindemuth], aged fifty-five years. Deceased had been for many years a resident of this province, having come from Pennsylvania. For some time past, he has been stopping at Boston Bar and, being ill of late, came down to see the doctor. It is said heart disease was the cause of death. Buried by Undertaker Budlong at Yale Cemetery."[209]

Lindemuth's burial service was held the day after he died, officiated by Reverend Edwin Wright of St. John the Divine. The location of his grave is no longer known.

Carlo, Castiglioni

1841 - 1884

An Italian labourer for the Canadian Pacific Railway, Castiglioni Carlo passed away in 1884 and was buried in Yale.

"Died —On the 8th inst. (March 8, 1884), Castiglioni Carlo, a native of Italy, aged forty-three years. Deceased was a blacksmith by trade and worked upon the railroad for some time. Last fall, he came down to Messrs. Bossi and Velatti, where he was attended by Dr. Hanington, who pronounced the ailment consumption. Every care possible was given him, but he gradually sank and passed away as stated. He was known as a kind-hearted, quiet man and his premature death is deeply regretted, especially by his associates. Sunday afternoon, his remains under charge of undertaker Budlong were removed to Yale Cemetery, when a large number attended. Reverend Mr. Wright officiated."[210]

Bossi and Velatti ran the Miner's Saloon in Yale, located at the corner of Front Street and the Cariboo Road, ran a grocery store, and were involved in the shipping trade. It seems that they also reached out to the Italian railway labourers and could be the reason that at least some of them have grave markers that have survived until today.

GREAT BARGAINS!

WINTER TRADE!

THE ROMANO HOUSE

Has now the Largest and most complete Stock of Fall and Winter Goods ever Exhibited in this Market. Speciality in Gents' Fine

CLOTHING, AND UNDERWEAR.

A WELL SELECTED STOCK OF

Dry Goods, Fresh Groceries, Provisions, and Liquors of Best Quality.

We Keep the Best Goods in the Trade and Sell at Wholesale and Retail at the

LOWEST PRICES.

Parties desiring to purchase Goods in our Line would find it to their interest to call and examine our stock and prices; all are invited.

J. QUAGLIOTTI ROMANO,
East End, Front Street, Yale.

Gordon, Courtney C.

1863 - 1884

Gordon, an American railroad conductor for the CPR, died in an accident on June 23, 1884. He was born in Alabama at the height of the American Civil War; how and when he came to the Fraser Canyon to work for the Canadian Pacific is a mystery. The twenty-one-year-old was buried in the Yale cemetery the day after his death. Reverend Horlock of St. John the Divine in Yale officiated the service. The location of Gordon's grave is not known.

Tupper, James Benjamin

1855 - 1884

Tupper was a CPR brakeman born in the Musquodoboit Valley of Nova Scotia in 1855. He was twenty-nine years old when he was killed while at work on August 23, 1884. Tupper was laid to rest in Yale by Reverend Darrell Horlock of St. John the Divine.

Dickie, David

1859 - 1884

Dickie was a railway brakeman born in Moncton, New Brunswick, in 1859. He seems to have had some experience in the trade before coming west to work for the CPR in Yale, as he was listed as such in the 1881 census while still living in his home province. Dickie's time was short in the Fraser Canyon, as he was fatally injured by a moving train on October 2, 1884. Dickie was buried two days later in the Yale cemetery, where today no monument to him exists.

Kimball, Daniel

1814 - 1884

Daniel Kimball was an American labourer for the Canadian Pacific railway. Kimball, unlike many of his fellow countrymen who came to build the railway, was not a young man. At seventy years old, he held the job of carter, shuttling goods back and forth. He passed away on October 26, 1884, from what Reverend Wright termed "decay of nature."[211] Wright recorded Kimball's first name in the church register as "William," although that is the only place it is written as such. Amazingly, Kimball's grave marker has survived, and although faded, can still be read today.

McCarthy, John

1852 - 1884

Canadian Pacific bridge carpenter John McCarthy was born in New Brunswick in 1855. He was one of the seven children of Jeremiah and Mary McCarthy, and was raised on the family farm in the small town of Port Elgin in the eastern part of the province. On November 23, 1884, McCarthy was killed while at work along the line near Ashcroft.

"Crushed by a Log. —On Monday morning, six miles below Ashcroft, John McCarthy, a native of New Brunswick, aged thirty years, was killed by a log which rolled down the mountain side and crushed him."[212]

McCarthy was brought to Yale for burial, and in the ensuing years the location of his grave has been lost.

Rycroft, George Patrick

1830 - 1884

The Irishman George Rycroft was killed in a gruesome railway accident on November 28, 1884. Deceased was a labourer for the CPR and that day was run over by a train. Reverend Wright of St. John the Divine noted that the accident occurred near "the mission" while Rycroft's death certificate claims the accident happened in Mission, a town on the CPR in the Fraser Valley. Wherever the mishap took place, Rycroft's legs and one hand were severed and he died instantly. His burial in the Yale cemetery was just as swift, as he was laid to rest the same day he was killed.

Willis, James

1839 - 1884

Willis was a subcontractor, born in Ireland and likely working for the CPR north of Yale when he died in November 1884. His body was found on the west bank of the Fraser River near Keefers, a whistle post on the railway north of North Bend, British Columbia. Willis's body was spotted by W. H. Holmes, who was working as a watchman on the steamer Skuzzy, and who in the past had worked for Andrew Onderdonk in many different capacities (see Rombrot, Vincent and Tuttle, Viola). Frederick Hussey estimated that

Willis was about forty-five years old at the time of death, and the Irishman was interred in Yale on November 29, 1884.

Gibbons, Thomas
1864 - 1885

Born in Illinois in 1864, Thomas Gibbons worked as a fireman for the Canadian Pacific Railway when he was killed on the job at Spences Bridge. Only twenty-one years old, Gibbons suffered a fatal blow to the base of his skull on January 9, 1885, nearly eleven months before the last spike was driven. Gibbons died after suffering for about six hours; he was buried two days later in the Yale cemetery by Reverend Wright.

Willey, George
1849 - 1885

George W. Willey was a road engineer's assistant for the CPR. The native of Magog, Quebec, had been a farmer in his younger years, tending the family acreage with his father Lyman in the town seventy-five miles from Montreal. His mother, Olive, passed away when George was four years old, and by the age of twelve, he was attending a boarding school near his hometown. When he came west to British Columbia is not known, but he was working for the CPR when he was found deceased on January 25, 1885. Willey died by his own hand in the Maple Ridge area, and his body was transported to Yale for burial. Today, his grave marker can be seen in the Yale cemetery, located to the left when facing the Fraser River, surrounded by ferns and towering fir trees that have grown in the years since his death. His headstone was placed in the cemetery as a tribute by his older brother, Dr. Oscar Willey, and the trees that have sprung up over the grave in last century almost seem to be dedicated to its protection.

Wild, William

1855 - 1885

Wild was a thirty-year-old carpenter likely working for the CPR as the construction phase drew to a close in the mid 1880s. On February 23, 1885, while performing maintenance work along the line, Wild fell to his death from a bluff. He was brought to Yale for a burial service conducted by Reverend Henry Edwards of St. John the Divine.

Wood, R. P.

1862 - 1885

Wood was a brakeman for the newly completed CPR. The twenty-three-year-old native of Brantford, Ontario, was killed near Hope on April 8, 1885, when he was accidentally run over by a ballast train. He was attended by Dr. Ernest Hanington, but quickly succumbed to his injuries. Wood was buried in Yale by Reverend Wright of St. John the Divine in what is today an unmarked grave.

Pease, William

1853 - 1885

Pease was a brakeman for the CPR who was killed on the job on May 15, 1885. He was born in the village of Melbourne, Quebec, in 1853, the sixth of George and Mary (Nicholson) Pease's nine children. The thirty-two-year-old was one of the early casualties of operating the railway, following the scores killed during its construction. Pease worked in a time before the air brake was introduced, and so his job as a brakeman put him in almost constant danger, as one misstep could send him down into the wheels of the train, which in the end is exactly how he met his fate. His working conditions would have been similar to this:

"Prior to 1888 when Westinghouse developed a reliable air brake, stopping a train or a rolling car was very primitive. Iron wheels, located atop cars, were connected to a manual braking system by a long metal rod. The brakemen, usually two to a train, would ride on top of the car. On a whistle signal from the engineer, the brakemen, one at the front of the train and one at the rear of the train, would begin turning the iron wheels to engage the brakes. When one car was completed, the brakeman would jump the thirty inches or so to the next car and repeat the operation to apply the brakes on that car. The brakemen would work toward each other until all cars had their brakes applied. Tightening down too much could cause the rolling wheel to skid, grinding a flat spot on the wheel. When this happened, the railroad would charge the brakeman for a new wheel. New wheels cost $45, which was exactly what a brakeman earned a month. In good weather, the brakemen enjoyed riding on top of the cars and viewing the scenery. However, they had to ride up there in all kinds of weather—in rain, sleet, snow, and ice, as well as good weather. Jumping from one car to the next at night or in freezing weather could be very dangerous, not to mention the fact that the cars were rocking from side to side.[213]

Pease was killed "accidentally by cars" according to Yale's Dr. Langis. He was interred in the Yale cemetery by Reverend Wright two days after his death, and the exact location of his grave is not known.

Stayton, L. G.

1861 - 1885

Stayton was a fireman for the Canadian Pacific Railway who was killed on May 15, 1885. "Killed accidentally by cars" was the doctor's summary, echoed by Reverend Wright, who buried the twenty-four-year-old in Yale two days later.

Moore, James

1861 - 1885

After the Canadian Pacific Railway was completed, the dangerous work of operating the railroad commenced. There are many men buried in Yale who were killed while working as members of a train crew, or as maintenance workers along the line. One of these men is James Moore, a twenty-four-year-old Chicago native who was working as a CPR brakeman in the summer of 1885 when he was killed in a gruesome accident near Devil's Lake across the Fraser from Hope. The provincial police investigated the incident led by Frederick Hussey, who would go on to become superintendent of the provincial force a few years later. Hussey's report stated that Moore was run over by a locomotive and died instantly. The accident occurred on June 16, 1885, and the young railwayman's funeral was conducted by Reverend Edwin Wright the next day in Yale.

Wright, Joseph

1859 - 1885

Wright was born in the United States, and, like R. P. Wood, was a CPR brakeman. The two young men met almost identical fates while working on the train crews in the Fraser Canyon. Almost exactly three months after Wood was fatally injured by a ballast train, Wright fell between the wheels of a moving train and was instantly killed. Accidents that claimed the lives of so many railroad workers like Joseph Wright and R. P. Wood reminded those associated with the CPR that just because the dangerous years of construction were behind them, the perils of working on the rails were equally precarious. In late 1884 and throughout 1885, at least ten men were killed operating the railway along the relatively short stretch of track between Boston Bar and Hope. James Tupper and David Dickie were both run over by trains in June 1884; L. G. Stayton and William Pease died in the same accident in May 1885, when they were "accidentally killed by cars." The next month, James Moore was run down by a locomotive and a man named Colwell met a similar fate. While today a similar volume of such accidents would almost certainly be unthinkable, the CPR in the 1880s was able to shrug them off. It almost seems an affront to the men who died along the line that their final resting place in Yale today lies so near to the running wheels of the long freights that pass by on a daily basis.

Colwell, ?

???? - 1885

Everything about Colwell is mystery except for his gruesome cause of death. According to Reverend Edwin Wright, Colwell was "accidentally killed by cars"[214] on September 23, 1885. This would suggest that he worked for the CPR, but the *Inland Sentinel* had moved to Kamloops by this time, so there is no notice of the man's death. His grave is not marked.

Bateson, Henry Woodward

1854 - 1886

Henry Bateson was born in July 1854, in Greasbrough, Yorkshire, England, and christened on December 30, 1855, in Rotherham, York. He was married to Charlotte Shaw in the spring of 1878, and in 1880, they had a son, George. While growing up in Yorkshire, he became an apprentice blacksmith and soon searched overseas for opportunities to ply his trade. By 1886, he was in Yale working for Canadian Pacific in the machine shop. On November 8, of the same year Bateson was accidentally shot and killed by his hunting companion Charles Atherton at Harrison River, British Columbia.[215]

"Victoria, November 9. —Henry W. Bateson and Charles Atherton were hunting at Harrison Lake last Sunday when the latter turned his gun toward his companion. It exploded and the charge lodged in Bateson's stomach, from which he shortly after died."[216]

Also:

"New Westminster, November 13. —Henry W. Bateson, a young man employed in the blacksmith shop of the CPR at Yale, was accidentally shot at Harrison swing bridge on Sunday last. Bateson, Henry Schofield, and C. Atherton left Yale on Sunday morning for Harrison River on a shooting expedition. At the swing bridge, when Atherton was in the act of firing, Bateson spoke to him, which caused Atherton to turn around. As he did so, his gun exploded, and the contents entered the stomach of Bateson. Assistance was procured and the wounded man conveyed to the train, but before Hope was reached, he was a corpse. He leaves a wife and three children."[217]

He was thirty-two when he was buried in the Yale cemetery. Bateson has no grave marker.

Combe, Beaudine

1858 - 1888

Combe was born in Quebec and was working for the Canadian Pacific as a bridge carpenter when he was killed while at work on November 29, 1888. He and Peter McPherson were caught in a rockslide while working along the line that day and were both immediately killed. From Victoria's *Daily Colonist*:

"Land Slide on the CPR. —Two Bridge Carpenters Killed and One Injured —The Accident Occurs at Sailor Bar Bluff, Near Yale —The Eastbound Train

Delayed One Day and Passengers Brought Back to Vancouver —Vancouver, November 29. —An accident occurred today at 1:30 at Sailor Bar Bluff on the CPR, eight miles east of Yale, by which Peter McPherson and Coombes (sic) were killed and W. Geisler was fatally injured. All were bridge carpenters. This was an old slide, which has given trouble before, and is the one which the CPR are disputing about with the government with a view to having it cut down to a proper angle. There was but slight damage to the bridge. The train will go out on time tomorrow. Today's train was cancelled and the passengers were brought back to Vancouver. The train only went to Westminster junction. These slides are of common occurrence. No train was caught in the slide."[218]

Combe, thirty when he died, is buried in an unmarked grave in Yale.

McPherson, Peter

1856 - 1888

On November 29, 1888, Canadian Pacific bridge carpenter Peter McPherson was caught up and killed in a rock slide north of Yale at Sailor Bar. Killed in the same accident was fellow carpenter Beaudine Combe. McPherson was from New Brunswick and was thirty-two when he died. Both men were interred in Yale by Reverend Wright of St. John the Divine on December 1, 1888, and while Combe's grave has been lost, Peter McPherson's can still be visited in the Yale Pioneer Cemetery.

Geisler, Freidrich William

1845 - 1889

Geisler was born in Germany on May 8, 1846. After he immigrated to Canada, he was based in the Emory area throughout the 1880s. He was the owner of the Emory Hotel, and was caught up in the era of railroad land speculation that had Emory City becoming the hub for construction of the CPR through the canyon. Throughout 1881, Geisler ran advertisements for his business in the *Inland Sentinel*, and the paper noted on June 9 that year, "We learn that Mr. W. Geisler, the enterprising proprietor of the Emory Hotel, has opened a store adjoining his premises. This will be a great accommodation to the people of Emory and vicinity."[219] Unfortunately, the businesses failed when it became clear by late 1881 that Yale would be the CPR's base of operations, but Geisler remained in the area and took up work farming and building the railroad. On November 29, 1888, Geisler was working on the railroad at Sailor Bar Bluff, north of Yale, when he was caught in a rockslide and gravely injured. He lay paralyzed by a spinal fracture in a hospital bed for close to five weeks before he passed away on January 7, 1889, at the age of forty-two. Geisler was buried in Yale, where his grave marker can still be found.

> **EMORY HOTEL,**
> W. GEISLER, Proprietor.
>
> This House has been greatly enlarged and well finished up and furnished for both pleasure and comfort. The table will be supplied with the best the market affords.
>
> The Liquors of best quality, and Cigars of best brands. Terms reasonable.

Johnson, Gus

1842 - 1892

On the evening of February 21, 1892, a fire destroyed the remote cabin that was home to Swedish-born Gus Johnson. Johnson, a railway labourer, likely a track walker, was killed in the inferno. The coroner's inquest revealed the following:

"That Gus Johnson on the twenty-first day of February in ... aforesaid being intoxicated and lying himself down to sleep in a hut about two miles to the west of Yale. It so happened that the said hut took fire and was burnt to the ground and that accidentally, casually, and by misfortune, the said Gus Johnson was there suffocated and burnt of which said suffocation and burning the said Gus Johnson there instantly died."[220]

Johnson was said to be about fifty years old at the time of his passing in that lonely hut. David Creighton and Ned Stout were among those that served on the coroner's jury investigating Johnson's death.

Robertson, James

1852 - 1892

Hailing from Aberdeen, Scotland, James Robertson was a railroad labourer. He was near North Bend, riding on a handcar, when it collided with CPR steam locomotive 364, killing him instantly. The forty-year-old was brought to Yale and buried in the cemetery on December 20, 1892. His headstone is intact and was "erected by his friends." It includes the symbol of a hand with the finger pointing toward heaven.

Barnett, John Spence

1867 - 1895

Born in Kirkwall, County of Orkney, Scotland, Barnett was working as a labourer when he died near Spences Bridge, British Columbia, on April 22, 1895. One of eight children born to James and Mary, Barnett, a former Canadian Pacific ticket agent turned construction worker, was killed instantly while at work.

"J. Barnett, formerly assistant ticket agent in the CPR station, was killed this morning at Spences Bridge by a derrick falling on him while engaged in construction work. Mr. Barnett was a young Englishman and was well known in Vancouver, where he had many friends."[221]

Although it is fading, the writing on Barnett's headstone is still visible in the pioneer cemetery.

Calahan, Michael

1852 - 1897

Born in Ireland, Michael Calahan was a labourer, presumably for the CPR. He was killed when caught up in a rock and snow slide while working near North Bend on November 17, 1897. Due to the conditions and remote location of the accident, his body wasn't recovered until a week later, on November 24. His interment in the Yale cemetery shows that, despite the Church of England maintaining responsibility for it during the early years, it was indeed a non-denominational burying ground, as Calahan, being Roman Catholic, is included in its roll.

Ansellmi, Oliver

1862 - 1898

Oliver Ansellmi was born in Italy in 1862. The thirty-six-year-old was employed as a track-walker for the Canadian Pacific, responsible for a section of track between Spuzzum and Boston Bar, British Columbia. Before coming to the Fraser Canyon, Ansellmi lived for many years in Vancouver, where he was known as William Oliver and worked as a railway bridge inspector. In his role as a track-walker, Ansellmi would have been on foot along the line potentially at any time of day and in all kinds of weather. A sample of a nineteenth-century track-walker's job description was as follows:

"Each foreman (or his track walker) must pass over the section or sections under his charge every day, taking with him a track-wrench, two red flags, and four torpedoes, and carefully examine the track to see if it is safe for the passage of trains; and if any place is found unsafe, he must at once fix red signals on both sides of such place, at a distance of ninety rails (or fifteen telegraph poles). The flag-sticks must be firmly driven into the ground, and a torpedo fixed on the rail on the engineman's side."[222]

Naturally, this type of work, factoring in the rugged terrain and remoteness of the Boston Bar area, was dangerous at the best of times. Unfortunately, Ansellmi became a victim of his profession on June 10, 1898, when he was struck and killed by a passing train.

"Accidental casualty and by misfortune struck by a locomotive engine [owned] by CPR and, given the injuries received, died [approximately] one-and-a-half hours after."[223]

The details of Ansellmi's death were reported on by the *Daily Colonist* in Victoria on June 12, 1898:

"A Bridge Tender Meets Death on the Railway —Vancouver, June 11 —News of a shocking accident on the CPR was received in Vancouver this afternoon from North Bend. It appears that a man named William Oliver, well known in Vancouver, a caretaker of bridges, was literally cut to pieces by a train. He was at a siding near North Bend and one train had just passed when another came along. He could not get out of its way, and was dragged under the wheels, meeting death. The particulars are very meagre."

Ansellmi was buried in Yale on June 11, 1898, by Reverend Charles Croucher, and was given a grave marker that has survived the past century in remarkably good condition, although today there is a massive fir tree growing through the centre of his plot.

Brookfield, Alan

1865 - 1903

Brookfield was born in 1865 in Welland County, Ontario, one of the six children of Edwin and Priscilla Anne Brookfield. The 1891 Census of Canada lists his occupation simply as "servant," perhaps meaning that he worked on his father's farm. At some point in the late 1890s or early 1900s, Brookfield took a job with the CPR as a track watchman, which brought him to Yale. On September 5, 1903, he was killed while walking the track two miles west of Yale by engine 592. He was buried in Yale by authority of the coroner L. A. Agassiz two days later. He has no grave marker.

Kelly, Henry

1883 - 1911

Henry Kelly was born in England and came to Canada as a labourer for the Canadian Northern Railway. The twenty-eight-year-old was killed on March 18, 1911, when he was hit by a passenger train. His burial was officiated by Reverend Croucher and he was buried at Yale four days later.

Coganovie, Uras

1888 - 1911

The penmanship of the the local coroner leaves the spelling of this man's name in doubt. It is also in print as "Eras Cojanovic."[224] What is known is that he was born in Austria about 1888, and he was killed in an accident while helping build the Canadian Northern Railway near Yale. According to the coroner:

"The deceased came to his death by the premature discharge of a blast of powder set ... by himself while engaged with his ... in construction of a tunnel by contract for the Canadian Northern Railway about five miles east of Yale. We find that the death was accidental."[225]

The accident took place on October 27, 1911. Coganovie is another young European immigrant killed in the dangerous work of railway construction, labouring in unsafe conditions, killed violently and buried in an unmarked grave in a foreign land a long way from home.

Francesco, Serafino

1884 - 1911

Francesco was born in Italy sometime in 1890 and came to Canada to help build the Canadian Northern Railway. In the autumn of 1911, he became seriously ill and was sent to the CNR hospital in Yale, where he fought double pneumonia before passing away on October 29, at the age of twenty-seven. He was attended by Dr. Loring, who estimated that Francesco was battling the sickness for about two weeks when he died. He was interred at Yale the next day, with Reverend Croucher overseeing his funeral. Francesco's grave has long been lost.

King, Emanuel Henry

1887 - 1912

Also known as Harry, Emanual King was a long way from home when he took a job with the Canadian Northern Railway. He was born in Providence, Rhode Island, to Joseph (born in Portugal) and Mary (née Sullivan). In his youth, Harry worked as a store clerk in his hometown. Just after his twenty-third birthday, King came to Canada to seek employment, which he found in the kitchens of the camps that sprang up along the new railway built on the Fraser's opposite shore through the canyon. On January 4, 1912, while at work, King "received a cut while cutting meat four days previous,"[226] an injury that caused an infection and his death four days later. Dr. Loring of Yale wrote that, by the time he saw King, there was nothing that could be done to save him, and the twenty-four-year-old passed away in the early morning of January 8. He was buried the next day in Yale by Reverend Charles Croucher.

Mikelson, Edward

1879 - 1912

Mikelson was a Norwegian member of the International Workers of the World labour union that helped to build the Canadian Northern Railway through the Fraser Canyon in 1912. He had only been in the Yale area for about a month when he contracted pneumonia in the January cold. He was admitted to hospital across the river in Yale, where the railway's hospital was located, but the thirty-three-year-old succumbed to the illness five days later. Mikelson was buried in the Yale cemetery on January 12, 1912, in a grave that can no longer be found.

Fauske, Hans

1889 - 1912

Fauske, a Norwegian, was born in February 1889. In 1910 at the age of twenty-one, he came to Canada, first travelling to the Strathcona district of Alberta. While there, Fauske worked on a farm owned by a Swedish father and son. Late in 1911, Fauske came to work on the Canadian Northern. Eighteen days into 1912, Fauske was killed in a violent accident. Working three miles west of Yale on the railway grade, he died instantly when a rock fell on him from some height. Reverend Croucher officiated Fauske's funeral and burial in the Yale cemetery four days later.

Weir, James

1890 - 1912

Weir was a Scottish-born labourer on the Canadian Northern Pacific Railway during its construction through the Fraser Canyon. In Scotland, the twenty-two-year-old had worked on his family farm, leaving in 1911 to come to Canada to join the track-laying gangs of the CPR's competitor. Weir arrived in the canyon in the summer of '11 and was based in North Bend beginning in September, where he worked for the teamsters until the end of the year. As the calendar turned to 1912, Weir became ill with what was soon diagnosed as typhoid fever, an illness that was spread by poor hygiene and public sanitation conditions. Transmission of these types of illnesses would have been almost unpreventable in the remote camps of the CNPR. The disease followed its usual course with Weir, and he lingered in the CNPR hospital for about three weeks before succumbing in the middle of the night on January 23, 1912. Hope's *West Yale Review* gave a brief account of Weir's passing:

"On Tuesday morning, James Weir, aged twenty-six, died of typhoid fever in the local hospital."[227]

As was the case with most immigrant labourers in the area, Weir's body was transferred to Yale for burial, with the service taking place the next day, officiated by Reverend Croucher of St. John the Divine. Weir's grave is today unmarked.

Erickson, Gus

1870 -1912

Erickson, born in Sweden in 1870, was another European immigrant killed during construction of the Canadian Northern Railway. He was working about a mile east of Yale on January 31, 1912, on a tunnel-blasting crew when he, like many others performing such duties, was killed by an explosion. The official cause of death determined by coroner Agassiz was "explosion of dynamite from unknown causes," and "loss of arm and general concussion all over body," resulting in immediate death.

"Quite a number of accidents were reported last week. While working in the east end of Yale tunnel, Gus Erickson was killed instantly while his partner, Frank Olson, was severely injured about the face and head. The accident was due to premature explosion while springing a hold. On the 3rd inst. while working east of the 'Hole in the Wall' on Section 2, three Swedes were caught in a rockslide. One was severely hurt about the head, and succumbed to his injuries on the following day. The other two men were removed to the hospital at Yale and are now out of danger."[228]

The accident occurred around 4 a.m. at the Number 2 tunnel. Erickson had previously worked in the same dangerous capacity on the Grand Trunk Pacific Railway between Edmonton and Prince Rupert. He was buried at Yale on February 1, 1912.

Brink, Albert

1872 - 1912

Brink was one of the many European immigrant workers employed by the Canadian Northern Railroad as the rails were laid through the Fraser Canyon. He was born in Sweden in 1872, and he, along with the rest of his countrymen, soon realized that life and work upon the railway was going to be a challenge. In early 1912, in a series of events the *West Yale Review* blamed on the International Workers of the World labour union, several of the camps strung out along the canyon went on strike. The union, pointing to the long list of deductions on the workers' paycheques, had little trouble instigating the job action. The workers, blindsided by the amount of pay received after medical fees, board, lodging, and other luxuries had been subtracted, found themselves idle in a foreign land, and, after laying down their tools, had very little to do. Unfortunately for Albert Brink, his restless hands found the bottle, which proved fatal. On January 30, Brink was discovered passed out and injured six miles west of Yale on the Canadian Northern line. He was brought to the hospital in town, but passed away early the next morning. The coroner noted that Brink died from "several hours' exposure while under the influence of liquor."[229] No funeral service was held, but he was buried in the Yale cemetery by his fellow workmen on February 1, 1912.

Fahlman, Bror

1891 - 1912

Bror Amandus Fahlman was nineteen years old when he arrived in Boston, Massachusetts, on the SS Ivernia of the Cunard Line from Liverpool on October 11, 1910. He was born on September 14, 1891, in Pitea, Sweden, to John and Maria Fahlman, and was on his way to Spokane via Boston, presumably to work on the railway. It was this same line of work that would bring him north in August 1911, along with his brother Edward and two dollars in his pocket. The brothers crossed into Canada at Grand Forks, British Columbia, and made their way to Yale to join scores of their fellow countrymen, along with other European labourers, building the Canadian Northern Railway. Like many of them, Fahlman would die while toiling in the Fraser Canyon, pushing the CNR through the narrow space between the mountains and the river; however, Fahlman wasn't killed in an explosion or any other workplace accident. He contracted typhoid fever while on the job near Camp 4 along the line. He lingered at the CNPR hospital for eight days before passing away on February 2, 1912, at about 10:30 p.m. His brother Edward signed his death certificate. Twenty-two-year-old Bror Fahlman was buried two days later in the Yale cemetery, far from king and country.

Pocuca, Steven

1867 - 1912

Poor penmanship and a faded death certificate cast doubt on the exact spelling of this man's last name (it could be Pociica), but it is known that he was yet another immigrant worker for the Canadian Northern Railway. He was a native Austrian, born about 1867, and was a member of the International Workers of the World, the union representing the construction workers of the CNR. About those workers, C. E. Barry remembers, "In 1912, the International Workers of the World, known as the IWW, moved in, with one of their main branches to the town of Yale. And shortly afterward, a dispute arose over the conditions on the CNR—the Canadian Northern, as it was known then. And so we had a lot of excitement at that time. I particularly remember one night there were so many in front of the local saloon that they blocked the CPR mainline and it was some hours before they could get the trains moving again."[230] Early 1912 saw labour trouble on the CNR, as a lengthy strike, at times violent, halted construction and forced the workers to find other employment. By mid-February 1912, it seemed like work was soon to resume:

"Trouble On CNR Grade Appears to Be At An End —The trouble between the contractors and labourers on the CNR construction work between Hope and Yale appears to be over. Three camps were immune: No. 6, of the McGillivray Bros.; and two of Palmer Bros. and Henning—No. 8, their headquarters camp, and No. 12, the nearest to Hope. The chief storm centre was Camp 3 where, after attempting to discharge the company's cook, the strikers tried to intimidate the men who were willing to work by attacking them in their bunks. The sole cause of the outbreak, such as it was, was undoubtedly the visit of walking delegates of the Industrial Workers of the World. The workers, most of them unable to speak or read English, were not hard to persuade that they ought to be getting a lot more money. Out of their first paycheques they find, usually with a shock, that they have to pay for board and lodging, medical fees, and every little luxury they have indulged in. The balance is often disappointingly small and they cannot understand. The presence of Messrs. Henning and Pearson and Constable Gravenor was always enough to restore order. For a time, two special constables were employed to patrol the line. The necessity for even this precaution no longer exists." [231]

It was against this backdrop that Pocuca worked as a powderman for the CNR. He was working at the east end of the long tunnel that sits on the opposite shore of the Fraser from Yale on February 25, 1912, when he was killed by a premature explosion of dynamite. He had been in the Canyon about three months when the accident occurred, and had been living at CNR Camp 5. His body was brought across the river and buried in the Yale cemetery the next day.

Bergstrom, John

1879 - 1912

Bergstrom was a Swedish immigrant labourer, in Canada to help construct the Canadian Northern Railway. He came to British Columbia from California, where he had done previous railway work, and was one of a number of Europeans toiling in unsafe conditions pushing through what would become Canada's second transcontinental railroad. On the afternoon of April 17, 1912, two days after the sinking of the Titanic, Bergstrom was working as a grader five miles below North Bend, British Columbia, when he was caught in a rockslide and killed instantly. According to the coroner, Bergstrom was "crushed and nearly all of his bones broken by above rocks."[232] Killed alongside Bergstrom was fellow Swede Phillip Solderham, also buried in Yale. John Bergstrom was thirty-three years old when he was buried April 20, 1912, at Yale. His grave marker is lost.

Peterson, Paul

1885 - 1912

Peterson was a twenty-seven-year-old Swedish railroad labourer who died in the Fraser Canyon on the opposite shore of Keefers, north of Boston Bar, in 1912. He was working on the Canadian Northern Railway when he was caught in a rock slide and killed instantly, on May 10 of that year. His remains were brought to Yale where they were interred by Reverend Croucher soon after. Strangely, for an immigrant worker only two months in Canada and with no family nearby, his gravestone, likely paid for by his fellow workers, is still very much intact in the Yale cemetery.

Calderini, Tony

1888 - 1912

Calderini came from Italy to labour in the construction of the Canadian Northern Railway being built through the Fraser Canyon in the years leading up to World War I. He had been living in railway construction Camp 4 near Yale for eleven months when he was killed on the job on June 20, 1912. Calderini was caught up in a premature explosion of eleven kegs of black powder and died instantly, along with fellow Italian labourer Emanuel Denardo. He was twenty-four years old at the time of his death. He was buried at Yale under the authority of the provincial police, having no relatives or close friends nearby.

Denardo, Emanuel

1881 - 1912

Emanuel Denardo arrived in New York along with his brother Luigi on the SS Virginian in 1909. In search of employment overseas, the brothers left behind their wives in their hometown of Prata, Italy. Emanuel was twenty-eight when he arrived and Luigi was twenty-five. They came to Canada and hired on with Canadian Northern construction crews working through the Fraser Canyon. Like so many of the other European immigrant labourers, Emanuel was killed on the job. He had been living at Camp Four, just a few miles east of Yale, for about nine months when, on June 20, 1912, he was caught up in a premature powder explosion and killed instantly, along with fellow Italian Tony Calderini. According to the coroner, he suffered a massive brain injury and was "generally smashed up."[233] His brother signed as the informant on Denardo's death certificate and attended the burial on June 22. Emanuel Denardo's headstone is still visible in the cemetery, and although at one point it had broken apart and fallen backward, it has since been repaired.

Dugan, J. H.

???? - 1912

Dugan, like Daniel Donald (see below), was one of the many casualties of 1912 while building the Canadian Northern. He died about three weeks before Donald and was buried at Yale.

Donald, Daniel

???? - 1912

Daniel Donald was killed while working on the Canadian Northern Railway on June 21, 1912.

Hahhu, Matti

???? - 1912

The only record of this CNR labourer is given in Reverend Croucher's handwriting in the St. John's burial record book. The surname could be Hahhn, Hahhin, or Hahhu. All that is known is that he was killed during CNR construction and was interred at Yale on August 17, 1912.

Fransiscola, Louie or Luigi Francescutti

1885 - 1912

Just over a year after the death of his fellow countryman Serafino Francesco, Italian-born Louie Fransiscola was killed during construction of the CNR. Like so many of his European immigrant counterparts, Fransiscola suffered an accidental, yet violent, death while at work. He was born about 1885 in Casarsa, a town in northern Italy near the Austrian border. On November 24, 1912, he was working as a driller on the CNR when he fell over a cliff and was killed instantly. The accident occurred near CNR Camp 5, just east of Yale. Like fellow Italian Emanuel Denardo, Fransiscola's grave marker has survived. The two headstones are identical, suggesting that their fellow workers pooled money together to pay for the monuments.

Macintosh, Donald

1881 - 1912

Donald S. L. Macintosh was born in Scotland on December 17, 1881. He came to Canada about 1907, taking a job with the CPR. In 1909, he became a section foreman for the railway based in Camp 16, where death would find him on Christmas Eve, 1912. While at work along the line, Macintosh was struck by a westbound freight train near his post. He was brought to Yale immediately by the provincial police, but the severe trauma Macintosh suffered was proved to be fatal. He passed away at the CPR hospital and was buried on Boxing Day by Reverend Croucher. His grave marker can still be seen today in the Yale Pioneer Cemetery.

Mullin, Thomas

1853 - 1913

Mullin was about sixty years old when he died of heart failure while living at Camp 3 during construction of the Canadian Northern Railway on Yale's opposite shore. He was interred in the cemetery on March 3, 1913.

Puffer, Percival Harold

1874 - 1917

Percival Puffer was an agent for the CPR and later the Canadian Northern Railway. He was based in Spuzzum, but his work forced him to lead a transient lifestyle, requiring him to check in at different points up and down the line. He came to the Fraser Canyon from Minden, Ontario, around 1898. At the time, he was newly married to Cora Lofthouse, born in 1872 in Cincinnati, Ohio. It appears that he preferred the use of his middle name in his day-to-day life, although exotic-sounding names were something he and Cora seemed to celebrate. The couple had six children: Geneva Cora, Perci Esther, Percival Ian, Truro Anza, Harold Lofthouse, and Kipling Lofthouse. Percival passed away on August 12, 1917, at the age of forty-three of heart disease. His grave can still be viewed today in the Yale cemetery.

Tsing Wong

1851 - 1939

Tsing Wong came to British Columbia in 1884 as a railroad labourer, and like so many of his Chinese countrymen, he remained in the province after the track-laying was completed. In the years after the construction was done, he turned to placer mining, which he stayed at for the next half century. Tsing Wong was eighty-eight years old in 1939, and it appears that the winter of that year contributed to his demise. He was found deceased on the south bank of the Fraser near Yale by Tommy Joe, who alerted the authorities. Natural causes and extremely cold weather were given as the cause of death by the coroner at Hope, and the body was interred in the Yale cemetery.

Children

There are at least fifty-seven children buried in the Yale Pioneer Cemetery, some as young as one day old. In 1881, a scarlet fever epidemic swept through town, taking with it at least eight young lives.

Sympathy

Oh, mothers whose children are sleeping,
　　Thank God by their pillows tonight;
And pray for the mothers now weeping
　　O'er pillows too smooth and too white;
Where bright little heads have oft lain;
　　And soft little cheeks have been pressed;
Oh, mothers who know not this path,
　　Take courage to bear all the rest.

For the sombre-winged angel is going
　　With pitiless flight o'er the land,
And we wake in the morn, never knowing
　　What He, ere the night may demand.
Yes, tonight while our darlings are sleeping,
　　There's many a soft little bed
Whose pillows are moistened with weeping
　　For the loss of one dear little head.

There are hearts on whose innermost altar
　　There is nothing but ashes tonight;
There are voices whose tones sadly falter
　　And dim eyes that shrink from the light.

Oh, mothers whose children are sleeping
　　And ye bend to caress the fair heads,
Pray, pray for the mothers now weeping
　　O'er pitiful, smooth little beds.[234]

Browning, Mary E.

1863 - 1863

Miss Mary Browning was born in Yale on January 7, 1863, and lived for one week, passing away on January 14. Reverend Reeve, who succeeded Reverend Crickmer at St. John's, performed her funeral service. She was the sixth burial in the cemetery three years after it was established by Crickmer and Bishop George Hills.

Barlow, Gilbert

1867 - 1868

Gilbert Barlow passed away at Yale on June 8, 1868, at the age of sixteen months. His burial was officiated by Reverend David Holmes. His father was an A. Barlow, a freight forwarding agent and vice president of the Yale Literary Institute, a debating and literary society established in 1864. The infant Barlow's gravesite in the Yale cemetery is unmarked.

A. BARLOW,

YALE, B. C.,

MERCHANT

AND

GENERAL AGENT

All kinds of Colonial and other
**Produce Bought and Sold
on Commission.**

BILLS COLLECTED,
And a General Agency Business transacted.
jy20

Turk, Lee

1863 - 1868

The son of Cariboo Wagon Road teamster James Turk and Mina Jane, an Indian woman, Lee Turk passed away at the age of five on October 14, 1868, in Yale. Lee was born in 1863 in Fort Pemberton, British Columbia. No cause of death was given, and he was interred in Yale on the same day he died by Reverend David Holmes of the Anglican Church.

Good, Cyril Wordsworth

1869 - 1869

Born on September 28, 1833, at Wrawby, Lincolnshire, England, Reverend John Booth Good arrived on the mainland of the colony of British Columbia in 1866 after spending five years in Victoria. Good was sent by Bishop George Hills to Yale, where he quickly developed a heart for reaching not only his new community and its relatively young church, but also the Thompson Indians living near Lytton. Good spent the next sixteen years serving the area, staying until the early years of railway construction.

In 1869, the reverend and his wife Sarah welcomed a son, Cyril Wordsworth. The infant was baptized on June 7, at Sapperton, British Columbia. Sadly, the baby would pass away a little over two months later, on August 14. Reverend Holmes noted at the time that Cyril was "buried in cemetery, Yale, British Columbia. Infant of the Reverend J. B. Good." Young Cyril was the twelfth burial in the Yale cemetery. His cause of death and the location of his grave are unknown.

Ward, Albert

1868 - 1872

Albert Ward was the firstborn son of William "Johnny" Ward and his wife, Alice Squalabia. He was born in Yale on March 16, 1868, at a time when his father was making a name for himself as a teamster on the Cariboo Wagon Road, shipping goods and transporting people to the interior of the province. On May 14, 1872, Albert was fatally injured in a stagecoach accident, presumably in the company of his father. Reverend Holmes at St. John the Divine noted that the four-year-old was "accidentally crushed under a wagon two miles from Yale. Died a quarter hour afterwards."[235] He was laid to rest in the Yale cemetery the next day. His grave today is distinguished by a wooden marker.

Nelson, Franklin

1868 - 1873

It is not clear if five-year-old Franklin Nelson's family lived in Yale or the surrounding area. The boy was born in Bridge Creek, a now-defunct name for a settlement in the Cariboo region of the then United Colony of Vancouver Island and British Columbia, British North America. His father was Stephen Marden Nelson (1827-1886) of Penobscot, Maine, and his mother was Phoebe Persis Weld, Nelson's second wife. His first marriage produced two children before his wife Margaret passed away in 1860: Florence (born 1855), (Uriah, 1857] and not the same Uriah Nelson who was a longtime Yale merchant). Stephen and Phoebe were married in Maine in the early to mid-1860s and the family came to present-day British Columbia not long after. Son Augustus was born in Bridge Creek in 1867, followed by Franklin on April 23, 1868. Frederick, Blanche, and Flossie would join the family, as well, but, sadly, the latter two were born after Franklin's death. Reverend David Holmes, who served at St. John the Divine from 1867 to 1873, kept detailed records of the funerals and burials over which he presided, and his notation on April 26 of that last year reveals an accident that took the life of young Franklin. The family was travelling on that day when, Holmes wrote, "the whole family thrown over the bluff near Yale, and boy killed."[236] The official record states that Franklin was killed instantly in the accident; he was the only fatality. The boy was buried in Yale three days after his fifth birthday.

Sargison, Henry Barnard

1866 - 1876

Henry was the sixth child of George and Margaret Sargison of Chambly, Quebec. George was an accountant who worked in several different locations in British Columbia, and eventually became the chief census officer for the province. The family lived in the Cariboo for a time, and George wrote about a trip to 100 Mile House that was so cold even the brandy in his sled froze solid. In the late spring of 1876, the Fraser River spilled over its banks and a flood that was at the time the largest on record wreaked havoc along its course. At Yale that July, the temperature reached "96 degrees in the shade"[237] and it was reported that the nineteen-mile post on the Cariboo Wagon Road was twenty-five feet under water. Buildings were swept down the river and ranchers lost crops and livestock. Far north of Yale along the road, tragedy struck the Sargison family. While crossing the Fraser at Quesnel in a canoe that served as the town's ferry, ten-year-old Henry Barnard Sargison fell overboard and was lost. The accident was witnessed by the ferryman Charles Ross, and Alex Burnett, a packer working along the road. The boy's body wasn't recovered until later that year in November, when he was discovered in the Fraser between Lytton and Lillooet. The Reverend George Ditcham was serving at St. John the Divine at the time, and performed a burial service for Sargison on November 19, 1876, in the Yale Cemetery. The Sargison family had no connection to Yale, and an Anglican cemetery was established in Lytton in 1872, adding to the mystery of why Ditcham chose to bury Henry Sargison there. Unfortunately, the location of the boy's grave is today unknown.

Gladwin, James Charles

1861 - 1877

James Gladwin was the son of businessman Walter Baker (or Beiker) Gladwin. The elder Gladwin was a commission merchant and shipper, proprietor of Kimball & Gladwin, which had been established in Victoria and opened a branch office in Yale in 1863. James was the firstborn of Walter and Mary, joined in later years by Harriet, Walter Frederick, Mary Elizabeth, and Louisa Elizabeth. It seems that the family matriarch, Mary, had passed away by 1881, as she is not listed in that year's census, but there is no record of the year of her death. James was born in Yale on November 28, 1861, and passed away at the age of fifteen on June 10, 1877, after suffering from consumption (tuberculosis) for about a month. He was buried the next day in Yale by Reverend Ditcham of the St. John's Church. In later years, his father, Walter, would remarry and move to the Cache Creek area. His brother Walter Frederick Gladwin married in 1908 and settled on Nicomen Island in the Deroche area where he was a rancher. James Gladwin's tombstone can be seen to this day in the Yale cemetery.

Tuttle, Mabel

1868 - 1877

For all the information available concerning the passing of young Viola Tuttle in 1881, there is almost no surviving evidence of her older sister Mabel. Their young lives overlapped by only about a year, as Mabel, the oldest of Guy and Ada Tuttle's children, passed away on December 27, 1877, at the age of nine. Her cause of death is a mystery and there is no notation of her burial in the St. John the Divine register. This is probably because the reverend serving Yale at the time, Reverend George Ditcham, was often not in town and seemed only to record deaths that occurred out in the larger Yale District. Ditcham only noted five deaths between 1876 and 1878, and none at all between 1873 and 1876. This speaks to the lull in town between the gold rush and the beginning of railway construction, and suggests there was no need for a full-time reverend in Yale, as Ditcham spent much of his time further north in the Fraser Canyon, around Lytton. The only hint at the life of Mabel Tuttle resides to this day in the Yale cemetery, where the grave she shares with her sister Viola has survived the years.

Bailey, David Bertram

1879 -1879

David Bailey was born June 18, 1879, to Benjamin and Sarah Bailey. In fact, Sarah delivered twins that day, welcoming both David and his brother Arthur Tennyson Bailey. The boys' father came to Yale from San Francisco during the gold rush in 1858, while Sarah followed in 1860, with their two eldest children. According to Elizabeth Hamilton, a living relative of the Baileys, their next eleven children were all born in Yale.

"From 1864, Ben was in business with John Alway—Alway and Bailey Storage and Forwarding Agency—situated adjacent to the BC Express. From 1868, he was in business with a Mr. Lawrence—Bailey and Lawrence Forwarding Agency—on Front Street. In 1875, he is listed as a school trustee, Yale School.[238]

Sadly, young David passed away at the age of six weeks, on August 1, 1879.

Tragedy followed the Bailey family when they moved to Victoria in 1882, as Benjamin was directly involved in the Point Ellis Bridge disaster of 1896. A crowded streetcar crashed into Victoria's Upper Harbour from the bridge, killing fifty-five people on their way to celebrate Queen Victoria's birthday. Ben Bailey was aboard the streetcar and he survived the crash, helping pull survivors and bodies from the water.

Arthur lived until 1927, when he passed away at the Provincial Mental Hospital (later called Riverview) in Coquitlam, British Columbia.

Benjamin Bailey

Teague, Charlotte

1872 - 1881

Charlotte Teague was the eldest daughter of William and Alice Teague of Yale. Like her parents, Charlotte was born in the English village of St. Day, Cornwall. Her father, William, had left England several years before her birth to seek his fortune in the gold fields of California, and eventually Yale and the Cariboo. He returned to England to marry Alice Michell on April 19, 1871, and a year later the couple welcomed Charlotte. The three soon crossed the Atlantic and settled in Yale, where William prospected and acted as the town's government agent for revenue and vital statistics. When Charlotte was four years old, the family had another daughter, Alice, named for her mother. Brother Cundy was born in Yale in 1877, and Nannie followed in 1880. In the summer of 1881 in the midst of a scarlet fever outbreak, nine-year-old Charlotte fell ill and, after suffering for just over week, passed away, on July 28. She was laid to rest in the Yale cemetery by Reverend Good on July 29, and, unfortunately for the Teague family, the devastating event would be repeated not a week later, as Charlotte's brother Cundy also succumbed to scarlet fever. Reverend Good was again called upon to officiate, and William, who signed the death certificates of so many miners, railroad workers, and other citizens of Yale, was forced to sign those of his own children. Charlotte and Cundy Teague's shared grave is visible today in the Yale cemetery in the family burial plot.

Teague, Cundy

1877 - 1881

Cundy Teague was born in Yale on November 22, 1877. He was the third child of William, Yale's government agent, and Alice Teague, both of St. Day, Cornwall, England. Older sister Alice was born the previous year in Yale, while the Teagues' eldest daughter, Charlotte, was born in England and came to British Columbia in 1875 with her parents. Cundy was a family name; the surname of his paternal grandmother, Michel Cundy, also of St. Day, and the middle name of a younger sister he would never meet. In the summer of 1881, as the rails of the CPR were being laid through the heart of Yale and progressing up the narrow Fraser Canyon, many of the town's children became ill with scarlet fever. The disease, spread through the air or by contact with an infected person, was characterized by a sore throat, fever, and rash, and was exceptionally dangerous to children between the ages of five and fifteen. In 1881, an effective treatment of the disease was still two decades away; a largely ineffective vaccine didn't come to market until 1924. The results of scarlet fever's rampage through Yale in 1881 were devastating, with at least seven recorded cases of death that summer and probably many more that went undocumented. Just four months from his fourth birthday, Cundy Teague suffered with the illness from the middle of July until he passed away on August 6. His death followed by a week that of his sister Charlotte, who passed of the same disease, a double blow for the Teague family. In fact, all four of William and Alice's children were sick at the same time. Daughter Nannie, barely a year old, and five-year-old Alice were in serious danger but, mercifully, pulled through. Michael Hagan's *Inland Sentinel* shared the news of Cundy's passing with the town:

"(We regret to announce the passing of Cundy Teague, son of William) and Alice Teague, aged three years and eight months. It was only last week we recorded the death of the eldest girl of this stricken family and now a second beloved child is taken away by scarlet fever, while a third and younger child is very low. We, also, learn the infant (Nannie) shows symptoms of illness. Mr. Teague and his family have the deep sympathy of our whole people."[239]

He was laid to rest next to his sister in the cemetery overlooking the Fraser in a grave that can still be visited today.

Tuttle, Viola Nelson
1876 - 1881

Viola Tuttle was the daughter Guy and Ada Tuttle. The Tuttles, married in February 1867, in Pugwash, Nova Scotia, came to Yale via Victoria, where Guy had employment as a hostler for F. J. Barnard's shipping company. In the CPR construction years, Guy was in the hotel business and referred to as a "capitalist" in the local directory. Thanks to the memoirs of W. H. Holmes, the exact location of the hotel is given:

"We then (came) to a side street, Albert Street, leading to the town above, and to the boat landing below; where on the beach was built a freight warehouse for Messrs. Kimball and Gladwin, Forwarding Agents, whose place of business was across the street from the commissary. Next was the Bailey

Hotel, then Peter Claire's Bakery and Confectionery store. Then a few small houses, then Guy Tuttle's hotel, and after that, three saloons."[240]

The summer of 1881 was deadly not only for the scores of men dying on the railroad grade, but for a number of Yale's children, as scarlet fever swept the town and claimed many young lives. Unfortunately for the Tuttle family, five-year-old Violet was to be counted among them. Just a few weeks before, another five-year-old, Harry Elley of the nearby Railroad House Hotel, would also die of the disease, Viola passed away on August 16, 1881. News of her death was carried in the local *Inland Sentinel* and the *Daily Colonist* of Victoria. From the *Island Sentinel*:

"Scarlet Fever —The eldest child, a bright girl of nine (an error, as Violet was listed in the 1881 census as being five years old), of Mr. Guy Tuttle of Yale, died of scarlet fever on Tuesday. A child died at New Westminster on the same day of the complaint."[241]

From the *Inland Sentinel*:

"Died —On the 16th inst., after a short illness with scarlet fever, Viola Nelson, daughter of Guy and Ada Tuttle, aged five-and-a-half years. Funeral yesterday at 4 p.m. largely attended, Reverend Mr. Blanchard officiating.

> A cloud, illumed by a ray,
> Shines dazzling like the orb of day,
> When of the ray in is bereft,
> Naught but a melting vapor's left;
> Yet to the sun the ray returns,
> And brightly there forever burns,
> Thy body was that cloud, dear child;
> The ray, the spirit undefiled;
> Thy God, the sun: His radiant brow
> Pours heavenly glory on thee now."[242]

Compounding the immense loss to the family, Viola's burial on August 17, 1881, was followed only hours later by a huge fire that swept Yale and seriously damaged the family home on Douglas Street.

"The Fire Fiend at Yale —Further Particulars, Loot, etc., etc. —When the fire first broke through a garret window in the rear of the Caledonia Hotel, it seemed a small affair, so much so that people a short distance away were not at all alarmed, imagining that the fire brigade would extinguish it with a few buckets of water. The critical moment, however, was not seized upon and, in a short time, the building was enveloped in flames. Wind at the time was light and drawing down from the hills back of the town. It is said that two men made their way upstairs to a room occupied by the party who is supposed to have accidentally set the house on fire, in order to get him out. He was intoxicated and would not move and the men who were trying to rescue him had to leave to save themselves. Whether the man was burnt or not was not known yesterday; at any rate, no charred remains were discovered. It was supposed that two men lost their lives in the California Hotel; but a strict search among the ashes afterward failed to show any indications of human remains, so that probably there was no loss of life at all. One man got seriously hurt by the fall of a verandah which struck him rather heavily. He will, however, soon get over the injury. Mr. Charles Moore of this city had his right hand considerably burnt in endeavouring to save some of his goods from the flames.

"The fire leaped from building to building with amazing rapidity and soon jumped across the street to the houses on the river bank. It is the opinion of many that had the captain of the Wm. Irving taken the responsibility of setting his donkey engine to work, that side of the street might have been saved, as a powerful stream could have been kept playing on those buildings and another one if necessary on the steamer. Unfortunately, Capt. John Irving was not there or this would certainly have been done and much valuable property saved from the devouring element.

"The Oppenheimer firm and other threw a large amount of goods over the bank down to the edge of the river. Some of this stuff was stolen and carried off by Indians. One gentleman chartered a large canoe and filled it up with valuable goods. After the fire was over, he went down to look for his canoe-load of stuff but it was missing. Neither canoe nor crew has yet turned up and, as he is unable to identify the men, the probabilities are that nothing will be recovered. It is supposed that at least $4,000 worth of goods was stolen by thievish whites and Indians.

"Looting was not confined to the river bank. A very great deal of stealing was done in the upper part of town and down below where the fire started. Romano saw a man with a full suit of his clothes on, but could not give him into custody for the reason that there was no one to take charge of the thief. The Onderdonk Hospital took fire, but was fortunately extinguished by one of the patients who, with others, kept it from catching again. There were but few prisoners in the lockup, mostly for slight offences, and those were liberated when it was found that the gaol and courthouse must go. One of the prisoners afterward remarked that 'it was an ill wind that blew nobody good' for the fire had set him at large. The thick foliage and the low buildings mostly under the bank at the rear of it saved Mr. Tuttle's house, although it is seriously scorched and many of the windows were broken by the heat. Mr. T. is among the heaviest sufferers and, in addition to losing property for which he was offered $12,000 a few months ago, another of his children, a fine boy of eight or nine years, is dangerously sick of scarlet fever and not likely to recover. His little girl was buried a few hours before the fire broke out."[243]

"Mr. Tuttle's cottage close by was given up to the devouring element, most of the things removed to a distance, when a couple of heroines rushed to the rescue, and mostly from the exertions of Mrs. J. B. Harrison and Mrs. Pressey may be seen that solitary home in the block standing, and again occupied by Mr. Tuttle and family. These ladies ought to put masculines to shame for not making proper exertions to check the flames.[244]

The town shrugged off the second massive fire in as many years and sawmills from Yale to Burrard Inlet worked twenty-four hours a day to provide lumber to rebuild as quickly as possible. Viola's passing left Guy and Ada with two children, seven-year-old Frank Tuttle, who did recover from his bout with scarlet fever, and one-year-old Florence. In 1877, the family lost another daughter named Mabel to an unknown cause. The Tuttle sisters, Viola and Mabel, are buried together under an obelisk-shaped monument that reads "Erected to the memory of the darling children of Guy and Ada Tuttle." The grave marker has survived the years remarkably well and can be visited today in the Yale Pioneer Cemetery.

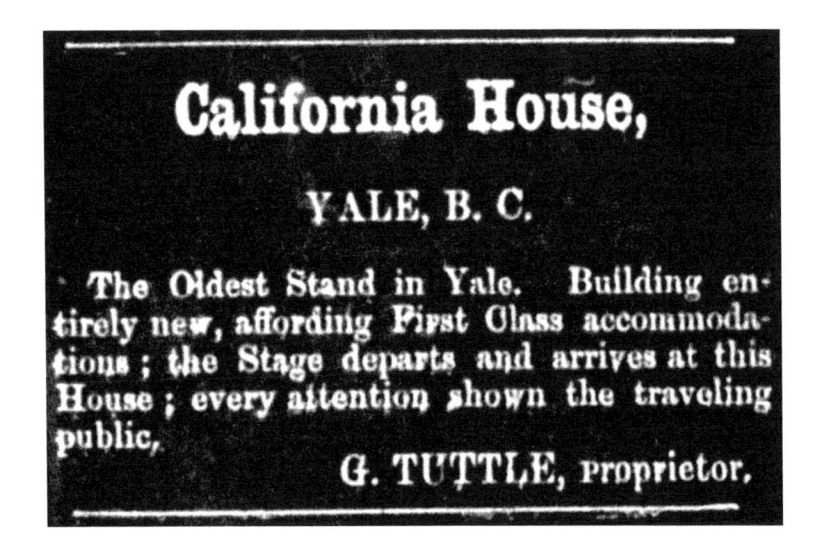

California House,

YALE, B. C.

The Oldest Stand in Yale. Building entirely new, affording First Class accommodations; the Stage departs and arrives at this House; every attention shown the traveling public.

G. TUTTLE, Proprietor.

McGirr, Howard John

1874 - 1881

Howard McGirr was the eldest son of William and Mary Jane McGirr who lived in Yale with his parents and four siblings in the early years of the construction of the CPR. His father, William, was a saloon keeper and tobaconnist; partner in the California Hotel on Front Street in Yale. On October 15, 1881, young Howard passed away from what Dr. J. D. Frickelton described as heart disease. Michael Hagan reported the death in the *Inland Sentinel* that week:

"Died —On the 15th inst., after a short illness, Howard John McGirr, aged seven years and five months.

'Happy is the tomb where the early dead
in the sleep of peace has pillowed his head,
Ere be felt the griefs of this dark abode
Or the world usurp'd what was made for God.'"[245]

Reverend Blanchard noted that Howard died of scarlet fever in the church burial record, making Howard one of several children in Yale who would die of the disease in 1881 and 1882. Howard, like his mother Mary Jane, were interred in Yale, but both of their graves are now hidden.

McDonald, David Pratt

1878 - 1881

News of the death of two-year-old David McDonald was carried in the *Inland Sentinel* on November 10, 1881.

"Died —on 7th inst., of brain fever, David Pratt, son of D. A. McDonald, aged two years and ten months. 'If not much of joy I knew, my griefs were light, and brief, and few.'"[246]

There was both a Douglas McDonald and a Donald McDonald living in Yale in 1879, one of which went by the name Alex and was the boy's father. Young David was buried on November 9, 1881, by Reverend Blanchard in the Yale cemetery.

> **TRAVELERS' REST,**
>
> Carlboo Street, East End, Yale, B. C.
>
> *The following are the rates of this House, which deserve attention:*
>
> Board, per month, - - - $20 00
> Board, per week, - - - - 5 00
> Board and Lodging, per week, - - 6 00
> Beds, - - - - 25 and 50 cents
>
> Alex. McDonald, - Proprietor.
>
> 35

Nelson, Abbe

1870 - 1881

While her name is absent in the St. John the Divine church burial records, it is highly likely that the daughter of Yale merchant Uriah Nelson is buried in the Pioneer Cemetery.

"Deaths —At Yale, on the 18th inst., Abbe, third daughter of Uriah and Annie Nelson, aged eleven years, four months, and twenty-eight days. The funeral will leave Thos. Story's undertaking rooms at 2:30 p.m., and from St. John's Church at 2:45 this afternoon (November 23, 1881). Friends and acquaintances are respectfully invited to attend."[247]

Elley, William (Willie), Reuben, and Harry

Harry - 1876 -1881
Willie - 1878 - 1882
Reuben - 1880 - 1882

The story of the Elley brothers is a sobering indication of what life was like in a frontier town with limited medical services where diseases that today are effectively treated with relative ease were often fatal. They were the sons of Reuben (1846-1922) and Catherine (1854-1940). Reuben Sr. was born in Wicken, England, and Catherine hailed from Hanover, Germany. They married on May 26, 1875, in Oakland, California, and welcomed their firstborn, a son, named Harry, on January 7, 1876. Their second son, Willie, was born March 7, 1878, also in Oakland. By the time Reuben Jr. was born on January 2, 1880, the family was living in New Westminster, British Columbia. Soon after, Reuben and Catherine moved their young family to Yale to run the Railroad House, a hotel located on Douglas Street across the tracks from the current location of the Yale Museum. The hotel was owned by Reuben's brother-in-law, Arthur Churton of Victoria.

Reuben and Catherine Elley

Not long after moving to Yale, five-year-old Harry got sick, and would die of what Dr. Hanington would call "eclampsia,"[248] a term that today is mainly associated with pregnancy. It is likely that Harry died suddenly from a series of seizures. Reuben and Catherine laid their firstborn in a grave on the hillside overlooking the Fraser on September 6, 1881.

"Died —After a short illness, on the evening of the 5th inst., Harry, son of Mr. Ruben (sic) Elley, of the Railroad House, Yale, aged five-and-a-half years."[249]

The late summer's trauma of losing their young son gave way to more sorrow when, only four months later, three-year-old Willie became ill and passed away. He died of what the doctor termed "bilious intermittent fever and by being allowed to remain in a draft, which produced congestion of the lungs" on his younger brother Reuben's second birthday. Reverend Good called it scarlet fever; Reuben and Catherine buried their second-born in the Yale cemetery.

"We regret to learn that Mr. Elley, of the Railroad House, who recently lost by death an interesting child, is again left to mourn for his little boy (Willie), aged three years, who died 2nd inst."[250]

The next week, on January 12, 1882, the *Inland Sentinel* ran this melancholy note:

"We regret to record that, since our last issue, Mr. Elley of the 'Railroad House' lost, by fever, his third and last child."[251]

The toddler Reuben succumbed to scarlet fever just four days after he turned two, and four days after his brother Willie had passed away. Reuben and Catherine's family of five was reduced to the grieving pair, losing them all in the space of four short months. Yet, out of the tragedy, ten months later, Reuben and Catherine had another son, George. The Elleys would go on to have at least five other children after the birth of George, all of whom would live to be at least forty. Their last son, James, lived to be almost 100 years old.

Unfortunately, the graves of the Elley brothers were likely lost in the flood of 1948, when the Fraser River covered most of the cemetery and washed away many of the historical grave markers.

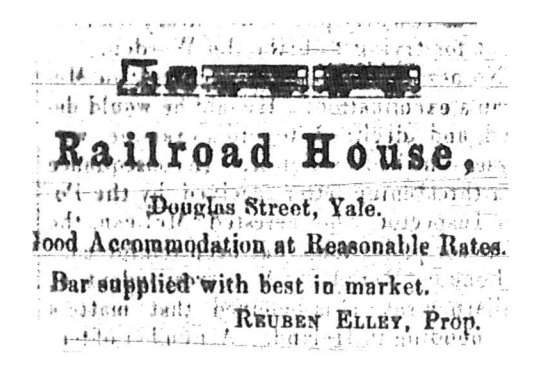

Railroad House,
Douglas Street, Yale.
ood Accommodation at Reasonable Rates.
Bar supplied with best in market.
REUBEN ELLEY, Prop.

Gladwin, Louisa Elizabeth

1881 - 1882

There is some mystery surrounding the birth and, shortly thereafter, death of little Louisa Gladwin. She was born on April 2, 1881, in Yale, and the church records state that she was the daughter of Walter Baker Gladwin, which would make her the sister of James Charles Gladwin (see above). If this record is accurate, she was born twenty years after her older brother.

She is not listed in the 1881 census, although she could have been born after the forms were filled out. There is also no mention of her mother on either the enumeration form or the baby's death certificate filled out nine months later. Adding to the perplexity that was her young life, her headstone in the Yale cemetery lists her last name as "Irving" and her year of birth as 1880. The latter seems to be a nineteenth-century typographical error, but the former raises questions as there were both Irving and Gladwin families living in Yale at the time. What is known, is that Louisa did not see her first birthday, as she passed away on January 25, 1882. Reverend Good and Dr. J. D. Frickelton both list the cause of death as "congestion of the lungs," with Frickelton noting that she succumbed to her illness "five hours from the time I was called."[252] Her grave marker can still be seen today in the Yale cemetery.

Lindsay, Annie Isabella

1876 - 1882

Alexander and Emma Lindsay were residents of Yale during boom years of railway construction. Lindsay was born in Glasgow, Scotland, in 1848, and came to Canada in the early 1870s. Emma (Parker) Lindsay was born in Victoria in 1855, one of the first white babies born in that city. The pair were married on June 25, 1876, in Emma's hometown. Alexander had been living in the mining settlement of Van Winkle, not far from Barkerville, at the time of his marriage to Emma, and they returned to the area following their wedding. By the time the pair were lured to Yale by the CPR a few years later, they had three children: Annie Isabella, born August 31, 1875; and sons Alexander (born 1877) and Robert (1880).

Emory City SAW MILL.

We beg leave to announce that we are NOW READY TO CUT TO ORDER, Rough and Dressed LUMBER Of All Descriptions!!

And hope by strict attention to the wants of the trade to receive a share of public patronage.

Office—Corner of 3rd & Lisgar Streets

GRAY, HOY & Co.

Annie was born in Stanley, British Columbia, another small mining town near Van Winkle in the Cariboo. Lindsay, a telegraph operator by trade, also served as Yale's postmaster, a position he held from 1881 to 1884. He was also a freemason, and a founding member of Cascade Lodge No. 10, acting as its Worshipful Master and Grand Standard Bearer in 1880-81. His masonic contemporaries included Drs. Hanington and Frickelton, William Teague, Isaac Oppenheimer, Thomas Gray, and Henry Hoy. The latter two men were owners of the sawmill at short-lived Emory City, which supplied lumber to the railway. It was against this backdrop that the Lindsay family suffered the tragic loss of their firstborn Annie on April 4, 1882. The *Inland Sentinel* carried the sad news:

"Died —Here, April 4, of paralysis of the heart, ANNIE ISABELLA, eldest child of Alexander and Emma Lindsay, aged six years and eight months.

> "'My Lord has need of these flowers gay,'
> The reaper said, and smiled.
> 'Dear tokens of the earth are they
> Where he was once a child.'
> 'They shall all bloom on fields of light
> Transplanted by my care,
> And saints upon their garments white,
> These sacred blossoms wear.'""[253]

Young Annie's cause of death was attributed to her heart. Reverend Good recorded that she passed away from a "spasm of the heart,"[254] while Alexander Lindsay's fellow Mason Dr. Hanington called it "paralysis of the heart—sudden death,"[255] surely a shock to the family. Annie was buried on April 5, 1882, evidence of which is still visible today in the Yale cemetery, as her grave marker is in remarkably good shape. It reads, "Safe in the arms of Jesus."

Powers, Lucius George Freeman

1878 - 1882

Lucius Powers was the son of Hartwell and Emeline (McCoy) Powers (see above). The boy was born on August 11, 1877, in Clarke, Durham County, Ontario, where his father was a farmer, and his birth made a family of four as Lucius joined his sister Eva, who was five years his senior. Not long after Lucius was born, the family relocated to Yale to take advantage of the town's new status as the headquarters for Canadian Pacific Railway construction. Hartwell opened a general store called Powers Bros. on bustling Front Street. However, on the journey from Ontario, young Lucius fell ill, and his condition worsened as the family set up shop in Yale. It wasn't long before the toddler's condition was grave, and on May 22, 1882, he passed away. Michael Hagan broke the news to the town in the *Inland Sentinel:*

"Died —On the 22 inst., Lucius G. F., second child of Mr. H. A. Powers, aged four years and nine months. Mr. Powers with his family arrived lately from Newcastle, Ontario, and while crossing the plains on the cars, his child was taken ill. It was not considered by doctors at San Francisco or Victoria dangerous, and it was only on arrival at Yale that the worst symptoms of scarlet fever were discovered. Dr. Frickelton thought he could have saved the child if attended a few days sooner. Mr. P. and his family feel deeply their loss and receive the sympathy of our citizens."[256]

There was no effective treatment for scarlet fever in the 1880s; a serum wouldn't be introduced until about 1900, and it was only then that mortality rates significantly declined. The disease claimed a shocking number of Yale's children in 1881 and 1882, including Harry, Willie, and Reuben Elley; Charlotte and Cundy Teague; and seven-year-old Viola Tuttle. The epidemic forced the temporary closure of Yale's school, only recently rebuilt after it was destroyed in the fire of 1880. The *Daily Colonist* of December 18, 1881, makes mention of a scarlet fever epidemic in Victoria and Nanaimo that claimed many young lives; this was not a contagion isolated in Yale. Young Lucius was laid to rest in a town he and his family barely knew. Tragically, his mother, Emeline, who had suffered with heart problems for many years, died the next year. Mother and son are buried next to each other in the Yale cemetery; their graves marked by a double headstone that has survived the last 130 years. The inscription on his marker reads: "Our boy has gone before us."

Sumner, Daisy

1877 - 1883

Daisy Sumner was born in London, Ontario, and moved west with her family to take advantage of the railroad construction boom enveloping the

Fraser Canyon in the early 1880s. The family was living at a remote point along the line in the Boston Bar area when young Daisy became seriously ill with croup in the winter of 1883. The *Inland Sentinel* carried the sad story of the conclusion of Daisy's short life:

"Died —At Yale, on the 19th inst., Daisy, aged six years, daughter to James Sumner, of 36-Mile Post. About a week since deceased experienced an attack of croup and was slowly recovering; it was deemed advisable, however, to seek medical aid, and the lamented one was carefully wrapped up and brought to Yale. Dr. Hanington was called in and expressed a fear for recovery; an hour-and-a-half elapsed when dear little Daisy breathed her last.

O, lost too soon! O, loved too well—
Too dear for earth—farewell, farewell!
One solace yet is given
Tho' lost on earth, thou'rt saved in Heaven.

The funeral took place here Wednesday afternoon, Rev. Mr. Horlock officiating, when a large number of friends attended."[257]

Though Michael Hagan in the *Sentinel* said Daisy was six years old, she in fact passed away three days shy of her sixth birthday in the Yale CPR hospital on February 19, 1883. Her grave marker is still standing in the Yale cemetery today, and is a testament to the grief her parents experienced as a result of her death.

McDonnell, Gertrude May

1878 - 1883

A faded headstone with the name "Gertrude" in the Yale Pioneer Cemetery may belong to five-year-old Gertrude McDonnell, who passed away on October 13, 1883. There is no record of a McDonnell family in the area, lending some mystery to the identity of the young girl. There was a brief mention of her passing in the *Inland Sentinel*:

"Died —At Texas Lake, 31st ult., after a short illness, Gertrude May, youngest daughter of Mr. James R. McDonnell, in her fifth year."[258]

Irwin, Lydia Elizabeth

1883 - 1883

There are marked similarities between the cases of Louisa Elizabeth Irving (or Gladwin) and Lydia Elizabeth Irwin, names aside. Both were born and died in Yale, neither saw a first birthday, and both passed away suddenly. Miss Irwin was born on September 3, 1883, and lived three short months, passing from the world on December 11.

"Died —On the 11th inst., Lydia Elizabeth, only daughter of Mr. Joseph Irwin, schoolteacher, aged three months and seven days. The funeral took place Wednesday at 2 p.m. and was largely attended by our citizens and the schoolchildren."[259]

She was the firstborn child of Joseph Irwin (1856-1918) and Alice Ann Woodward (1859-1938). They were married on August 8, 1882, in the Nicola Valle,y about a year before Lydia's birth. Construction of the CPR brought the family to Yale, where Joseph was a schoolteacher, and where they stayed until the railroad was finished in 1885; moving on to the Cache Creek area in the following years. After the loss of Lydia, Alice gave birth to two more children in Yale: Eleanor in 1884, and a daughter known only as R. E. Irwin. As for Lydia, Dr. Ernest Hanington noted the sudden nature of her death on the infant's death certificate, going on to write, "this infant was a weakly child, and was found dead in bed in the morning. Appearance showed no signs of violence."[260] Reverend Edwin Wright also wrote that Lydia was unbaptized, and that a short service was held at her grave site twelve days before Christmas, 1883. The next year, Joseph Irwin wrote a letter to *Inland Sentinel* editor Michael Hagan, which gives an interesting glimpse into life in Yale in those years.

"Letter from Mr. J. Irwin —Yale, May 27, 1884. For the *Sentinel*.

Sir: —Having been considerably annoyed during the past week by the actions of our chief magistrate, with your permission, I shall expose some of them to the public. One evening last week while passing along the street with a friend, Mr. A. C. Elliott called out the words 'blackguard, sneak,' etc. Learning that these expressions were, in all likelihood, intended for me, I sent him a note next morning asking him to be manly enough to give me his signature if he meant these remarks to apply to me, or I should publish the affair and let the public decide to which of us they really belonged. I have not heard from him since, but I have found out that lately he has been using considerable choice language with reference to myself and others, in hearing of my friends passing along the sidewalk. For instance, he has stated he would like to see me hung. Just imagine how his very soul would gush forth in a paroxysm of excessive joy to see me dangling at the end of a rope! But I am afraid there is no such soul-inspiring scene in store for him. As I have never been in court, either as plaintiff or defendant, that rope idea, however sweet to contemplate, had better be abandoned for the present. I beg also to inform him that any little satisfaction he may get by this 'new method' he is welcome to, but that I consider any man, who dare not put his signature to his language when called upon to do so, is no man at all—no matter what position he may occupy. As you are aware, Mr. Editor, he has been forcing me into this controversy from the first, and now if it turns out that he 'has been climbing the wrong tree,' he has himself to blame.

I am, sir, yours truly,

JOSEPH IRWIN
Teacher Public School, Yale.

The conclusion of the disagreement between the teacher and the local magistrate will likely never be known, but it was enough to stir up controversy at least for a short while. As for baby Lydia, her grave in the Yale cemetery is now lost.

McDonald, Alexander

1884 - 1884

Alexander McDonald was the infant son of hotel operator Alexander and Mary Jane McDonald. Alex Sr. owned and operated the Traveler's Rest Hotel on Cariboo Street (today the Trans-Canada highway). Young Alexander was born in Yale, but, tragically, he passed away just eighteen days after his birth.

Reverend Darrell Horlock made the sad notation in the church record that the baby had a "lay baptism in extremis," meaning he was likely baptized by his father or mother who knew their son would not survive long enough to have a church baptism. Alexander was laid to rest in the Yale cemetery on June 15, 1884.

Hayes, Edith May

1879 - 1885

The daughter of cabinetmaker William Henry Hayes and his wife, Margaret, Edith May was born in 1879 in Napanee, Ontario. She was the older sister of Clarence, born in 1881. The young family moved west in the early 1880s to Yale, where Henry worked during the boom years of CPR construction. Tragically, their young daughter Edith, by then six years old, died on February 11, 1885, of unknown causes. She was buried in Yale and the family moved back to Ontario sometime in the next few years. William passed away in 1899, and Clarence became a sailor. In his later years, he worked as a truck driver in Cordova, Alaska, where he would live the remainder of his days.

Pickles, Sarah

1881 - 1885

Sarah Pickles was the daughter of Abram and Elizabeth, the first child of the farming couple from Comox, British Columbia. She was born on January 3, 1881. How and why the family was in Yale in 1885 is no longer recorded, but four-year-old Sarah was laid to rest there on March 9, two days after her death from what Reverend Edwards called "infantile paralysis," otherwise known as polio. In the years after the toddler's death, the family continued to farm on Denman Island, near Comox.

Castle, Alph and Castle, Robert

Alph - 1891 - 1892
Robert - 1886 - 1886

These two baby boys are difficult to trace as they don't register in any of the Castle family trees. They are buried together in the Yale cemetery. Robert was born May 11, 1886, and died August 15 of the same year, while Alph lived from August 9, 1891 until February 1, 1892. Their shared headstone reads, "I know that you are waiting for me, darling" and is a sad reminder of a time of high infant mortality that affected many of Yale's families. Although there still stands a monument to the Castle boys, their names do not appear in St. John the Divine's burial register, adding to the mystery of their short lives.

Michell, David William

1883 -1886

By 1886 the railway was completed through the Fraser Canyon and the population of Yale had plummeted as those associated with railroad construction had moved on. However, the town remained an important stopping point for the CPR, with train crew members, dispatchers, track foremen, and maintenance workers still calling Yale home. Thomas Michell was an engineer based in the town in the 1880s and remained after Onderdonk's crews had moved on in 1884. He and wife Rebecca (née Reseigh) were born in England and had lived in the United States, where son Thomas was born in Grass Valley, Nevada, in 1873, then moved on to British Columbia, where at least five other children joined the family: John (1877), Stephen (1879), Jane (1880), David (1883), and Julia (1885). The latter four were all born in Yale. The family would endure tragedy, when, on July 3, 1886, young David was involved in a terrible scalding accident. He would suffer with his injuries for four days before passing away on July 7. He was buried in the Yale cemetery the next day; the location of his grave is today unknown.

McFarland, Margaret

1872 - 1888

Miss McFarland was listed as both a domestic servant and a pupil at the All Hallows School in Yale. She was likely from the Lytton area. On April 11, 1888, when she was sixteen years old, McFarland died of pulmonary tuberculosis at the school. She was interred at Yale by Reverend Richard Small, who also served as the All Hallows chaplain, two days later.

Webb, Peter

1887 - 1889

The son of a Boston Bar farmer and merchant, Peter Webb was only two years old when he died in an unfortunate accident involving some medicine that had been left within his reach. The toddler had been sick at the time, and had been administered "Fellows' Syrup of Hypophosphites," a medicine used at the time to treat a wide variety of illnesses, but that also contained strychnine and was thus dangerous in large quantities. His father, John, noted, "We had been giving the boy this medicine as he was sick. He climbed up on a chair and took it off a shelf in the store and drank a half bottle of it. No one in store at time."[261] The accident took place three days before Christmas, 1889, and the boy was brought to Yale for burial.

Shepherd, Carrie Muriel

1891 - 1891

Carrie Shepherd was the infant daughter of Yale teacher Samuel Shepherd. She was born in April 1891, to Samuel and his wife, Caroline, and was their fifth daughter. Unfortunately, young Carrie passed away in at home in Yale on November 24, 1891, with the cause of death given as congestion of the lungs.

Creighton, Amy Lillian

1896 - 1896

Amy Lillian was born to David and Mary Alice Creighton in Yale on January 28, 1896. She died the next day and was laid to rest in the Yale cemetery. In the late nineteenth century, between ten and twenty percent of all children born would not live until their first birthday.[262] Many factors worked against Yale and babies like Amy. The town's relatively remote location and the fact that it was in a period of decline, sparse to almost non-existent medical care, home births, and in Amy's case, the fact that she was born in the winter, all made it difficult on both mother and child. She was David and Mary Alice's fifth child, and was their second to die in infancy.

Coppen, Albert Arthur

1896 - 1897

Young Albert Coppen was born sometime in the late summer of 1896, the third son of bookkeeper Ambrose and wife Ada Mary (née Poston) at Spuzzum, British Columbia. Ambrose, born in Marylebone, London, England, in 1865, and Ada had been married on May 30, 1891 also in London. Ambrose had previously served as Hope's assistant postmaster in 1893, when the population of the town was around eighty. Baby Albert was baptized in Yale at St. John's Church on September 12 of the same year. Sadly though, Albert would pass away on May 25, 1897, when he was only nine months old. His cause of death is unknown. Tragedy would strike the family again in the next few years, as, by 1901, Ada had also died, leaving Ambrose and his sons Richard and Edmund without their wife and mother. Ambrose would remarry in 1907 to Agnes Pill of Nelson, British Columbia, and Richard and Edmund would both go on to fight for Canada in the First World War.

Choate, Frederick Zaccheus

1898 - 1898

Frederick Choate was born in North Bend, British Columbia, on March 27, 1898, to James Zaccheus and Alice Choate. His father, James, worked for the CPR, and when Frederick was born, the family already had two other children, three-year-old Edward and two-year-old Edith. James Choate was Andrew Onderdonk's trusted bridgebuilder during construction through the Fraser Canyon in the early 1880s. From 1880 until the end of construction in the area nearly five years later, the Choate family ran a farm between Hope and Yale that supplied produce to the railway. As a tribute to the family, the area is known to this day on the map as Choate, and a building on the land, currently occupied by a church camp, is called Choate Lodge. Sadly for James and Alice, baby Frederick died on September 8, 1898 when he was not quite six months old. His cause of death is listed as gastroenteritis. After Frederick died, the couple had two more children, William in 1899 and Arthur in 1900. The family's firstborn son, Edward Walter Choate, served overseas during World War I.

Arnott, John Harold

1900 - 1905

Five-year-old John Arnott lived in North Bend with his father, William, and mother, Anne, the youngest of their six children. William ran a general store and was the town's postmaster while Anne, twenty-two years his junior, stayed home with their family. On February 16, 1905, John died of diphtheria. He was buried near the creek in the Yale Cemetery, where his fading grave marker can still be seen today.

Flann, Arthur Thomas

1905 - 1905

Young Arthur Thomas Flann was the son of Thomas and Jane Flann, making him the brother of Susanna and James (see above). He was born in early 1905 in North Bend, British Columbia. Sadly, his life was short; he passed away July 10 of the same year; the cause of death was listed as "gangrene of the lungs."[263] He was buried by Reverend Croucher in Yale, interred in the family plot. His gravestone reads:

"Our Baby
Arthur T
Son of T & J Flann
Died July 17, 1905
Aged 10 Months

I know that our darling
is safe in the arms of Jesus"

Davis, William

???? - 1906

There is little information about young William Davis save for Reverend Croucher's note in the St. John the Divine parish register. He was just eighteen months old when he passed and he was the "child of Annette."[264] Davis was buried on May 22, 1906, in the Yale Cemetery.

Turner, Myrtle Violet and Winifred
Turner, Norman and Clifford

Myrtle - 1897 - 1898
Winifred - 1900 - 1900
Norman - 1906 - 1906
Clifford - 1906 - 1906

The young daughter of CPR fuel man John Turner and his wife Margaret of North Bend, British Columbia, Myrtle Turner was born on April 29, 1897, and passed away only ten months later, in March 1898. The Turner family was large, with at least five other children when young Myrtle made her brief appearance. Another daughter, Winifred, was just five weeks old when she died in early June 1900. Reverend Croucher laid the infant to rest in the Yale cemetery, just as he did for her sister Myrtle two years earlier. In January 1906, Margaret gave birth to Clifford, followed by the arrival of his brother Norman, on December 14 of the same year. Tragically, a bout of whooping cough claimed the lives of both boys, one-year-old Clifford on Christmas Eve, and fifteen-day-old Norman only five days later. The boys were added to their family's sad plot in the Yale cemetery soon after.

Flann, Susanna Irene

1906 - 1911

Susanna Flann was likely the daughter of Thomas and Jane Flann of North Bend, British Columbia. She died of diphtheria on January 27, 1911, at the age of four. She is buried in the combined Paffard/Flann family plot, where her grave marker exists to this day.

Paffard, Florence Alena

1890 - 1911

Florence was the daughter of Thomas and Jane Flann of North Bend, British Columbia. Thomas was a CPR stonemason who stayed in the area to raise his family even after construction was complete. Florence was born on July 28, 1890, and married railroad man Frederick Paffard in July 1907, in Vancouver. Preferring to be called by her middle name, Alena, she lived with her husband alongside her parents in North Bend, where they would have three children: Florence (born 1907), Winifred (1908), and Thomas (1910). On March 27, 1911, Florence succumbed to meningitis, leaving Fred and her three young children behind. According to the census that year, Fred was living in North Bend with his in-laws and their still growing family after the death of his young wife. Sadly, Florence's four-year-old sister had predeceased her by a few months, dying of diphtheria in January, and her young son Thomas died the following April, also from meningitis. The three are buried together in the Yale cemetery in a family grave.

Paffard, Thomas Fredrick Dyland

1910 - 1912

"Tommy" was the son of Frederick and Florence Paffard of North Bend, British Columbia. He passed away on April 20, 1912, about a week after the sinking of the Titanic. The boy's death from meningitis came a little over a year after his mother passed away, meaning Fred Paffard lost his wife and son in about thirteen months. Thomas is buried alongside his mother and his four-year-old aunt Susanna who had died in 1911 (see Susanna Flann).

Cox, Arthur

1900 - 1912

Arthur Frederick Cox was the son of Sunset and Annie (Foster) Cox. He, like his parents and most of his siblings, was born in Quebec. On August 20, 1912, at about five o'clock in the afternoon, eleven-year-old Arthur drowned in the Fraser River. The *West Yale Review*, published at Hope, carried the news:

"Yale In Mourning for Sad Drowning Fatality —(Special Correspondence) —Yale, August 24. —The deepest sympathy from Yale and district goes out to Mr. and Mrs. A. W. Cox and family in their sad bereavement. On Tuesday while bathing in the Fraser near Yale Creek along with some of his little playmates, their little son, Arthur, went out beyond his depth and before help could be summoned the current had carried him out and drowned him. The burial service on Wednesday (August 12, 1912) was conducted by the Reverend C. Croucher in St. John's Church, and was attended by everyone in Yale. The spirit of the sad event was noticed in everyone present, and when the organ played that beautiful hymn, "Safe in the arms of Jesus," tears were shed by everyone present. Nearly all mourners followed the cortège to the graveyard and saw the remains put to rest of what was the day before a bright and happy little lad. Floral offerings and messages of sincere sympathy were sent by nearly everyone in Yale. The honorary pall-bearers were four playmates, Masters Crann, Castle, Gadossic, and Vicars; the casket was carried by Messrs. Creighton, Egan, Drybury, and Barry. Mr. and Mrs. Cox wish to express their heartfelt thanks for all the kindness and sympathy shown them. The boy was not quite twelve years old, having been born on September 2, 1900, in Megantic County, Quebec."[265]

Coroner L. A. Agassiz gave his cause of death as "drowning through being unable to swim."[266] He, along with his brother Everett and his father, are interred at Yale. Arthur's grave is still visible, although the years have taken their toll on it.

Sawyers, Reginald Stanley

1912 - 1913

Reginald Sawyers passed away at about one month of age on January 16, 1913, at his home in North Bend, British Columbia. The infant succumbed to bronchial pneumonia and was brought to Yale for burial. Reverend Croucher at St. John the Divine performed the burial service in the Yale cemetery.

Castle, Frank August

1900 - 1915

Frank Castle was the son of August and Margaret (McLinden) Castle, born in Yale in February 1900. On June 6, 1915, the teenager was "trying to swim in the Fraser River,"[267] but drowned. The coroner noted that Frank was "buried by his father August Castle"[268] two days later in the Yale Cemetery.

Lovell, Doris May

1915 - 1916

Doris was the firstborn of Canadian Pacific section foreman Clarence Lovell and Charlotte (Smith) Lovell. Clarence and Charlotte were married in Agassiz in late 1914, and after Doris was born on October 20, 1915, in Harrison Hot Springs, the family moved to Clarence's childhood home of Spuzzum. In the middle of the night on March 7, 1916, baby Doris passed away from convulsions related to a gastrointestinal problem. The family laid their four-month-old daughter to rest three days later in the Yale cemetery, with Reverend Croucher officiating. In the years after Doris's passing, Clarence and Charlotte relocated to the Deroche area where Clarence continued his employment with the CPR. They would have five more children.

Garraway, Evelyn Ruth

???? - 1917

Little information is available about baby Evelyn Garraway other than that she died from pneumonia as an infant, and that her body was brought to Yale from Regina, Saskatchewan, where she was buried sometime in late 1917. Reverend Yates noted that her father was a railway employee, who may have been based in Yale at the time.

Wo, Wing Howe Fook

1916 - 1918

Of the scores of Chinese who died in the Fraser Canyon between the gold rush and the railway construction years, it is an almost certainty that only a very small handful were buried in Yale's public cemetery. In fact, the Chinese had their own burial grounds on the eastern end of town, where those who were not simply buried where they fell in the canyon were transported for interment. It is a strong possibility that two-year-old Wing Wo was buried in that graveyard as well; his death certificate only indicates "Yale, BC" as the place of burial. No cause of death is given because the toddler saw no doctor. A note scribbled on the side of the document reads "called but could not go as too many were sick at home."[269] What is remarkable about the young boy's death was the date and time of its occurrence: November 11, 1918, at 11 a.m. Armistice Day.

Rickarby, Harold

1921 - 1921

Harold Rickarby was born on December 7, 1921, in North Bend, British Columbia, and passed away the next day. The baby boy was the son of Great War veteran Richard and his wife Violet-Maud Rickarby, both born in England. A carpenter by trade, Richard moved to Keefers in the postwar years and he and Violet started their family, welcoming a daughter named Joan in 1918. Harold arrived when Joan was three years old, but he survived only one night, dying of a convulsion on December 8, 1921. The grieving family had their son buried in the Yale cemetery two days later on December 10. Richard died in 1941 and Violet lived to the astonishing age of 105, passing away fifty years later, in 1991.

McEwan, Norman Ken

1927 - 1928

Yet another baby boy interred in Yale is Norman McEwen, born in North Bend, British Columbia, on May 6, 1927. He was the son of CPR employee Andrew, and his wife, Marion Ada (Kerr) McEwen. On March 19, 1928, at the age of ten months, Norman succumbed to influenza-induced convulsions. He was buried on March 21, 1928, but the whereabouts of his grave are no longer known.

Creighton, Thelma Eris
1923 - 1929

Thelma Creighton came into the world in Yale on a summer's day in 1923 and left it only six years later. She was the second of four daughters born to Francis and Margaret Pearl Creighton, and the only of their children to die at a young age. Her death was tragic and accidental, made even more so by the sad notation on her death certificate where it lists her occupation as "schoolgirl."[270]

"Struck down by a car driven by A. L. Greenhalgh [of] ... Vancouver, Thelma, the six-year-old daughter of Mr. and Mrs. Frank H. Creighton, Yale, died while being taken to the Chilliwack Hospital Sunday night. The little girl, who was a member of a picnicking party near the Cariboo Highway, is said to have dashed across the road and run directly in front of the Greenhalgh car. Mr. Greenhalgh rushed her to Hope but, finding no physician available, he transferred the child to another car which set out for Chilliwack. Mr. Creighton, the father of the girl, was a member of the board of trade party that visited the mines near Jessica (a station on the Kettle Valley Railway). He was informed of the accident on his return to Hope, where he expected his wife and children to meet him. Mr. Creighton operates the general store and post office at Yale. His father, Mr. David Creighton, is a pioneer of the district. At an inquest held on Tuesday afternoon in connection with the death of the little girl, a verdict of accidental death was brought in by the jury, it being proved that it had been an impossibility for the driver to have avoided the accident under the existing circumstances."[271]

The tragic accident occurred on June 23, 1929, four months before the beginning of the Great Depression, and barely a year before her grandfather's mysterious death in Yale Creek. She was two months shy of her sixth birthday. Her grave is found in the Castle/Creighton family plot.

Gennard, Marian

1923 - 1932

Marian Gennard was the daughter of Benjamin of Brierley Hill, England, and Helen (Price) of Toronto. She was born on October 6, 1923, in England and came to Canada with her parents, leaving from Liverpool and landing at Quebec City in June of 1928. The family made their way to British Columbia and settled in Yale soon afterwards, where Benjamin took various jobs with the railway. In 1932, Marian was stricken with typhoid fever, an infectious disease that, in the 1930s, was preventable by vaccine, but in Miss Gennard's case, was fatal. She died on February 19, 1932, at the age of nine. Benjamin and Helen remained in Yale for many years after the death of their daughter, with Benjamin working as a watchman for the CPR in his later years.

Angus, Donald

1921 - 1934

Born on April 25, 1921, to Felix Angus of Boothroyd and Sarah McMillan of Chilliwack, Donald died of tubercular meningitis at the Chilliwack General Hospital at the age of thirteen on February 28, 1934. He was the youngest of Felix and Sarah's children. His grave marker in the Yale cemetery has been lost.

Post 1960 Burials

Passing Away

We dream and lo! our lives flow on,
We dream and lo! our dream is gone,
We rock the cradle of our days,
From morn till night we sing life's lays,
We stretch our hands across the years
That bind our hearts with joys and tears,
And dreaming kneel and kneeling dream
How swift they flow, how fast the stream!

We climb the hills by morning light
And gaze into the shades of night,
The sky above, the waste below
Are vestments of the years that flow,
We lock our hearts with iron bands,
But ah! the work of unseen hands,
Our hearts must flow, our years must go

And roses bloom beneath the snow.
We stand where burn'd the lights of youth,
We kneel before the shrine of truth,
We feel the breath of love and grace
Steal o'er our brow, anoint our face,
Beside the fire that warms our heart
We sit and watch the flames depart,
And rock the cradle of our years,
And dream our days in joys and tears.

-Thomas O'Hagan, published in Yale's *Inland Sentinel, January 3, 1884*

Deegan, Patrick

1940 - 1959

Eighteen-year-old Patrick Deegan perished in a car accident on June 28, 1959. The accident occurred near Hope, and the young highway worker was rushed to St. Paul's Hospital in Vancouver where he passed away. Deegan, who lived in Yale at the time, was buried in the Pioneer Cemetery. Unfortunately, flooding the next year destroyed many graves including Deegan's. The plaque from his grave marker was saved, however, and is housed in St. John the Divine to this day.

Seaberg, Gudrun Anna

1912 - 1971

Mrs. Seaberg was the daughter of Louis and Helga Fagervik, Norwegian immigrants to Canada in about 1910. Anna was born in Yale on January 2, 1912, although it appears that the family moved frequently in those years as, by 1921, they were living in Alberta tending a farm. The Fagervik family was back in Yale by 1931, where Anna's father, Louis, had taken a job with the CPR. She married William Seaberg and moved to Vancouver Island, settling in the village of Cedar, near Nanaimo. Anna Seaberg passed away on August 7, 1971, at the age of fifty-nine. Her cremated remains were buried in the Fagervik family plot at Yale, and her grave can still be seen today.

Barry, Mary Ellen

1876 - 1972

Mary Ellen was born in Yakima, Washington, to Edward (Ned) and Mary Stout on March 27, 1876. She was about four years old when her mother passed away in 1880, and her father returned to Yale from Washington, Mary and her sisters Daisy and Margaret soon after. In 1882, six-year-old Mary Stout had a brush with royalty, and received a gift that she kept for the rest of her life:

"There are still a few personal links with the fabled past of Yale if one really looks hard enough. Not far from the church in a cottage by the railway tracks, a gentle little old lady sits with a book on her lap. It's a typical Victorian children's book, titled *Papa's Little Daughter*, and it's a bit the worse for wear and tear. On the flyleaf is the inscription, 'To Miss Mary Stout. From the Governor-General and the Princess. Yale, BC, 1882.' The Governor-General was the Marquis of Lorne. The Princess was Queen Victoria's daughter, Princess Louise. And the little old lady who holds the book in her hands is Mrs. Mary Ellen Barry, who was little Miss Mary Stout back in 1882. Mrs. Barry recalls the vice-regal visit, how the princess arrived from New Westminster in a stern-wheeler, and how she and her sister, two little girls in crinolines, presented Lord Lorne and the princess each with a Fraser River nugget. Mrs. Barry is the daughter of Ned Stout, Indian fighter and prospector, who followed the call of gold to California in '49 and to Yale and the Cariboo in '58. He lived to be nearly 100, dying at Yale in 1924, still full of wonderful tales of the gold rush."[272]

The census in both 1891 and 1901 list Ned and Mary Ellen as a single family residing in Yale. As a young girl, Mary attended All Hallows in the West, a boarding school established in Andrew Onderdonk's former residence and administered by the Church of England. Miss Stout married Charles Barry in Yale just after Christmas in 1904, and they had one son, Charles Edward Barry, the next year. The couple raised their son in Yale, where Charles Sr. was an employee of the CPR. He passed away in 1928, and Mrs. Barry remained a widow for the last forty-five years of her life. She died on February 23, 1972, in Coquitlam, at the age of ninety-five, and was buried next to her husband in the Yale Pioneer Cemetery.

McLinden, Fredrick Thomas

1912 - 1974

Fred McLinden was born in Yale on March 12, 1912, to James and Emma (McMillan), the last of their five children. The family—which included Jeanette (born 1898), Minnie and Charlotte (1902), and Earnest (1906)—had been residents of Yale for many years. Fred's parents were both born in the Yale district, James in 1879 and Emma in 1885. James's father, Arthur, was a teamster on the Cariboo Wagon Road and his mother hailed from the Boothroyd area near Boston Bar. The McLindens were married in Yale on May 25, 1906, but by 1914, had separated and both had remarried. Fred would later be joined by half sisters and brothers from his parents' new relationships. McLinden would remain in and around Yale for most of his life. He was a logger and married Geraldine (Hughes). He passed away on May 25, 1974, when he was sixty-two years old. McLinden was cremated and buried in the Yale cemetery where his mother and other members of his family also rest.

Doern, Richard Wade

1970 - 1974

Richard "Dunky" Doern was born on August 4, 1970, and lived in Quesnel, British Columbia. His family has a long history in Yale: his great-great-grandfather was William Teague, and his great-grandmother was Gladys Chrane, both of whom are buried at Yale. Tragically, he drowned in the Fraser River on March 19, 1974, and his body was never found. To honour their son's memory, Richard's family placed a headstone in the family plot in the Yale cemetery.

Richard "Dunky" Doern

Barry, Charles Edward

1905 - 1979

Charles Edward Barry was born August 29, 1905, in Yale to Charles and Mary (Stout). Charles Sr. was a bridgeman for the Canadian Pacific Railway during the construction years. Barry grew up in a time of decline for the town, its streets quiet in the years since the building of the CPR, but he nonetheless found Yale an exciting place to grow up, and shared some of his memories in an interview with the CBC's Imbert Orchard, conducted at his home in 1965. "At the time of my boyhood, there was a large Chinatown here in Yale," remembered Barry. "These people (the Chinese) were always very nice to the children. In fact, many of us children looked forward to Chinese New Year much more than we did some of our own holidays. It always meant fireworks and presents for all of the schoolchildren."

Between 1911 and 1913, the young Barry witnessed the town come alive as railway construction once again boosted the local economy when the Canadian Northern Railway was built across the river from Yale. "The population of the town at that time rose to 2,000 people," Barry remembered.

"It was the largest I guess since the '58 gold rush, when it was reputed that there were over ten thousand people in the town." Barry remembers the International Workers of the World labour union setting up a branch office in Yale and the excitement that occurred during the acrimonious strike of 1912. "I particularly remember one night there were so many in front of the local saloon that they blocked the CPR mainline and it was some hours before they could get the trains moving again."

Other favourite childhood memories of Barry's were seeing the last sternwheeler arrive at Yale in 1911, with a load of black powder for the CNR, and the burning of the old Hudson's Bay Fort building that same year. "You can be sure," he said, "that on both of those occasions, all of us children were there." C. E. Barry became involved with the local school board in 1926 and served the local educational system for over forty years. When he took up with the board, Yale had only a one-room schoolhouse; but by 1965, he was proud to proclaim that the district spanned sixty miles and had a million dollars' worth of schools. He took immense pride in his involvement with the education system, and was rewarded when, in 1973, a brand new middle school opened in Hope bearing his name.

Barry married Lilly Dennis in 1930 and owned a general store in Yale. The couple had two sons, Robert and William. Robert carried on the family business, operating Barry's Trading Post until he was no longer able. In fact, the business is still in Yale, and remains in the Barry family. C. E. Barry became a magistrate serving the Fraser Canyon in 1941, something he called his "most important occupation." Most satisfying for the judge was working with juveniles, especially to have "had the opportunity on several occasions to start boys out on the right track in life by handling them carefully when they appeared in court. And I will say that many has been the sleepless night that I've put in on thinking of some boy that was coming up in the morning and what I should do to put him right in life. Of course there have been many unsuccessful attempts, too, but I think the successful ones overshadow the losses." Judge C. E. Barry passed away September 7, 1979, in Vancouver at the age of seventy-four and was buried in the Yale Pioneer Cemetery.

Bjerky, Verna Susan

1964 -1981

Verna was the daughter of Clara Algie (Bjerky) Chrane and Gordon Gervil Bjerky, the son of Norwegian homesteaders of Saskatchewan, Minnesota, and Norway. Her mother Clara is of Spuzzum native descent (N'Laka'pamux), and has connections to Yale and the Fraser Canyon that stretch back many generations. Remembered by her sister Irene, Verna was bright and sunny, tanned in a minute, and the only blonde in the family. She led an active life, and worked as a forest fire fighter and carnival worker during her teen years. One May 2, 1981, sixteen-year-old Verna went missing while traveling to Kamloops. She had been working at a restaurant in Hope, and due to a bus strike, found her only option was to hitchhike. Sadly for the family, Verna's remains have never been found, although some of her personal effects were recovered from the Fraser River when the water receded later in 1981. The family has never stopped looking for closure in her disappearance, and remain hopeful that the mystery will one day be solved. Her parents, Walter and Clara, added a pink granite memorial stone for her in the Yale Cemetery at the same time they put one in for Verna's sister, Glennie; and to simplify things; they inscribed "Glennie, daughter of Walter and Clare," and "Verna, daughter of Clare and Walter."

Chrane, Gladys

1889 - 1981

Gladys was the youngest daughter of William Teague and Alice Michel, both born in St. Day, Cornwall, England. William came to the Fraser River with the horde of gold seekers, and busied himself panning for gold at Cornish Bar in Hope before moving on to Yale and becoming the Government Agent in Yale during the Fraser River Gold Rush. Once he had established himself, he went back to Cornwall for his bride, Alice Michel, and they bought the former Trutch residence in Yale. They had many children, and several of the youngest attended All Hallows Canadian School as day students. They also boarded some of the extra (British) girls at their home, which was located beside the school.

Gladys was born on June 24, 1889, in Yale, and attended the day school. In 1918, Gladys married a charming man, Raymond Lindell Chrane, who hailed from St. Louis, Missouri. They lived in Ruby Creek for a while, but returned to Yale, where they lived with their five children, Glenn, Walter, Eleanor, June, and Norma. Soon, however, Raymond deserted the family, leaving Gladys and the children alone. A persevering woman with a strong spirit, Gladys was devoted to the history of Yale. She had her own small museum in later years, and devoted herself to recording local aboriginal history, including important family connections with Chief Liquitum, also known as the last great leader of the Fraser Canyon indigenous people; Chief James; and Chief Jimmy Charlie. She contributed volumes of information to historical researchers who came to interview her and was a valuable source of local knowledge and family. Gladys lived to the ripe age of ninety-two. She is remembered by family for her most excellent bread, baked in the oddest pans that made round bread with ridges perfect for cutting. One of the best-known and proudest pioneers of Yale, Gladys passed away on September 2, 1981, and was interred in the Teague family plot in the Yale Pioneer Cemetery.

Hayward, Dollie

????-1985

Chrane, Glynnis (Glennie)

1970 - 1989

Glennie is remembered by her family as an absolutely sweet, charming, gorgeous tomboy. She and her sister, Glady, being only a year apart, grew up almost like twins. They graduated together because Glady spent one year in Denmark as an exchange student. Glennie grew to be long, lanky, and beautiful. Her sister Irene reminisced that Glennie's mother, Clara, witnessed one man walk straight into a pole while staring at her.

Glennie wanted to be a fashion designer, and made her own grad dress when she graduated from Hope Secondary School in 1988. Glennie was also into mechanics, especially interested in motorcycles, and she eventually bought her own bike, a Honda 500. This is how she died. She crashed her bike in Abbotsford, on a long curve near Mount Lehman Road. An investigation was held, and it was determined that she had been run off the road, by accident. She passed away on May 31, 1989, and was interred in the Teague family plot by her parents, Walter and Clara.

Cox, Everett

1902 - 1989

Everett Uberta (also recorded as Roberts) Lemuel Cox, the son of Samuel and Annie Cox in St. Johnsbury, Vermont, was born on January 13, 1902. He came with his family to Yale from Strathcona, Alberta, in 1910, and he was a schoolmate of C. E. Barry, referring to his friend in interviews about childhood in Yale as "Eddie." The family also lived in Hope for a short period of time, where his father was a carpenter; however, most of Everett's years were spent in Yale, where he helped to establish the Yale Museum, and was an honourary member of the Yale Historical Society. His candid stories from his younger years when Yale still had distinct Chinese and White neighbourhoods are recorded in Andrea Laforet's doctoral thesis called, "Folk History in a Small Canadian Community." In one example, he remembers Yale's drinking establishments and the fascination they held for the town's boys:

"Before I was there—during the gold rush—Yale had lots of bars. All that Front Street was nothing but bars. I never got in Mrs. Revesbeck's bar, but I looked in lots of times. Underage—they wouldn't let you in. They sold whiskey in little square bottles you could put in your hip pocket. You could buy one and take it out. They used to give us a nickel for one of those bottles. You didn't see many beer bottles in those days."

Cox goes on to explain what he did with those nickels:

"If you had a nickel, what would you buy with it? Package of gum, chocolate bar, all-day sucker, apple, orange—each a nickel. Couple of pennies were all you needed. There was a great big jar full of penny candies. Round ones. Something like jawbreakers."

Later in life, Everett worked for the Department of Highways. He passed away September 22, 1989, at Fraser Canyon Hospital in Hope at the age of eighty-seven, and was buried in Yale near his father.

Orlando, Marianne Ward

1918 - 1990

Marianne Edelstein was born near Berlin, Germany, in 1918. Her parents were Julius and Margarete Edelstein, factory owners who manufactured porcelain goods and bicycle chains. Marianne and her brother Werner spent many of their summers with their grandmother, who emphasized "the importance of seriously applying oneself in order to realize success," which served Marianne well in the turbulent years that followed her idyllic childhood.

Marianne was fourteen years old in 1933, when life changed for her family. The Edelstein family was Jewish and soon came under persecution by the ruling Nazi party that had swept to power that year. Marianne and her family were uprooted and sent to live on the grounds of the porcelain factory that they no longer owned as it was confiscated by the Nazis, who kept her father, Julius, on as manager. Marianne attended the local school and was the only Jewish child in the class, an arrangement that held until a member of the Nazi party became her teacher. Her parents soon sent her to school in Switzerland to avoid the dark cloud of persecution they sensed coming. Marianne's brother Werner had been spirited out of the country after assaulting a member of the Nazi part on a Berlin street, and other members of her family were soon to follow. Marianne, however, returned to Germany from Switzerland and was in Berlin on the night of November 9, 1938, now known to history as Kristallnacht (Crystal Night) in which over 7,000 Jewish businesses and 1,000 synagogues were damaged or destroyed. Marianne, who had attended the Berlin Opera that night, "instinctively understood that she was witnessing an event of unbelievable horror." Her father, Julius, was picked up by the police soon after, and Marianne endangered herself by spending hours at the police station demanding his release. She managed to escape Germany to England where she served as a cook, nanny, and housekeeper, even though she had no experience in domestic work due to her comfortable upbringing. She married in 1940 to a British man, and automatically received British citizenship, putting an end to her days as a domestic. Around this time, Marianne lost contact with her remaining family in Germany, learning years later that her grandfather died in a Nazi concentration camp in Czechoslovakia, and her grandmother perished in the infamous Auschwitz-Birkenau extermination camp.

On November 27, 1941, Julius and Margarete Edelstein were deported to the concentration camp at Riga, now part of Latvia. They did not survive this experience. Marianne spent the remaining years of World War II in England, where she rode out the Blitz under her neighbour's kitchen table. After the war, she was determined to find out the fate of her family, and returned to Germany, where she worked as an interpreter. She was fluent in German and English, and possessed a working knowledge of French and Italian, which led her to some high-profile assignments, including translating for Konrad Adenauer, the first post-war chancellor of West Germany. She was able to visit a house in Berlin where her father had hidden from the Nazis, and learned that her mother and grandmother had, years before, buried a trunk in the yard filled with family photo albums and other heirlooms. Miraculously, she was able to recover the contents, despite the lid of the trunk being pierced by shrapnel.

In 1950, Marianne visited her brother Werner, who had immigrated to the United States some years before. She hadn't seen him for close to seventeen years, and upon seeing him, decided to stay. She found work at a publishing house, and when it was bought out by John Wiley and Sons, she became an executive and vice president of sales at the multinational corporation. The company is famous today for their "For Dummies" series of technical books. Marianne, who had divorced after the war, married Phillip Orlando in 1956 and the couple lived in Queens and Westchester, New York. Phillip died in 1987, and Marianne followed three years later, passing away on April 11, 1990, in Vancouver. How she came to be buried in the Yale Pioneer Cemetery is a mystery.

Autenrieth, Diane

Autenrieth, Karl
Diane - 1943 - 1991
Karl - 1932 - 2003

Diane Autenrieth was born February 2, 1943, in Truro, Nova Scotia. She was the daughter of Yale residents Phil and Annie Acar and worked as a nurse's aide. Autenrieth passed away January 9, 1991, at MSA hospital in Abbotsford, British Columbia, from lung cancer. She is interred in the Yale cemetery because of her family's long connection with Yale.

Karl Autenrieth was from Germany, born on December 6, 1932. He and wife, Diane, lived and raised their family near Abbotsford, British Columbia. He survived Diane by twelve years, passing away on July 12, 2003. His ashes were interred in his late wife's burial plot in the Yale Cemetery soon after.

Shilson, James and Verna

James - 1907 - 1991
Verna - 1919 - 2004

Jim Shilson was born in Folkstone, Dover, England, on March 25, 1907. He and his parents moved to Canada in 1913, settling near Fleming, Saskatchewan, where his father took up farm labour. Jim served with the Royal Canadian Engineers in World War II, and, after his discharge in 1947, Shilson, his wife, Verna, and their two daughters moved to Yale, where he was employed by the CPR until his retirement in 1972. Mr. Shilson loved Yale and its history and was happy to share his knowledge with tourists to the area. He was a founding member of the Yale and District Historical Society and was instrumental in the founding of the Yale Museum, dedicating many hours to its operation and upkeep. He passed away in 1991 and was laid to rest in the Yale Pioneer Cemetery.

Verna Jessop was born in Welwyn, Saskatchewan, in 1919. After marrying James Shilson, the family moved to Yale, where she would spend almost fifty years as an active community member and a champion of the town and its history. She obtained a licence to operate a movie projector and would screen films in the Yale Hall. She also worked in the local general store, the telephone exchange, and Yale's post office. In 1985, Mrs. Shilson was involved in the creation of the Yale Museum, and spent many years on the Yale Historic Society. She also did her best to see that the Pioneer Cemetery was cared for. She passed away in 2004 in Penticton, but was brought back to her adopted home of Yale for burial. She is buried alongside her husband, Jim, and the results of the work the Shilsons helped to start can be seen in visiting the museum and walking through the cemetery.

Goodwin, Robert

1913 - 1991

Goodwin was born on May 4, 1913, in Pilkington, Wellington, Ontario, the son of Richard and Annie. He was a private in the Royal Canadian Army Service Corps during the Second World War, a division that served as the transport corps for the army. After the war, Goodwin married Marjorie Kemsley, on February 16, 1946 in Sarnia, Ontario. The family moved west to Burnaby by the 1960s, where Goodwin worked for the highways department. In the 1970s, the couple relocated to Yale and lived on a small hobby farm on Front Street overlooking the Fraser River. Goodwin was the self-proclaimed "mayor of Yale" for many years, and passed away on September 30, 1991. His ashes were interred in the Yale cemetery.

Willock, Hector and Mary

Hector - 1917 - 1995
Mary - 1922 - 1992

The connection to Yale with the Willocks lies with Mary. She was the daughter of Margaret Pearl and Frank Creighton, born on April 9, 1922, in Vancouver. She spent her formative years in Yale, and worked for the On Lee family in their hotel, where she would eventually meet her future husband. Hector "Scotty" Willock was a native of Young, Saskatchewan, born there in 1917. Scotty came to Salt Spring Island, British Columbia, at the age of seventeen and ran a general store for a time. He later moved to Vancouver and hired on with the Canadian Pacific Railway on a track maintenance crew. He was stationed at Yale and lived on a work train parked on the siding near town. In search of food and entertainment, the work gangs invaded the local hotels and saloons, which set up the meeting between Mary Creighton and Scotty at On Lee's hotel in 1936. The couple soon married and took up residence in a cabin near Clara Clare's property just north of town near the Number One Tunnel, and lived in the area until about 1942. Railway maintenance work took Scotty from Yale, to the Coquihalla subdivision of the Kettle Valley Railway between Hope and Brookmere, to Port Coquitlam. The family also lived in Walhachin and Mission, where they spent the rest of their lives. During the years in Mission, Scotty continued to work for the CPR, and was employed as a light maintainer on the Mission bridge.

Before 1972, the CPR bridge functioned as both a rail and vehicle crossing, and passing trains created long lines of traffic waiting to cross. Scotty was responsible for traffic flow on the bridge, and kept a baseball bat with him to encourage overzealous drivers to keep clear when a train was approaching. He was also an operator for the swing-span, opening and closing the bridge for boat traffic on the Fraser. Mary worked as a water tester for the federal government, dropping bottles into the river, retrieving them, and sending them to the Fisheries Department in Ottawa. The couple had four children and seventeen grandchildren and were beloved by their family and community. Mary Willock passed away on December 6, 1992, in Mission, followed by Scotty on June 16, 1995. Although the couple had not lived in Yale since the 1940s, their wish was to be buried in the pioneer cemetery.

Goodwin, Marjorie

1921 - 1993

Marjorie Kemsley was born on January 12, 1921, to Ernest and Kate in Coquitlam, British Columbia. She married Robert Goodwin on February 16, 1946, in Sarnia, Ontario, and in the following years they would welcome seven children. They lived in the Lower Mainland of British Columbia and retired to Yale where Marjorie and Bob had a small hobby farm and garden. Marjorie was also a bowler and competed for Yale at the bowling alley in Hope. She passed away on November 16, 1993, in Langley and was buried next to Bob in the Yale cemetery.

Chrane, Glen

1918 - 1995

Glen Chrane was the oldest son of Raymond and Gladys Chrane, and the grandson of William and Alice Teague. Chrane lived in Yale in his early years, and during World War II, the twenty-year-old went overseas where he saw action in Sicily. After the war, Chrane spent many years living and working in Toronto. He returned to Yale for a time before moving to Hope where he lived his last years. He passed away in 1995, and was interred in the Teague family plot in the Yale Pioneer Cemetery.

Boyd, Evalyn Annie

1932 - 2002

Cox, Evelyn

???? - 2002

Evelyn Cox was the granddaughter of Everett Uberta Cox, who came to Yale in 1910 and lived most of his life there. After her death in 2002, Evelyn's ashes were interred in her grandfather's grave in the Yale cemetery.

Conrad, Karl and Queenie

Karl - 1908 - 2003

Queenie - 1915 - 2006

Karl Conrad was born in Obermoschel, Germany, on August 28, 1908, and immigrated to Canada when he was twenty-one, first settling in Manitoba and then in British Columbia. He found work at the British Columbia nickel mine between Hope and Yale, where he met Queenie Smith, herself an immigrant from England. Queenie, born on December 1, 1915, was twelve years old when she arrived in Canada. She eventually left Alberta and hitchhiked to British Columbia, where she found work in the kitchen at the same mining camp. Though the facility was remote, it didn't stop Karl and Queenie from skiing out to attend the dances held at the Yale Community Hall. The couple soon relocated to Prince Rupert, British Columbia, where Karl looked for work on the docks, sometimes finding it hard to do so during the war years because of his German heritage. During this time, Karl began taking action to realize a long-held dream of becoming an architect, and while formal training was not to be, Conrad studied feverishly and read book after book on the subject. The first project the self-taught builder completed was a barn in Prince Rupert, built to the extreme satisfaction of the owner. The Conrads moved from the north coast of British Columbia to Vancouver, where Karl honed his craft as a housebuilder. In 1947, after a few years in construction and having saved up some money, Karl, Queenie, and their two daughters moved back to Yale, the town they loved. Karl bought a share in the Canyon Hotel, then located across the railway tracks from where the museum stands today. He and a partner rented the hotel to workers constructing the highway through the Fraser Canyon. In later years after the hotel was demolished, he built a new incarnation of the establishment not once, but twice after it burned to the ground. The new location was at the corner of Victoria Street and the Trans-Canada Highway, the footprint of which can still be seen today next to Barry's Trading Post.

Karl also built several houses in Hope, some of which are still inhabited to this day. Queenie, mother to three daughters, loved their plot of land on the mountain overlooking Yale, and was a one-time owner of the house built by Johnny Ward across the railroad tracks from the Creighton house. The construction of the BC Hydro transmission lines through Yale in the early 1960s forced the Conrads, now with three daughters, to sell their property and relocate to Hope, although they retained a lot near the cemetery, where Karl built a cabin for the family to spend vacations in Yale. The Conrads spent their later years in Hope, where Karl continued to build, before finally retiring to Chilliwack, where Karl passed away on January 30, 2003, at the age of ninety-four. Queenie followed on December 9, 2006, having just turned ninety-one. The couple's wish was to be buried in the Pioneer Cemetery in Yale, which their family honoured.

Chrane, Walter Lindell
1921 - 2005

Throughout his long life, Chrane was a logger, an expert faller, gold miner, bookie, and WWII veteran soldier. He was from one of Yale's old families, being the son of William Teague's youngest daughter, Gladys, and her husband, Raymond. Raymond's family resided in St. Louis, Missouri, and had connections to Jesse James and the famed Pinkerton family. The family was extremely poor for most of Walter's formative years, compounded by the absence of his father, who left early in Walter's life. He became an excellent hunter and gardener. Everyone worked hard to survive, but much of it fell to him as the eldest son.

Chrane's adolescent years coincided with the Great Depression, and he remembered a large work/relief camp in Yale. He and his young partners would pan and sluice for gold on the sandbars of the Fraser between Yale and Hope, just like his grandfather had done when he first came to the area. Eventually, Chrane found work as a logger, a job he held until he joined up when the Second World War broke out.

Then nearing twenty, Chrane sailed for England on a troop ship for training and worked as a part-time messenger, completing his rounds on a Harley-Davidson. Chrane was wounded by suspected friendly fire and sustained multiple injuries, including a broken leg which required a long stay in hospital. Upon his recovery, he was sent to Europe, and was in Germany when the fighting ceased in 1945. Like so many others coming home after the war, Chrane was reluctant to talk about his experiences with his friends and family.

Yale was a welcome sight for Walter Chrane, and he quickly resumed his logging career, becoming known as one of the best tree-fallers in the business. He continued to support his mother and sisters and, in the late 1960s, he renewed his acquaintance with his soon-to-be wife Clara, seventeen years his junior, and whom he had held in 1937 when she was a baby. They married in 1969 and gave birth to Gladys Mae Chrane. The following year, 1970, they welcomed Glynis Sandra Chrane, fondly known as Glennie, and embarked on raising a family of his own in the town where his family roots were so deep.

Tragedy struck the family when, in 1989 Chrane's daughter Glennie lost her life in a motorcycle accident. Chrane, looking with dismay on the state of the Yale Cemetery, wanted it to be a place worthy to remember Glennie, and so with the help of other members of his family, went to work digging, smoothing, and landscaping the grounds. Much of the credit for the current pristine state of the cemetery can be credited to Chrane and his work, which included cleaning up a mess of bush, thorns, slide alder, and small invasive trees. Together with wife, Clara, and their family, Chrane removed over 150 small trees and stumps, along with boulders that had likely been deposited during the great Fraser River flood of 1948. After the clearing was done, the family faithfully mowed the grass and held back the encroaching greenery until the Yale and District Historical Society assumed control with an endowment from the estate of Dr. Hayashi. Walter Chrane passed away on October 30, 2005, and his monument was added to the Teague family plot, along with the memorial stones of his daughter Glennie, stepdaughter Verna, nephew Dunky Doern, brother Glenn, mother Gladys Teague Chrane, and the various Teague family members, including his aunt and uncle who died as children before his mother was born.

Royal Canadian Air Force Plane Crash

On September 21, 1941, an Avro Anson bomber en route from Kimberley, British Columbia, to Vancouver crashed in the mountains above Yale. All three men on board were instantly killed in the accident, which occurred in such a remote area that rescuers were unable to reach it for four days. Passing away were Sergeant Lloyd Poston Britland, First Officer Lloyd William Brooks, and Aircraft Second Classman Douglas Buchanan Wortley. Britland was twenty-one years old, born on January 9, 1920, in Birkenhead, England. Brooks, a native of Joplin, Missouri, was thirty-seven at the time of the crash, and the twenty-three-year-old Wortley was from Saskatoon.

"Plane Crew Unreported —No Word from Rescue Party After Bomber Discovered Down Near Yale —Fate of F. O. L. W. Brooks and two companions, whose lost Royal Canadian Air Force plane was sighted in rough timbered country near Yale, about eighty miles northeast of Vancouver, yesterday, was unreported late last night, according to Western Air Command officials. The plane, a twin-engine Avro Anson bomber, was forced down or crashed early Sunday afternoon on a flight from Kimberley to Vancouver. Besides F. O. Brooks, whose wife lives on East Saanich Road (in Victoria), the ship carried Sergt. L. P. Britland and AC-2 (Aircraftman Second Class) D. B. Wortley, both of Vancouver.

 A ground searching party was sent out from Hope, about fifteen miles from the scene, early yesterday afternoon, travelling through a rugged terrain, after the bomber had been discovered in the morning by searching

RCA planes, sweeping low over the southwest boundary country. Reporting by radio, searchers said they were unable to make a landing because of the nature of the country. The report did not say if the bomber had crashed and made no mention of the three-man crew. Western Air Command officials believed it would be some time before the ground party reached the plane. The missing plane was last seen over Princeton at 12:30 p.m. (PDT), Sunday, flying at about a 14,000-feet altitude, according to a report from that interior town. Princeton is approximately fifty miles from where the plane was discovered. The report added that the downed ship was one of two making the flight, and that they had picked up ice at high altitude. One of the planes returned to Princeton, but the other was unreported until found yesterday.[273]

The wreck was sighted by a Royal Canadian Air Force search flight on September 23, but it was another forty-eight hours before the site was reached by rescuers on foot.

"Plane Dropped Thousand Feet in Treacherous Air —Down in the valley, a warm autumn sun bathed Chilliwack in warmth and a gentle northeast wind rolled across the flat land. Seventy-five-hundred feet over Yale, our plane swirled and spun and dropped a thousand feet at a crack in the down draft; the cold cut through the fur-lined flying suit, leather jacket business suits we each wore. That was a Tuesday morning and Saturday, a plane with three young Vancouver air force men had dropped, crashed into the hillside below us. Downdrafts, the kind our little plane was fighting and ice, not cold, probably caused the wreck of that big Avro Anson bomber and carried its crew to death. We were looking for that plane. Down below us a rescue party was within a quarter of a mile of the wrecked machine. And up there, among the craggy, scarred mountain tops, our machine, a fraction the size of the big bomber, was being buffeted by the winds. Every time we tried to gain altitude a downdraft suck us toward earth. Once we fell a thousand feet. The next time it was seven hundred feet. We twisted and turned to escape the clutches of the treacherous wind. Off on one side was historic old Yale, basking in the sun. On the other were the milk-green waters of Harrison Lake. Below us were buildings which once hummed with activity—the BC Nickel mine. Old Settler mountain, all eight thousand feet of it, was dangerously close. We could get above it only once. Snow-capped and forbidding it was. And the wrecked plane and the dead men were below us. It's a rough and tough country, that sea of mountains behind Yale. Jagged peaks and granite-like patches of bare rock, with a few gnarled trees here and there. The Cheam range behind us, snow-capped and towering, wasn't inviting. Huge draws, heavily forested, with streams rushing down them, separated the peaks. Little lakes dotted the tops of mountains. Earl Brett, as capable and shrewd a pilot as ever, skinned a mountain top in this part of the country, cruised over the wreck area for over an hour, his machine buffeted every minute of the time. Once he sighted the wrecked machine and pounded on the fuselage. I got the glasses out but the shining wreck was gone and we couldn't get back. Finally, aware that the hundred horsepower engine probably would not take us down the draw where the wreck was and out again without suffering the same fate as the bomber, he turned his machine in the direction of Harrison Lake. We dropped 6,500 feet in what seemed like a few seconds. Cold faces were soon beaded with perspiration. A gentle wind still blew and up there, in the hell-hole where those men died, it was blowing and cold."[274]

The *Chilliwack Progress* held out hope that the bodies of the men who perished in the accident could be brought down from the mountain:

"To Bring Out Air Crash Victims —Hope and Chilliwack men are playing a prominent part in efforts to bring the bodies of three RCAF men who crashed in an Avro Anson bomber Saturday out of the mountainous country northwest of Yale. A trail is being brushed out today in an effort to take horses to the scene of the wreck, 5,400 feet up a mountain, Sergeant W. J. Thomson, head of the Chilliwack detachment of BC Police, said this morning. Sergeant Thomson directed the search for the missing men, who were found dead beside the plane yesterday at 4:30 p.m. The finding of the wreck after it had been sighted by an RCAF observer, came after two days of struggling through heavily forested country and steep mountainsides. First to discover the machine were Game Warden Percy Cliffe, Mission; Pilot officer Black, RCAF; and four Hope men who acted as guides—Bill Richmond, Allan Bears, Bert Scott, and Ed Bailey. Food is being dropped to the advance party by parachute. Further down the trail were Constable Lionel Miller and Game Warden Art Butler, who first caught the smoke signal that the men were dead. Other local policemen aiding in the search were Constable Bert Dillabough and Constable Dobell. The latter is in charge of a receiving set at Yale which is in constant communication with the advance camp. Fred Martin, Cultus Lake, is also assisting."[275]

On September 24, *The Daily Colonist* reported:

"Three Found Dead in RCAF Wreck —All Aboard Aircraft in Crash Near Yale on Way to Vancouver Killed —Bodies Discovered in Steep Mountainside

Forest —Provincial Police headquarters here announced late today that all three occupants of a Royal Canadian Air Force plane, which crashed Sunday on Old Settler Mountain near Yale, British Columbia, were dead. Word of the tragedy was received from Sergeant W. J. Thompson of the Provincial Police, who reported to headquarters direct from the scene of the crash 100 miles northeast of Vancouver on a portable radio transmitter. The victims were P.O.L.W. Brooks of Saanichton, and Sergeant L. P. Britland and AC-2 D. B. Wortley, both of Vancouver. The crash occurred after the plane left Kimberley, British Columbia, on a flight from Macleod, Alberta, to Vancouver. 'All occupants of the plane are dead,' was the terse message Sergeant Thompson sent out today when the searchers reached the wreckage after toiling for hours up the sheer slopes of the mountain. Reports to police headquarters later described the trip in from Spuzzum as 'pure hell.'

"'We established radio headquarters at West Nickel Mine at 4,000 feet elevation, seven miles in from Spuzzum,' radioed Sergeant Thompson. 'Men who went in over the terrain told of a climb of 1,500 feet from the camp, then down 2,500 feet and up the same distance to the wrecked plane, a distance of seven miles. It took nine hours to get from West Nickel Mine, where our party camped last night, to the wreckage. 'Both engines and the wings were smashed. The pilot, F. O. L. W. Brooks, was thrown twenty-five feet clear of the plane, while the other two members of the crew, Sergeant L. P. Britland and AC-2 D.B. Wortley, were found in the front end of the smashed fuselage.'

"'It will take probably four days to bring out the bodies and salvageable parts of the machine.' Sergeant Thompson reported that Pilot Officer Black, with Game Warden P. M. Cliffe and Guide William Richmond, was staying with the plane last night. Three other guides—Betts, Bailey, and Scott—went in with them, but returned on an easier route and made the return journey in four hours of fairly easy-going. Stretcher-bearers will go in tomorrow via the newly discovered route to bring out the bodies. Other members of the Provincial Police with the party were Constable L. G. Miller, Chilliwack, and Constable H. J. Engleson, of Coquitlam, who was rushed to the radio camp with a portable transmitter, keeping headquarters here in touch with developments."[276]

The rescuers battled the weather and terrain for days in an attempt to reach the crash site and recover the bodies of the three airmen:

"Leaving Yale at three o'clock yesterday afternoon, a party of RCAF officers, Provincial Police, guides, and forest rangers late last night had reached a point 3,000 feet up the rugged sides of Old Settler Mountain, where lay a wrecked twin-engined Avro-Anson bomber and the bodies of F. O. L. W. Brooks, Saanichton; Sergeant L. P. Britland; and AC-2 D. B. Wortley, both of Vancouver. The plane was wrecked Sunday afternoon on a flight from Macleod, Alberta, to Vancouver, at a spot 5,400 feet up the mountain. Forest rangers and a crew had brushed a trail to the 3,000-foot level. They had eight miles farther to go, but were faced with a six-mile rockslide. Sleeping bags were dropped from a Patricia Bay plane to the party this afternoon and the advance guard is expected to reach the wrecked plane by noon today. This guard will include Provincial Constable H. J. Engelson, with a portable radio transmitter, Constable A. J. Sutherland, and Flight Sergeant Kernaghan, of the RCAF. Trailblazers will follow, clearing a path for horses which will be taken in as far as possible. The party has three days' supply of food. Another RCAF plane from Patricia Bay will fly over the scene this morning, dropping other supplies required for the work of rescue and salvage."[277]

The story of the onerous journey continued in *The Daily Colonist* the next day, and described a new hurdle the rescuers faced: bears.

"Party Reaches Bomber Wreck —Air Force Officials and Provincial Police Arrive at Scene of Crash —Hampered by rain, fog, high winds, and black bears, the advance guard of RCAF officers and Provincial Police sent to bring out the bodies of three men killed in the crash of a twin-engined Avro-Anson bomber on Old Settler Mountain, near Yale, last Sunday, reached the scene of the wreckage at the 5,400-foot level at five o'clock yesterday afternoon after an arduous climb of eleven hours. 'It is raining, blowing heavily, and foggy, and the black bears are increasing in number and can't be frightened away,' radioed Provincial Constable H. J. Engelson, in his report to Provincial Police headquarters here. 'Please drop some ammunition in the morning, as well as food for six men,' he asked. 'Ten men and three horses are on their way up, having passed Fire Lake. The going is extremely difficult, however, and we cannot hazard a guess as to when they will reach here.'"[278]

Finally, on the night of September 25, the decision was made to bury the three men at the site of the crash:

"Airmen Buried Atop Mountain —Victims of Crash Near Yale Laid at Rest on Old Settler Mountain —With snow covering the bleak mountainside to a depth of one inch and still falling, prayers for the dead were said 5,400 feet up the side of Old Settler Mountain, near Yale, at 12:30 o'clock yesterday (September 26), as the bodies of three airmen, killed in the crash of a twin-engined Avro Anson bomber last Sunday, were buried and cairns, erected to mark their graves. The burial service was read by Pilot Officer

Black, of Patricia Bay, with members of the Provincial Police, other RCAF officers, guides, game wardens, and packers standing by with bared heads. The decision to bury the bodies at the scene of the crash was made late last night, owing to the extreme difficulties encountered in reaching the wreckage and the knowledge that a return trip with the bodies would be almost impossible."[279]

The Daily Colonist provided more information on the three airmen:

"An outstanding American flyer before the war, when he was well-known on the Pacific Coast, Flying Officer Brooks was born in Joplin, Missouri, thirty-seven. After joining the Royal Canadian Air Force, he was stationed at the Central Flying School, Trenton, Ontario, until transferred to the Ucluelet airport in 1940. He later returned to Trenton, but was transferred again to the West Coast, coming to Patricia Bay. He is survived by his wife and two children—Robert, fourteen, and Diana, eleven—at the family residence, East Saanich Road, Sidney. Sergeant Lionel Poston Britland came to Vancouver in 1930 from Birkenhead, England, where he was born. He was educated in Vancouver schools and worked as a delivery boy there before joining the Royal Canadian Air Force as a wireless operator in September 1939. He served the 111th Squadron, Vancouver, and with No. 3 Coastal Army Co-operation Squadron at Patricia Bay. He was twenty-one years old. AC-2 Wortley was a member of No. 7 Service Flying Training School, Macleod, Alberta. Western Air Command reported no further information concerning him on record here."

Brooks became a member of the RCAF under a program that allowed American pilots to join due to a shortage of trained Canadian pilots. The crash occurred just over two months before the Japanese attack on Pearl Harbor, and the United States was still officially neutral in the conflict at the time. Taking an oath of allegiance to King George VI could have led to forfeiture of citizenship for an American; however, the Canadian government waived this requirement for foreign nationals, requiring instead that they swear the Oath of Obedience. Though these three are not buried in the Yale cemetery, and they had no connection to the town itself, it is important that their names, and the circumstances in which they lost their lives, should not be forgotten.

About the Author

The Author and His Grandfather Lloyd Brown in Yale, 1980.

Ian Brown was born in Hope, BC, but considers Yale an important part of his upbringing. His grandparents, Lloyd and Dorothy Brown, lived in Yale for over forty years, and their love for the town was always evident to those around them. Lloyd stoked the same fondness for Yale and its storied past in his grandson Ian by reminiscing in the restaurant at Barry's Trading Post, digging in the backyard with the help of a metal detector, and taking trips to local historic sites.

So keen was the interest Ian developed in history that he earned a degree in the subject. He found his focus in 2010 when the idea to research the Yale Pioneer Cemetery took shape in his mind. He launched the project in 2014 and, with the considerable assistance of Debbie Zervini at the Yale Museum and a number of supportive others, he finished it in 2017.

Ian lives in Abbotsford, BC with his wife, Anita, and their three children, Nathan, Laura, and Jillian. He returns to Yale whenever he can.

Endnotes

1. Williams, David R. "… The Man for a New Country"—Sir Matthew Baillie Begbie (Sidney: Gray's Publishing Ltd. 1977), 149

2. Ibid. 155

3. Begbie, Sir Matthew Baillie Letter to Governor James Douglas, 1859

4. Bagshaw, Roberta L. No Better Land: The 1860 Diaries of the Anglican Colonial Bishop Geroge Hills (Victoria: Sono Nis Press 1996), 20-21

5. Ibid. 142

6. Ibid. 143

7. Ibid. 145

8. Ibid. 146

9. British Columbia Tribune, 7 May, 1866

10. Inland Sentinel, 11 May, 1882

11. Inland Sentinel 8 June, 1882

12. Barry, Charles Edward. Interview by Imbert Orchard. *Canadian Broadcasting Corporation* Yale: 25 October, 1965. Radio

13. Correspondence from Rosemary Wilson to Yale & District Historical Society, June 2, 1980

14. Higgins, David Williams. Tales of a Pioneer Journalist: From Gold Rush to Government Street in 19th Century Victoria. Heritage House, 1996

15. Ibid

16. Ibid

17. Ibid

18   British Colonist, 15 July, 1861

19   British Colonist, 16 July, 1861

20   British Colonist, 26 August, 1861

21   BC Tribune, 23 July, 1866

22   St. John's Church burial records

23   St. John the Divine burial records

24   St. John the Divine burial register

25   British Colonist, 15 March, 1871

26   Charles Evans's Obituary; obtained on www.ancestry.ca

27   "British Columbia Death Registrations, 1872-1986," index and images, FamilySearch (https://familysearch.org/ark:/61903/1:1:FLKX-JN5 : accessed 7 April, 2015), George Dunbar, 01 December, 1872; citing , British Columbia, Canada; British Columbia Archives film number B13114, Division of Vital Statistics, Victoria; FHL microfilm 1,927,142.

28   Daily Colonist, 22 January, 1873

29   Cariboo Sentinel, 14 January, 1873

30   W. H. Holmes memoir

31   Cariboo Sentinel, 18 January, 1873

32   "British Columbia Death Registrations, 1872-1986; 1992-1993", database with images, FamilySearch (https://familysearch.org/ark:/61903/1:1:FLKX-KZR : accessed 11 April, 2016), David Oney, 1873.

33   Coroner's Inquest into the death of David Oney, January 14, 1873, Yale, British Columbia

34   Ibid

35   St. John the Divine burial records

36   British Columbia Death Registrations, 1872-1986," index and images, FamilySearch (https://familysearch.org/pal:/MM9.1.1/FLKX-JWP : accessed 22 March, 2015), William Cline, 22 January, 1873; citing British Columbia, British Columbia, Canada; British Columbia Archives film number B13114, Division of Vital Statistics, Victoria; FHL microfilm 1,927,142

37   "British Columbia Death Registrations, 1872-1986; 1992-1993," database with images, FamilySearch (https://familysearch.org/ark:/61903/1:1:FLKX-KJQ : accessed 29 May, 2016), William Reeds Or Baxter, 1873.

38   Cariboo Sentinel, 1 February, 1873

39   Daily Colonist, 12 April, 1874

40   "British Columbia Death Registrations, 1872-1986," index and images, FamilySearch (https://familysearch.org/ark:/61903/1:1:FLKX-JJ7 : accessed 4 May

2015), Robert I Foster, 22 Jun 1873; citing , British Columbia, Canada; British Columbia Archives film number B13114, Division of Vital Statistics, Victoria; FHL microfilm 1,927,142.

41 "British Columbia Death Registrations, 1872-1986; 1992-1993," database with images, FamilySearch (https://familysearch.org/ark:/61903/1:1:FLKX-VJ2 : accessed 24 January, 2016), Ann Mcintee, 1876.

42 St. John the Divine burial records. Accessed at BC Anglican Archives

43 Daily Colonist, 16 October, 1873

44 Daily Colonist, 6 September, 1878

45 Daily Colonist, 8 September, 1878

46 St. John's Church burial records

47 "British Columbia Death Registrations, 1872-1986; 1992-1993," database with images, FamilySearch (https://familysearch.org/ark:/61903/1:1:FLKX-VNR : accessed 8 December 2015), John Lewis, 1878.

48 "British Columbia Death Registrations, 1872-1986," Database with images, FamilySearch (https://familysearch.org/ark:/61903/1:1:FLKX-JTY : accessed 22 June, 2015), Dominique Geordique, 29 Sep 1878; citing Yale, British Columbia, Canada; British Columbia Archives film number B13114, Division of Vital Statistics, Victoria; FHL microfilm 1,927,142

49 Daily Colonist, 25 July, 1875

50 Ibid

51 Daily Colonist, 30 July, 1880

52 Ibid

53 Inland Sentinel, 29 July, 1880

54 Daily Colonist, 30 July, 1880

55 Ibid

56 Ibid

57 Inland Sentinel, 25 November, 1880.

58 Inland Sentinel, 6 January, 1881

59 Inland Sentinel, 28 April, 1881

60 Inland Sentinel, 11 August, 1881

61 Inland Sentinel, 28 September, 1882

62 Ibid.

63 Inland Sentinel, 26 October, 1882

64 Ibid

65 "British Columbia Death Registrations, 1872-1986; 1992-1993," database with images, FamilySearch (https://familysearch.org/ark:/61903/1:1:FLKX-KNY : accessed 8 May, 2016), Edwin Peck, 1882.

66 Personal Correspondence, 5 May, 1878

67 Inland Sentinel, 9 November, 1882

68 Inland Sentinel, 1 March, 1883

69 Inland Sentinel, 17 May, 1883

70 Inland Sentinel, 31 May, 1883

71 Inland Sentinel, 30 August, 1883

72 Daily British Colonist, 23 September, 1873

73 Inland Sentinel, 6 September, 1883

74 Inland Sentinel, 13 September, 1883

75 Inland Sentinel, 20 September, 1883

76 Inland Sentinel, 13 December, 1883

77 Laforet, Andrea and Annie York Spuzzum: Fraser Canyon Histories, 1808 - 1939 UBC Press, Vancouver, 1998

78 Vancouver Daily World, 7 May, 1890

79 British Colonist, 13 January, 1892

80 British Columbia Death Registrations, 1872-1986; 1992-1993," database with images, FamilySearch (https://familysearch.org/pal:/MM9.3.1/TH-267-12385-121608-86?cc=1538285 : accessed 31 October, 2015), 004437840 > image 366 of 3136; Division of Vital Statistics, Victoria

81 Winnipeg Tribune, 13 September, 1893

82 Vancouver Daily World, 12 September, 1893

83 Paterson, Thomas William British Columbia Ghost Town Series: Fraser Canyon Sunfire Publications Limited, Langley, 1985

84 Annual report of the Minister of Mines, 1896, Province of British Columbia. Cited from https://open.library.ubc.ca/collections/bcsessional/items/1.0063783

85 Victoria Daily Colonist, 18 August, 1898

86 Victoria Daily Colonist, 11 May, 1899

87 George Webster Anderson fonds, BC Archives

88 Victoria Daily Colonist, 7 February, 1899

89 "British Columbia Death Registrations, 1872-1986; 1992-1993," database with images, FamilySearch (https://familysearch.org/ark:/61903/1:1:FL2M-6QM : 30 September, 2015), Mary Alice Creighton, 1900

90   Thomas, Fran *Forging a New Hope: Struggles and Dreams, 1848-1948* Friesen Printers, Cloverdale, 1984

91   "British Columbia Death Registrations, 1872-1986; 1992-1993", database with images, FamilySearch (https://familysearch.org/ark:/61903/1:1:FLKX-V4Z : accessed 3 October, 2015), Mary Ann Jackson Bee Jackson Beattie, 1906.

92   British Daily Colonist, 9 December, 1869

93   Inland Sentinel, Spring, 1881

94   Laforet, Andrea Lynne *Folk History in a Small Canadian Community*, 1969

95   Hope Standard, 25 May, 1977

96   Chilliwack Progress, 10 March, 1909

97   British Columbia Coroner's Report. Births, Deaths and Marriages Registration Act. Number 69623

98   Castle Family Notes, page 1

99   Year: 1901; Census Place: Yale (West/Ouest), Yale & Cariboo, British Columbia; Page: 2; Family No: 15

100 Victoria Daily Colonist, 21 November, 1911

101 Chilliwack Progress, 12 March, 1913

102 St. John the Divine burial records

103 Chilliwack Progress, 1 June, 1916

104 Chilliwack Progress, 15 June, 1916

105 The Chilliwack Progress, 18 October, 1917

106 Victoria Daily Colonist, 25 May, 1913

107 Laforet, Andrea and Annie York *Spuzzum: Fraser Canyon Histories, 1808-1939* UBC Press, Vancouver, 1998

108 Victoria Daily Colonist, 25 May, 1913

109 Paterson, Thomas William *British Columbia Ghost Town Series: Fraser Canyon* Sunfire Publications Limited, Langley, 1985

110 West Yale Review, 2 September, 1911

111 Orchard, Imbert - CBC radio interview with Charles Barry, 25 October, 1965

112 Chilliwack Progress, 24 January, 1924

113 Vancouver Daily World, 19 January, 1924

114 Orchard, Imbert - CBC radio interview with C. E. Barry, 25 October, 1965

115 Chilliwack Progress, 3 January, 1929

116 The Chilliwack Progress, 18 September, 1930

117 St. John's Church burial records

118 Bjerky, Verna www.virtualmuseum.ca - First Peoples of Yale and Spuzzum

119 Government of Canada - Personnel Records of the First World War - http://central.bac-lac.gc.ca/.item/?op-pdf&app=CEF&id=B1573-S013

120 Ibid

121 Wrigley's British Columbia Directory, 1918

122 Anderson, William P. *Science* Vol. 5, No. 110 (March 13, 1885), pp 214

123 The Chilliwack Progress, 13 December, 1944

124 Millar, Nancy. Once Upon a Wedding. Bayeux Arts Inc., 2000

125 Laforet, Andrea and Annie York Spuzzum: Fraser Canyon Histories, 1808-1939 UBC Press, Vancouver, 1998

126 Ibid

127 Inland Sentinel

128 Inland Sentinel, 9 September, 1880

129 "British Columbia Death Registrations, 1872-1986," index and images, FamilySearch (https://familysearch.org/ark:/61903/1:1:FLKX-JJW : accessed 25 April, 2015), William Finn, 28 May, 1880; citing Yale, British Columbia, Canada; British Columbia Archives film number B13114, Division of Vital Statistics, Victoria; FHL microfilm 1,927,142.

130 Indiana Archives and Records Administration - Digital Archives

131 "British Columbia Death Registrations, 1872-1986; 1992-1993," database with images, FamilySearch (https://familysearch.org/ark:/61903/1:1:FLKX-VNT : accessed 8 December, 2015), Nathan Lincicum, 1880.

132 Inland Sentinel, 28 October, 1880

133 Ibid

134 Memoirs of Walton Hugh Holmes

135 Ibid

136 Inland Sentinel, 20 May, 1880

137 "British Columbia Death Registrations, 1872-1986," database with images, FamilySearch (https://familysearch.org/ark:/61903/1:1:FLKX-JYV : accessed 21 July 2015), C F Haband, 08 October, 1881; citing , British Columbia, Canada; British Columbia Archives film number B13114, Division of Vital Statistics, Victoria; FHL microfilm 1,927,142.

138 Inland Sentinel, 13 October, 1881

139 "British Columbia Death Registrations, 1872-1986; 1992-1993", database with images, FamilySearch (https://familysearch.org/ark:/61903/1:1:FLKX-V48 : accessed 16 October, 2015), Daniel Kennedey, 1880.

140   Inland Sentinel, 20 January, 1881.

141   Robertson, Ian Bruce. The Honourable Aleck Friesen Press, Victoria, 2013

142   Daily Colonist, 27 January, 1881

143   Daily Colonist, 23 December, 1882

144   Inland Sentinel, 31 March, 1881

145   Daily Colonist, 7 May, 1881

146   Register of Enlistments in the US Army, 1798-1914; (National Archives Microfilm Publication M233, 81 rolls); Records of the Adjutant General's Office, 1780s-1917, Record Group 94; National Archives, Washington, DC

147   Inland Sentinel, 19 May, 1881

148   Inland Sentinel, 26 May 1881

149   Inland Sentinel, 2 June 1881

150   Charles Kerr Death Certificate

151   Inland Sentinel, 2 June 1881

152   Daily Colonist, 4 June 1881

153   Inland Sentinel, 9 June 1881

154   Daily Colonist, 11 June, 1881

155   Inland Sentinel, 9 June, 1881

156   "British Columbia Death Registrations, 1872-1986," index and images, FamilySearch (https://familysearch.org/pal:/MM9.1.1/FLKX-JWR : accessed 24 March, 2015), Michael Corbitt, 23 June, 1881; citing British Columbia, British Columbia, Canada; British Columbia Archives film number B13114, Division of Vital Statistics, Victoria; FHL microfilm 1,927,142.

157   "British Columbia Death Registrations, 1872-1986," index and images, FamilySearch (https://familysearch.org/ark:/61903/1:1:FLKX-JTB : accessed 24 May, 2015), Peter Galaway, 12 July, 1881; citing , British Columbia, Canada; British Columbia Archives film number B13114, Division of Vital Statistics, Victoria; FHL microfilm 1,927,142.

158   Brooklyn Daily Eagle, 23 February, 1850

159   Inland Sentinel, 11 August, 1881

160   Inland Sentinel, 11 August, 1881

161   Inland Sentinel, 27 September, 1881

162   Inland Sentinel, 27 October, 1881

163   Ibid

164   Ibid

165 Ibid

166 "British Columbia Death Registrations, 1872-1986; 1992-1993," database with images, FamilySearch (https://familysearch.org/ark:/61903/1:1:FLKX-KNL : accessed 11 April, 2016), Patrick O'Brien, 1881

167 St. John the Divine burial records

168 Inland Sentinel, 24 November, 1881

169 Inland Sentinel October 1881

170 St. John's Church burial register

171 Inland Sentinel, 21 December, 1881

172 Inland Sentinel, 23 February, 1882

173 Inland Sentinel, 9 March, 1882

174 Ibid.

175 Inland Sentinel 16 March, 1882

176 Inland Sentinel, 13 April, 1882

177 British Columbia Death Registrations, 1872-1986; 1992-1993", database with images, FamilySearch (https://familysearch.org/ark:/61903/1:1:FLKX-VN1 : accessed 7 December, 2015), David Lenihan, 1882.

178 Inland Sentinel, 4 May, 1882

179 Inland Sentinel, 2 September, 1880

180 Inland Sentinel, 26 October, 1882

181 Inland Sentinel, 7 December 1882.

182 Inland Sentinel, 4 January, 1883

183 Inland Sentinel, 11 January, 1883

184 Register of Enlistments in the US Army, 1798-1914; (National Archives Microfilm Publication M233, 81 rolls); Records of the Adjutant General's Office, 1780s-1917, Record Group 94; National Archives, Washington, DC

185 Berton, Pierre. *The Last Spike - The Great Railway 1881-1885* pp 194

186 Hansard, 1882, p 1477

187 Ibid

188 Inland Sentinel, 1 February, 1883

189 Inland Sentinel, 29 March, 1883.

190 "British Columbia Death Registrations, 1872-1986; 1992-1993," database with images, FamilySearch (https://familysearch.org/ark:/61903/1:1:FLKX-JJC : 30 September, 2015), Thomas Alexander Frazer, 1883.

191 Inland Sentinel, 3 May, 1883

192 Daily Colonist, 13 May, 1883

193 Inland Sentinel, 28 June, 1883

194 Inland Sentinel, 30 August, 1883

195 Inland Sentinel, 28 June, 1883

196 Berton, Pierre. The Last Spike—The Great Railway 1881-1885, McLelland and Stewart, 1971

197 Inland Sentinel 23 August, 1883

200 Inland Sentinel, 20 September, 1883

201 Inland Sentinel, 27 September, 1883

202 Inland Sentinel, 18 August, 1881

203 Royal Commission of the Liquor Traffic - Minutes of Evidence - Volume III, Provinces of Manitoba, North-west Territories and British Columbia, 1894, pp 600

204 Ibid, pp 607

205 Ibid

206 "British Columbia Death Registrations, 1872-1986; 1992-1993," database with images, FamilySearch (https://familysearch.org/ark:/61903/1:1:FLKX-KJC : accessed 1 June, 2016), Edward Roody, 1883.

207 Inland Sentinel, 15 November, 1883

208 Inland Sentinel, 6 December, 1883

209 Inland Sentinel, 10 January, 1884

210 Inland Sentinel, 13 March, 1884

211 St. John's Church burial records

212 Daily Colonist, 26 November, 1884

213 http://www.usgennet.org/usa/ne/topic/railroads/job.html

214 St. John's records

215 The Dominion Annual Register for the Twentieth Year of the Canadian Union, 1886 - Record of Accidental Deaths, Suicides, Etc.

216 Daily Alta California, Volume 41, Number 13586, 10 November, 1886

217 Manitoba Free Press, 15 November, 1886

218 Victoria Daily Colonist, 30 November, 1888

219 Inland Sentinel, 9 June, 1881

220 British Columbia Coroner's Report - 23 February, 1892

221 Victoria Daily Colonist, 23 April, 1895

222　Southern Pacific Co. (Pacific Systems), Rules and Regulations for the Government of Employees of the Operating Department, July 1, 1892

223　British Columbia Death Registrations, 1872-1986; 1992-1993", database with images, FamilySearch (https://familysearch.org/ark:/61903/1:1:FLKX-NZ6 : 30 September ,2015), Oliver Anselmi, 1898

224　"British Columbia Death Registrations, 1872-1986; 1992-1993," database with images, FamilySearch (https://familysearch.org/ark:/61903/1:1:FLKX-JNP : 30 September 2015), Eras Cojanovic, 1911.

225　"British Columbia Death Registrations, 1872-1986," index and images, FamilySearch (https://familysearch.org/pal:/MM9.1.1/FLKX-JNP : accessed 22 March, 2015), Eras Cojanovic, 27 October, 1911; citing Yale, British Columbia, Canada; British Columbia Archives film number B13114, Division of Vital Statistics, Victoria; FHL microfilm 1,927,142

226　"British Columbia Death Registrations, 1872-1986; 1992-1993," database with images, FamilySearch (https://familysearch.org/pal:/MM9.3.1/TH-267-12397-54554-50?cc=1538285 : accessed 21 October, 2015), 004437641 > image 356 of 2938; Division of Vital Statistics, Victoria

227　West Yale Review, 27 January, 1912

228　West Yale Review, 17 February, 1912

229　"British Columbia Death Registrations, 1872-1986; 1992-1993," database with images, FamilySearch (https://familysearch.org/ark:/61903/1:1:FL29-MNT : 30 September, 2015), Albert Brink, 1912.

230　Charles Edward Barry interview.

231　West Yale Review, 24 February, 1912

232　British Columbia Coroner's Report. Births, Deaths, and Marriages Registration Act. Number 64229

233　"British Columbia Death Registrations, 1872-1986," index and images, FamilySearch (https://familysearch.org/ark:/61903/1:1:FL29-96Y : accessed 4 April, 2015), Emanuel Denardo, 20 June, 1912; citing Yale, British Columbia, Canada; British Columbia Archives film number B13112, Division of Vital Statistics, Victoria; FHL microfilm 1,927,140.

234　Inland Sentinel 27 September, 1883

235　St. John the Divine burial records

236　St. John the Divine burial records

237　Daily British Colonist, 30 June, 1876

238　Personal correspondence Elizabeth Hamilton 21 April, 2014

239　Inland Sentinel, 11 August, 1881

240　W. H. Holmes memoir

241 Daily Colonist, 18 August, 1881

242 Inland Sentinel, 18 August, 1881

243 Daily Colonist, 21 August, 1881

244 Inland Sentinel, 25 August, 1881

245 Inland Sentinel, 20 October, 1881

246 Inland Sentinel, 10 November, 1881

247 Daily Colonist, 23 November, 1881

248 "British Columbia Death Registrations, 1872-1986; 1992-1993," database with images, FamilySearch (https://familysearch.org/ark:/61903/1:1:FLKX-JJ9 : 30 September, 2015), Harry Elley, 1881.

249 Inland Sentinel, 8 September, 1881

250 Inland Sentinel, 5 January, 1882

251 Inland Sentinel, 12 January, 1882

252 St. John's Church burial records

253 Inland Sentinel, 6 April, 1882

254 St. John's Church burial records

255 "British Columbia Death Registrations, 1872-1986; 1992-1993," database with images, FamilySearch (https://familysearch.org/ark:/61903/1:1:FLKX-VNB : accessed 12 December, 2015), Annie Isabella Lindsay, 1882.

256 Inland Sentinel, 25 May, 1882

257 Inland Sentinel, 22 February, 1883

258 Inland Sentinel, 1 November 1883

259 Inland Sentinel 13 December, 1883

260 "British Columbia Death Registrations, 1872-1986; 1992-1993," database with images, FamilySearch (https://familysearch.org/ark:/61903/1:1:FLKX-V4S : accessed 3 October, 2015), Lydia Elizabeth Irwin, 1883.

261 "British Columbia Death Registrations, 1872-1986; 1992-1993," database with images, FamilySearch (https://familysearch.org/ark:/61903/1:1:FLKX-2WB : 30 September, 2015), Peter Webb, 1889

262 CIA World Factbook

263 "British Columbia Death Registrations, 1872-1986; 1992-1993," database with images, FamilySearch (https://familysearch.org/ark:/61903/1:1:FLLV-ZJM : 30 September, 2015), Arthur Thomas Flann, 1905.

264 St. John the Divine burial records

265 West Yale Review, 24 August, 1912

266 "British Columbia Death Registrations, 1872-1986," index and images, FamilySearch (https://familysearch.org/pal:/MM9.1.1/FL29-M5V : accessed 25 March 2015), Arthur Frederick Cox, 20 Aug 1912; citing Yale, British Columbia, Canada; British Columbia Archives film number B13112, Division of Vital Statistics, Victoria; FHL microfilm 1,927,140.

267 "British Columbia Death Registrations, 1872-1986; 1992-1993," database with images, FamilySearch (https://familysearch.org/ark:/61903/1:1:FLKX-B4R : 30 September 2015), Frank August Castle, 1915.

268 Ibid.

269 "British Columbia Death Registrations, 1872-1986; 1992-1993," database with images, FamilySearch (https://familysearch.org/ark:/61903/1:1:FLKF-3HF : 30 September, 2015), Wing Howe Fook Wo, 1918

270 "British Columbia Death Registrations, 1872-1986; 1992-1993," database with images, FamilySearch (https://familysearch.org/ark:/61903/1:1:FLK2-8V8 : 30 September, 2015), Thelma Iris Creighton, 1929.

271 The Chilliwack Progress, 27 June, 1929

272 The Province, 6 June, 1960

273 The Daily Colonist, 23 September, 1941

274 The Chilliwack Progress, 24 September, 1941

275 Ibid.

276 The Daily Colonist, 24 September, 1941

277 The Daily Colonist, 25 September, 1941

278 The Daily Colonist, 26 September, 1941

279 The Daily Colonist, 27 September, 1941

Printed in Canada